W9-BBW-843

the NEW Breastfeeding DIET PLAN

Breakthrough Ways to Reduce Toxins & Give Your Baby the Best Start in Life

Robert Rountree, M.D. and Melissa Block, M.Ed.

Mc Graw Hill

New York   Chicago   San Francisco   Lisbon   London   Madrid   Mexico City
Milan   New Delhi   San Juan   Seoul   Singapore   Sydney   Toronto

The McGraw·Hill Companies

Library of Congress Cataloging-in-Publication Data

Rountree, Bob.
    The new breastfeeding diet plan : breakthrough ways to reduce toxins & give your
    baby the best start in life / by Robert Rountree and Melissa Lynn Block.
        p.   cm.
    Includes bibliographical references.
    ISBN 0-07-146160-4
    1. Breastfeeding.   2. Mothers—Nutrition.   3. Infants—Nutrition.
    I. Block, Melissa.   II. Title.

    RJ216.R59   2007
    649'.33—dc22   2006024941

1 2 3 4 5 6 7 8 9 0   FGR/FGR   0 9 8 7 6

ISBN 13: 978-0-07-146160-3
ISBN 10:   0-07-146160-4

McGraw-Hill books are available at special quantity discounts to use as premiums and sales promotions, or for use in corporate training programs. For more information, please write to the Director of Special Sales, Professional Publishing, McGraw-Hill, Two Penn Plaza, New York, NY 10121-2298. Or contact your local bookstore.

This book is printed on acid-free paper.

To all mothers, everywhere

Contents

Acknowledgments

FIRST AND FOREMOST, I would like to thank my coauthor, Melissa Block, for all of the tremendously hard work she put into this project. I have been equally impressed with her brilliant observations as I am by her willingness to evaluate challenging controversial issues with an open mind. It has been a joy to work with someone who shares the same passion for getting this message out, and I feel that we have both learned a lot from the collaboration. I would also like to thank our editor, Natasha Graf, for her insight, skill, and support.

I want to thank Karen Olsen for her grounded perspective and constructive advice on the manuscript. She has repeatedly helped me develop a deep respect and appreciation for the wonderful and invaluable resource provided by La Leche League to breastfeeding mothers all over the world. After all has been said and done, I trust that both Karen and the League will recognize our unwavering commitment to the clear and powerful message that breast is best. It goes without saying that scientific knowledge is continually built on the shoulders of those who have boldly gone before. This book could never have been written without the courageous efforts of Rachel Carson, a true pioneer who built the first lamppost in a dark and unfriendly wilderness. Every bird that chirps and every frog that still croaks loudly and noisily in the spring night owes a debt to her. Although many researchers have continued her legacy, I am especially appreciative of the excellent research and eloquent voices of Sandra Steingraber, Theo Colburn, John Myers, Philip Landrigan, Herbert Needleman, Devra Davis, Buck Levin, Paula Baillie-Hamilton, and Kim Erickson.

Finally, I want to thank my mother, Dorothy Rountree, for bringing me into the world and nurturing me until I was ready to take flight out of the nest; my father, Jeff, for his guidance and compassion; and my dear sister, Lynn, for her love and her laughter.

—ROBERT ROUNTREE, M.D.

THANKS TO DR. ROUNTREE for an effortless collaboration; Virginia Hopkins for her mentorship; my parents and siblings for their support and encouragement; Amanda, Julian, and Tristan Lake for unconditional love; Nicola Gordon for the dancing and remembering to breathe; Nirav Sumati and Nancy Michelson, anchors in the storm; the Santa Barbara Midwives and Fredda Spirka for ably guiding me into motherhood, the best place I've ever been; my husband, Patrick, my most helpful critic and a constant source of inspiration and laughter; and, finally, to our children, Sarah and Noah, whose combined five-plus years camped out at my breasts inspired me to join Dr. Rountree in writing this book.

—MELISSA BLOCK

Preface

DURING MY PREGNANCIES, I read a lot of books and talked to a lot of wise women—most notably, the midwives who helped me birth my children—to try to prepare myself for nursing and other experiences of motherhood. I also turned to books and tried to get at least an intellectual grasp of what to expect, what could go wrong, and how to troubleshoot.

Of course, no amount of "book-learning" could completely prepare one for any aspect of motherhood, but it did give me a place to begin. And it inspired me to begin working on the seeds of this book.

As I gathered information, I had nagging doubts. "Is this necessary?" I asked myself. "All this science to get women to nourish themselves and their babies in the way nature appears to have intended?" The more I delved, the more I realized that *yes, it is necessary*. Our food supply and environment have changed since this whole mammalian thing first evolved.

Modern life has moved us away from instinct and the patterns of nature. Part of the purpose of science, I believe, is to lead us back there again. Today, we need to know how our bodies work in order to make conscious choices that will best support our health. Knowing that an enormous body of scientific evidence supports on-demand, long-term nursing will help us stay the course when it gets hard. Understanding the connection between the way we nourish ourselves during pregnancy and the nursing years—

and the foods we give to our young children—and their lifelong health will motivate us to make the best possible food choices day after day.

Today, we can use our instincts along with our knowledge to keep ourselves and our children as well-nourished as possible in both body and soul.

—MELISSA BLOCK, M.ED.

Introduction

OVERALL, THE INCREASE in the number of women who breastfeed their babies is heartening. Some 68 percent of new mothers breastfeed their newborns, and 31 percent are still nursing at six months. That's a huge improvement since 1970, when only 25 percent of new moms put their babies to the breast at all.

On the other hand, we are still quite a ways from meeting the WHO/AAP recommendations that every woman breastfeed exclusively until the child is six months of age and then continue to make breast milk a part of the child's diet up until the child is aged two or beyond.

These figures are even less positive than they seem at first glance. First, keep in mind that these are national averages, and that breastfeeding rates have a lot to do with the age of the mother and with the mother's marital status, socioeconomic class, and level of education. Women of lower socioeconomic classes, including immigrants who are low on the socioeconomic scale, are more likely to formula-feed than women with higher incomes. This is likely due, at least in part, to the formula that WIC buys for them each year, spending $578 million in federal funds to do so. Formula is expensive—about eighty dollars per month for regular formulas and much more for specialized nonallergenic formulas that may be needed by some—but when WIC hands it out for free, the choice to use it is much simpler.

If women are serious about following the WHO guidelines for extended breastfeeding, the world is going to change. We'll see women nursing in public a lot more often. Women will spend two or more years of their lives breastfeeding, and those with several children will do so for much longer. We'll see more stores selling nursing bras and clothing that is nursing-friendly.

If women are going to go this route, they deserve the most current information about a diet they can adhere to during the nursing years that will optimize both their own health and their baby's—a diet that works with the hectic life of the nursing mom.

In these pages, my coauthor and I explore the scientific support for a particular way of eating during the nursing months or years. We have created an eating plan for new mothers to try to ensure that their milk is as nutritious and as free of contaminants as possible. This eating plan will benefit both mother and child in the short and long term.

When mothers have to turn to formula, exclusively or as a supplement, they need unbiased information about how to choose the right one. Back in medical school in North Carolina, a professor told my colleagues and me how to make baby formula. I don't recall the exact composition, but it was a mixture of Karo corn syrup and Carnation evaporated milk. This mixture was state-of-the-art twenty-six years ago. Today, formulas are far superior to what they once were, and we will help mothers to make the important decision of which to try—and how to know if they should try something else.

There are (approximately) three billion diet and nutrition books on the shelves today. A lot of them contain valuable information and guidance on how to eat right for long life or for weight loss, or offer ways to get children to eat greens and other good things without gagging. But there is precious little of this literature directed specifically to nursing women. These women need their own diet book with information on foods, food preparation, supplements, medicines, and environmental toxins that is written specifically for them.

The book you hold in your hands is that book.

—ROBERT ROUNTREE, M.D.

1

Congratulations, You've Decided to Breastfeed

You have decided to breastfeed your baby. Congratulations! Now that you have made this choice, you may have a lot of questions. *Will I have enough milk? How will I nurse in public? How will I return to work and continue to breastfeed? What if I want to leave my baby for a few hours and she won't take a bottle?* One question that soon-to-be nursing mothers rarely ask is, *What should I eat to make sure my milk contains the best possible nutrition?*

Strong scientific evidence suggests that, like the milk of any mammal, a woman's breast milk is powerfully affected by her diet. Cows fed on green grasses yield more wholesome milk than cows fattened on grain and dosed on antibiotics and hormones. It follows that women who plan to breastfeed need the best possible information about what to eat—and what to avoid—before and during the nursing months.

Why not do your best to offer your nursling premium dairy *before* he's weaned? Why not do all you can to ensure that you're giving her the purest and most nutritious breast milk possible?

Is Breast Always Best? The Benefits of Breastfeeding

Most pregnant women hear over and over again that the best thing for their babies is to breastfeed exclusively for at least the first six months of life and continue to nurse and feed with supplemental solids from six months of age until baby is at least one year old, preferably two.

The benefits of breastfeeding are multifold for both mom and baby. The more breast milk a baby gets, the better; and the benefits of nursing are greater for babies nursed for a year or more than for babies nursed only a few weeks or months. Partial breastfeeding—along with formula—protects babies against disease, but exclusive breastfeeding does so better.

The benefits of nursing extend well beyond the actual nursing period, protecting babies against diseases like type 1 diabetes, lymphoma, allergies, asthma, and Crohn's disease (an inflammatory disease of the colon) during childhood and potentially protecting them against these and other illnesses in adulthood. A breastfed infant has better immunity against childhood diseases, especially respiratory diseases, gastrointestinal infections, and ear infections. Breast milk strengthens a baby's immune system in responding to any challenge. Because of the superior bioavailability of the nutrients in human milk, she will absorb and utilize more of the nutrients in her food than the formula-fed child. Breast milk is cheap (free), always sanitized, always warm, and matched to the day-to-day, hour-to-hour needs of the nursling.

A breastfed child is likely to perform better on tests of intelligence and visual acuity than a child who has never been breastfed. There is some evidence that breastfeeding reduces risk of SIDS. According to Naomi Baumslag and Dia Michaels' book *Milk, Money, and Madness* (Westport, CT: Bergin & Garvey, 1995), "bottle-fed [American] infants were 14 times more likely to be hospitalized than breastfed infants."

On Mom's end of things, there are many benefits to exclusive breastfeeding for at least six months. Her fertility is reduced, with the chances of conceiving again during the period of exclusive, on-demand breastfeeding reduced to about 2 percent. This is nature's way of creating a healthy interval between pregnancies. A non-nursing mother can be fertile again within fifty days of giving birth.

A mother who nurses will see her long-term risk of breast cancer and osteoporosis fall, and her bonding with her baby is improved. Hormonal changes linked with lactation aid her in making good mothering choices and weathering the inevitable storms that come with having a new baby.

How the Nursing Mom's Diet Affects Her Baby's Health

We have made a troubling discovery about breastfeeding. In the past, a woman's diet hasn't been considered to vary milk composition very much, but current research shows that human milk's composition depends strongly upon the diet of the nursing mother. If the nursing mother does not eat right, neither does her nursling. A mom who eats a steady diet of low-protein, low-fat, processed, sugary foods, or foods that contain unhealthy fats or toxic chemical additives, may be giving her child nourishment that isn't all that superior to that found in the best modern formulas.

The milk of a mother who adheres to a strict vegetarian (vegan) diet—especially if she eats a lot of processed food rich in hydrogenated oils and sugar—will have lesser nutritional value than the milk of a mother who eats an omnivorous or lacto-ovo vegetarian (vegetarian with eggs and dairy) diet composed of the kinds of foods we'll recommend in later chapters of this book.

Breast milk is a living, changing food that contains immune components, growth factors, and friendly bacteria that formula does not. But in terms of the balance of fats and certain vitamins and minerals, formula may be a more reliable source of nutrition than the breast milk of a woman who isn't eating well.

Reducing Toxins in Breast Milk

In their first draughts of breast milk, nurslings swallow dozens of synthetic and potentially toxic chemicals in concentrations that we do not know to be safe. Ironically, as a woman lactates, her own

What This Book Is Not About

This book is not *about how to breastfeed. If you are looking for a book on how to breastfeed successfully, please turn to the Resources section in Appendix B for our recommendations. We have also compiled a list of terrific websites that can answer any and all questions you may have about the "how" of breastfeeding. At the end of Chapter 10, we offer resources for finding a lactation consultant (LC) to help you through whatever obstacles you encounter in your breastfeeding adventure. (Why in that chapter? Because mothers who wean their babies and decide they want to bring their milk back again usually need the help of an LC.) And La Leche League groups can be an enormously helpful resource for nursing mothers; you can find a chapter in your area at their website, lalecheleague.org, or in your local phone book.*

This book is also not about medications and how they affect mothers' milk. The premier expert on breast-feeding pharmacology is Thomas Hale, R.Ph., Ph.D., a professor at Texas Tech University. For comprehensive information on drug safety for lactating mothers, look at his website, http://neonatal.ttuhsc.edu/lact, or his book, Medications and Mothers' Milk *(Amarillo, TX: Pharmasoft Medical Publishing, 2000).*

This book is also not a thorough treatment of the use of herbal medicine during the nursing months or years, although we do recommend some herbs for specific indications, such as helping to promote better milk production or helping to solve some breastfeeding problems (see Chapter 10). For a thorough look at using herbal medicine during the postpartum months, refer to Susan Weed's Herbal for the Childbearing Year *(Woodstock, NY: Ash Tree Publishing, 1985).*

toxin levels fall. The longer she nurses, the less toxic she becomes. And as one might predict, her own risk of various toxin-related diseases (most notably cancer) falls when she breastfeeds, and the longer she nurses the better.

Those toxins go right into the little body of the babe she would, without a second thought, throw herself in front of a speeding truck to protect. What will the consequences of this be? No one knows for sure. Are there steps we can take to minimize the impact of breast milk toxins? Although the science on this is young, we share ideas throughout this book on how women might be able to do this with specific foods, supplements, and other practices.

It is safe to conclude that unbalanced nutrition during the first weeks, months, and years of life—whether it comes from food, breast milk, or formula—does have consequences for the short-term and long-term health of the child. And when a woman consumes the standard American diet, her own nutrition and that of her nursling will be compromised.

The question, then, is, *What should I be eating to improve the quality of my breast milk?* That's what the New Breastfeeding Diet (NBD for short) is all about.

Limiting Risk for Chronic Illnesses

Children today are at greater risk of chronic diseases (allergies, asthma, eczema, cancer, type 2 diabetes) than they have ever been. Twice as many preschoolers and adolescents are obese as they were thirty years ago, and kids aged six to eleven are more than three times as likely to be obese today as they were in the 1970s. The number of children with behavior problems (ADHD, autism) or learning disabilities has also shot up over the past few decades.

Scientists, educators, and parents have offered up a lot of explanations about the precipitous rise in childhood chronic diseases. Toxins in the environment, poor childhood diets, poor prenatal nutrition, an overhurried, overscheduled way of life, overuse of antibiotics and vaccines in small children, and too much time spent with electronic media are only a few. Many of these explanations are compelling, and each of these factors is likely to play at least a partial role. No one factor can be teased out from the huge number of environmental and genetic influences that make and mold our children. Dietary change in the nursing mom or formula/diet changes in the nonnursing infant will certainly help, but it fits into a larger spectrum of issues that can have powerful effects.

Growing evidence suggests that nutrition during infancy—particularly, prenatally—affects a child's developing cardiovascular and hormonal systems in ways that directly influence risk of disease later in life. D. J. P. Barker, M.D., and his colleagues at the University of Southampton, in the United Kingdom, have spent decades doing research into the so-called *fetal origins hypothesis*. This theory proposes that heart disease, stroke, high blood pressure, osteoporosis, and diabetes in later life are directly linked to poor nutrition in the womb.

The seeds of this research were planted when Dr. Barker found that several large studies, involving thousands of people followed for much of their life spans, showed a correlation between birth weight and risk of heart attack later in life. Men with lower birth weight had significantly higher risk of heart disease in their later years, as did men whose mothers were overweight during pregnancy. Boys with higher body mass index (BMI—the more overweight the person, the higher the BMI) during childhood were found to have higher risk of coronary heart disease later in life— especially if they had low birth weights. In girls, the shorter their *length* at birth, and the faster their weight gain during infancy, the higher their risk of heart attack after middle age. The same or similar connections were seen with risk of type 2 diabetes and hypertension (high blood pressure), both risk factors for heart disease.

When Mom eats poorly and doesn't take prenatal vitamins, the fetus gets inadequate nutrition and makes certain physical adaptations to compensate. In essence, her body changes in utero structurally and metabolically to prepare for a lack of food on the outside. She's born—in many cases, below optimal birth weight— and when her body doesn't encounter a food shortage, she gains weight rapidly. This is seen as a great sign of a healthy baby, but Barker's research suggests that this dissonance between what the baby's body grew to expect and the reality of the overabundant food supply it encounters predisposes it to obesity and disease later in life.

Nutrient intake during infancy—especially that magical "fourth trimester," the first three months of life—is bound to have an effect here, too.

Giving You and Your Child a Nutritional Boost

We can begin to prepare our children for the challenges they face by ensuring that breast milk is as nutritious and pure as possible and transitioning into a diet that teaches good lifelong eating habits. Supplements and highly nutrient-dense "super foods" can safely boost the nutritional value of the foods moms eat and feed to their kids.

The likelihood of a poor diet in the mother being harmful to the infant is higher during pregnancy than during breastfeeding. Breastfeeding experts tell mothers that they shouldn't worry too much about their diets, that they can make perfectly good milk as long as they follow some loose dietary guidelines.

Although levels of certain nutrients in breast milk are fairly constant no matter what Mom eats, it has been found that others can vary dramatically depending on the mother's diet: certain fats, vitamins B_6 and B_{12}, and the mineral selenium, for example. Nutrients like these play pivotal roles in the physical and psychological well-being of adults and infants both. It isn't much of a leap to conclude that a carefully designed diet that yields grade A premium breast milk can make a difference in the health and happiness of both halves of the mother-infant dyad.

As Finnish breast milk researcher Ulla Hoppu and colleagues write in the medical journal *Allergy*, "Breastfeeding mothers . . . do not constitute a uniform group. The composition of breast milk shows marked individual variation and so, consequently, does the success of breastfeeding in reducing the risk of disease."

Throughout the rest of this book, you will read about research that supports this argument for optimizing breast milk quality through the diet of the nursing mother. Diets that raise levels of vitamins, minerals, and specific fats in Mom's milk have been found to impact the health of both mother and child in the following ways:

- A Centers for Disease Control study found that two breastfed babies with marked neurological impairment were deficient in vitamin B_{12} because their mothers were vegetarians who did not get adequate amounts of this vitamin in their diets.
- The ratio of beneficial to less beneficial fatty acids can differ almost *one hundred times* in the breast milk of women who eat different foods. Growing evidence indicates that this ratio impacts infant brain development.
- When the mother has a high intake of "bad" fats and low intake of the beneficial fats, her milk reflects this, and both baby and mom are more susceptible to eczema, asthma, and allergy.
- Our previous book, *A Natural Guide to Pregnancy and Postpartum Health* (written with Dean Raffelock and Virginia Hopkins; see Appendix B), dealt with the link between the mom's intake of fats and her risk of postpartum depression (PPD). The fats best for PPD prevention are the same fats known to increase intelligence and improve vision in nursing infants.
- New research indicates that a specific fatty acid that is abundant in breast milk—lauric acid—has important antiviral and antibacterial roles in a baby's body. Increasing lauric acid in Mom's diet increases it in her milk.
- A study of nursing mothers in Iceland found that supplementing with cod liver oil greatly enhanced the amount of vitamins A, D, and E in breast milk.

With *The New Breastfeeding Diet Plan*, we intend to help new moms

- Enrich their breast milk with the best possible combination of fats, vitamins, minerals, and accessory nutrients
- Aid their bodies in eliminating toxins that might otherwise go into breast milk

- Optimally nourish themselves and cleanse their bodies of toxins to help prepare for the next round of pregnancy and nursing
- Shift their baby into a healthful solid food diet and, if needed, add nutritional supplements

Today: A Changed, More Balanced Climate—or Is It?

A big push in breastfeeding education and advocacy has had major impact on women's willingness to nurse their babies. In 1970, only 26.5 percent of new mothers attempted to nurse, and virtually none were doing so when their babies reached their sixth month; by 2001, however, 69.5 percent of new mothers did at least some breastfeeding in the hospital, and 46.5 percent exclusively breast-fed in the hospital. Figures from 2001 show that 31 percent of mothers were still nursing when their children were six months old.

The goals of the U.S. Surgeon General's Healthy People 2010 are to have 75 percent of new mothers breastfeeding their newborns; 50 percent at six months; and 25 percent at one year. This would have us approaching the 79 percent of women worldwide who breastfeed their babies until they are at least one, and the 50 percent of these who nurse up until or past their children's second birthday.

On the other hand, some women feel the pressure to breast-feed—if it's against their own desires or comfort level—is overwhelming and damaging. There's talk about the "breastfeeding police," "boob zealots," "breastfeeding Nazis," and getting looked down on for not breastfeeding. Some women say they tried their best and formula was the right choice for them. Others choose formula for other reasons. Either way, they are tired of being guilt-tripped by the lactation cops.

This is a point worth considering. It's safe to assume that mothers who feel judged and pressured for choosing to formula-feed want the best for their babies just like any mom, but they don't feel they can give their babies their own best when they are breast-feeding and hating it, not making enough milk, or having other problems.

Women who firmly believe that all it takes to master breast-feeding is some good old-fashioned self-sacrifice know that there may be more to that formula-feeding woman's story than you know. Approaching this issue in the spirit of education and mutual support, not judgment, is best for the well-being and health of all babies and moms. The more breast milk you can feed your baby, the better. But you can also rest easy that formula is better than it has ever been.

2

The Fat of the Land: Does Your Breast Milk Contain the Right Fats?

A lot about breastfeeding is counterintuitive. So many women go into it thinking that it's natural, women have done it since our species existed, what could be difficult? Picture this: An exhausted, frazzled mom tries to cram her engorged breast into baby's desperately rooting little mouth. OK, got that, after a few incomplete latch-ons. But the baby gags when the milk fully lets down and barfs out the entire feeding. Try again. Baby swallows air, needs burping, does so as milk sprays and dribbles out of both breasts. Baby still hungry, what a sport he is, pretty soon they're both gonna be crying, let's get him on there again. Mom's butt has fallen asleep, there's a cramp starting in the shoulder, need to reposition baby but don't dare now that he's finally on there and eating well. By the time this natural event has run its course a half-hour later, Mom is soaked in spit-up; the breast she hasn't fed with has a giant wet spot over it and is nearly twice the size of the other; and baby is asleep, but Mom doesn't dare lay him down for fear of him waking up and having to start all over again with the other breast. Next feeding, one and a half hours. No wonder we get discouraged.

Much like breastfeeding, the relationship between a mother's diet and the nutritional content of breast milk is also counterintuitive. Studies of populations in various spots across the globe have shown that the concentration of certain nutrients in breast milk depends heavily on the concentration of those nutrients in the body of the mother. This, in turn, depends on the concentration of those nutrients in the diet of the mother.

If you are what you eat, your nursling is also what you eat, at least for some of the nutrients she needs to survive and thrive. These nutrients include total fat content; the *omega-3 fatty acids— docosahexaenoic acid* (DHA), *eicosapentaenoic acid* (EPA), and *alpha-linolenic acid* (ALA); the B vitamins—especially B_6 and B_{12}; vitamin D; the carotenoids and other antioxidant nutrients; and the minerals calcium, zinc, selenium, and iodine.

The right balance of essential fatty acids in your diet as a post-partum and/or nursing mother sets the foundation for the New Breastfeeding Diet, so we've devoted this chapter to this topic. Then, in Chapters 3 and 4, we'll look at the vitamins and minerals that are affected by the mother's intake and the effects low levels in breast milk could have on the nursing baby.

All About Fats and Oils

The most basic element of fats are the *fatty acids*: chains of carbon molecules, one to twenty-four carbons long and capped at one end by a carboxyl group (a carbon, two oxygens, and a hydrogen). Throughout this book, you'll see fatty acids referred to as fats or oils. It's all the same stuff. When we get technical, we'll usually use the term *fatty acid*. (Fatty acids aren't acidic, and won't harm your stomach.)

The carbons are bound together by single, double, or (rarely) triple bonds. The names of the different fatty acids come from the length of the carbon chain and the location of double bonds along that chain. At the site of a double or triple bond, a fatty acid is bent. Hence, the more double bonds a fatty acid has, the more curvy it is. At the sites of double or triple bonds, the fatty acid is rigid. At room temperature, this rigid, curvy shape makes the fatty acids not stack up together in a line, as the straighter saturated fatty acids do.

Fatty acids can be saturated, monounsaturated, or polyunsaturated. Double bonds make a fatty acid unsaturated. A saturated fatty acid is all single bonds, which makes it stable and gives it a shape that enables it to pack in tightly with its brethren and make crystals: a solid fat. The more double or triple bonds a fat has, the less saturated it is.

- *Saturated fatty acids* have no double bonds and create solid fats at room temperature (think butter and lard)
- *Monounsaturated fatty acids* have one double bond and are liquid oils at room temperature (think olive oil and canola oil)
- *Polyunsaturated fatty acids* have more than one double bond and are liquid oils at room temperature (think soybean, sunflower, flaxseed, and corn oil)

Oils and fats always contain a mixture of saturated, monounsaturated, and polyunsaturated fatty acids, in varying proportions. The classification of the fat or oil is based on which type of fatty acid it contains the most of. More double bonds make a fatty acid more vulnerable to *oxidation*—having an electron "stolen" from one of these double bonds, creating harmful free radicals. We'll talk more about free radicals later on; for now, suffice it to say that they are up to no good. This explains why oils rich in polyunsaturated fatty acids like linoleic acid (predominant in soybean and corn oils) oxidize and go rancid when heated to high temperatures. The six unsaturated bonds in docosahexaenoic acid (DHA), which is a very-long-chain polyunsaturated fatty acid, create a unique spiraling shape that perfectly equips it to build nerve cell connections, the photoreceptors in the retinas of the eyes, and the tissues of the cerebral cortex, the part of the brain that does higher learning and reasoning.

Monounsaturated fatty acids, like those predominant in olive oil, have a single double bond, so they're relatively stable—the best of both worlds. This explains why you can fry at high temperatures with olive oil without creating stinky, rancid grease in the process. Monounsaturated oils are healthy for Mom, but they don't give your baby the same benefits as the polyunsaturated oils rich in the omega-3 fats DHA and EPA.

Olive oil is highly recommended as part of a healthy diet. Extra-virgin olive oil contains a high-powered antioxidant called hydroxytyrosol. Olive oil also contains a newly discovered compound called oleocanthal, which has anti-inflammatory effects similar to aspirin, without aspirin's side effects.

Avoid Hydrogenated Vegetable Oils

Solid vegetable-based cooking fats like Crisco are made by bombarding polyunsaturated oils with hydrogen atoms, a process called *hydrogenation*. This creates *trans-fatty acids*, which are (mostly) bad news and should be avoided by everyone, especially nursing mothers.

When you consume this fat, those unnatural trans-fatty acids are incorporated into your cell membranes, reducing the cells' ability to function at their best. And they also go right into your breast milk and into your baby, at levels proportional to your dietary intake. These fats have been found to be more dangerous to the health of your arteries than the previously demonized saturated fats. By overconsuming those fats, you could be putting your blood vessels and those of your baby at increased risk of damage that could someday lead to a heart attack.

Omega-3 and Omega-6 Fatty Acids: Include These in Your Diet

The fatty acids that are most important for pregnant and nursing mothers are special types of polyunsaturated fatty acids: the omega-3s and omega-6s. Although polyunsaturated fats are present in breast milk at relatively low concentrations, their roles in your baby's development are important. And the amount of omega-3 fats in your diet can make a big difference in the concentration of those fats in your breast milk. Human milk concentrations of docosahexaenoic acid (DHA) have decreased in recent years. This makes good sense, considering that the ratio of omega-6s to omega-3s in the human diet has gone from about 1:1 to up to 30:1. Some women's breast milk has a ratio of omega-6 to omega-3 as high as 175:1.

Studies of the milk of nursing mothers in different parts of the world have shown that the ratio of beneficial to less beneficial fatty acids (specifically, DHA to the omega-6 fatty acids) can vary by nearly one hundredfold, depending on the diet of the mother.

The omega-3s—docosahexaenoic acid (DHA), alpha-linolenic acid (ALA), and eicosapentaenoic acid (EPA)—have their first double bond at the third carbon, hence the name *omega-3*. The *omega-6s, linoleic acid* (LA), *gamma-linoleic acid* (GLA), and *arachidonic acid* (AA), have their first double bond at the sixth carbon. The configurations of omega-6 and omega-3 oils are different, and this makes a difference in how they are used by your body and your baby's body.

LA and ALA are *essential* fatty acids. This means that they are required for life—your body can't make them, and your baby's body can't make them. They must be consumed in the foods we eat.

Both the omega-6 LA and the omega-3 ALA can be converted into long-chain polyunsaturated fatty acids. LA becomes arachidonic acid (AA), and ALA becomes DHA and EPA. We can also consume AA, DHA, and EPA in the foods we eat: meats and dairy products tend to be rich in AA, while fish and fish oils are the best known dietary sources of DHA and EPA.

ALA, which is found in many vegetables and seeds—flaxseed is a particularly good source—can be transformed into long-chain omega-3s. Some people's bodies can build long-chain omega-3s better than others.

Both AA and DHA are abundant in the cells that make up the brain and the retina (the part of the eye that translates light energy into visual information). Unlike LA and ALA, the longer-chain fatty acids are resistant to being shuttled into energy-making processes within the cells. They are more building material than fuel. When they are incorporated into the membranes that surround most of our sixty trillion body cells, long-chain polyunsaturated fatty acids make those membranes more fluid, flexible, and permeable—desirable qualities for a cell membrane.

The amount of AA in your breast milk isn't affected by your intake of this nutrient, as long as you get enough. If you are a strict vegan (eat no animal-derived foods), you could be deficient in AA, but only extreme deficiency would adversely affect breast milk concentrations.

DHA (and EPA) status of human beings is highly sensitive to our intake of foods that contain this fatty acid. There is a huge difference in DHA levels between vegans and omnivores (people who eat both meat and plant foods).

Using supplements to change levels of AA in breast milk doesn't work. But eating fish or taking fish oil supplements quickly and significantly increases the amount of DHA and EPA in a mother's body cells and in her milk.

Humans' bodies are not good at making DHA from ALA. This conversion is improved in women during the childbearing years, but there is strong evidence that women should make efforts to consume more of this nutrient in its preformed state (preferably from fish or fish oil) during pregnancy and lactation.

The weight of the scientific evidence points toward making DHA a conditionally essential fatty acid during the first months of a child's life. At this writing, some formulas are fortified with AA and DHA. You can do the same with your breast milk—ensuring that your milk falls in the higher levels of DHA content—by following our guidelines in chapters to come.

A Big Fat Tutorial: The Long Course on Fats in Nutrition

The truth about fats is this: you need them, your nursling needs them, and some kinds are better than others for both of you. However, in order to convince you that carefully taking in certain fatty acids and avoiding others will improve the health of your nursing babe, we would like to offer a crash course on the nutritional aspects of fats and oils. There's a lot more to fat than how much of it is keeping you out of your favorite prepregnancy wardrobe items. Fats are major players in the physiology of your body.

Fats Are Food—and Vehicles for Vitamins

Fat in the diet provides the body with a source of slow-burning, long-lasting energy, metabolized within the cells to power their function. Whatever fat our bodies don't need for energy or to build tissues ends up in storage depots called fat cells. Collections of those fat cells on bellies, thighs, rear ends, upper arms, and elsewhere are what has given fat a bad name. Once you see how fats are helpful, supportive, and necessary, you will, hopefully, think of fat as your friend—at least, some *types* of fat.

Without fat in the diet, we couldn't absorb the fat-soluble vitamins, A, D, E, and K. Within the body, these vitamins coexist with fats—they link up with fats as they float around in the bloodstream and hop off wherever they are needed.

Fats Comprise the Membranes That Enclose Our Cells

In his book *Smart Fats* (Berkeley, CA: Frog, Ltd., 1997), Michael A. Schmidt writes that "if we took every cell of your body, opened them up and laid their membranes out flat, they would cover an area roughly the size of 10 football fields . . . . Each of those membranes is composed of fats from the foods you eat."

Cell membranes are fluid and flexible, with specialized channels and gates that let hormones, fuel, immune factors, vitamins, and other needed substances in and wastes out. Their function is affected by the types of fats that build them, which in turn is affected by the kinds of fats you take in when you eat. When scientists measure the amounts of specific fats in your body, they do so by measuring the content of those fats in your cell membranes.

The composition of fats in your breast milk will directly affect the building of cell membranes in your baby's body, and the right fats will positively affect the fluidity of cell membranes. This, in turn, is believed to affect the action of neurotransmitters—chemical conveyors of mood, energy, appetite, intelligence, and overall well-being.

Fats Build the Brain and the Rest of the Nervous System

Research shows that changes in the concentration of certain fatty acids in the brain are associated with changes in cognitive and behavioral performance. In other words: eating more or less of certain fats will affect how you think and behave. This is true for you and for your nursling.

Your brain is 60 percent fat. Every one of your nerves is coated with a fatty *myelin sheath* that's 75 percent fat and supports quick conduction of nerve impulses (two hundred miles per hour) through your body. (Multiple sclerosis is linked with deterioration of the myelin sheath, and it has been theorized that this deterioration has to do with inadequate fatty acid nutrition in infancy.)

In the months following birth, your baby's body uses specific fats to rapidly grow nervous system tissues. The branching of neurons—the process by which the brain makes new connections to hold onto new information and facilitate new, age-appropriate behaviors—depends in part on the fats you consume in your diet. By the time a child is eight months old, around 1,000 trillion synapses have formed in his brain, or around 7,500 per brain cell. Fats are required for this process; certain fats are believed to be superior to others in this regard.

Depression, attention deficit/hyperactivity disorder (ADHD), and autism have all been linked to low levels of these same fatty acids in the body. In the eyes, the making of a substance called *rhodopsin* that captures light and turns it into visual information also depends on adequate supplies of this same kind of fat. And no, we're sorry, it's not the kind of fat you find in Ben and Jerry's ice cream.

Your Baby's Needs for Fats and Oils Differ from Yours

An infant's requirements for fats and oils are quite different from those of older children or adults. Babies require plentiful cholesterol—for example, relatively, breast milk contains six times the amount recommended for adult daily consumption. They require plentiful arachidonic acid (AA), which their cells cannot yet manufacture on their own from the essential fatty acids. Older children and adults can make adequate AA from other fatty acids.

Eating too much AA-rich food won't harm your nursling, but it could make you more irritable, allergic, prone to infection, or vulnerable to high blood pressure and excessive blood clotting. This is because excess AA alters the balance of hormone-like chemicals in the body that modulate inflammation, blood vessel constriction, blood clotting, and immune responses. Mood can also be strongly affected by this shift, a point made repeatedly by biochemist and Zone diet creator Barry Sears.

Omega-3 Nutrition Promotes Good Health in Mom and Baby

Here's what some of the research shows about EPA and DHA—the two omega-3 fats that are most likely to be missing in the modern diet:

- Mothers whose bodies contain less DHA and EPA are more vulnerable to pregnancy complications. One study found that mothers with the lowest levels of EPA and DHA in their red blood cell membranes had eight times the risk of developing preeclampsia than women with the highest EPA and DHA levels.
- Women deficient in DHA and EPA have six times the risk of severe postpartum depression and postpartum obsessive-compulsive disorder. Scientists have successfully used high-dose fish oil to treat bipolar disorder (also known as manic depression), schizophrenia, attention deficit/hyperactivity disorder, and depression not related to childbirth.
- Babies whose mothers ate fish a few times a week during pregnancy score higher on intelligence and visual acuity tests.
- Children with attention deficit/hyperactivity disorder have lower levels of DHA in their bodies. Fatty acid analysis of children with aggressive or disruptive behaviors

demonstrate low DHA as well. Preliminary research suggests that supplementing these fats in the diets of children with ADHD or aggressive behaviors will eventually become standard therapy.

- Children born prematurely are deprived of needed DHA (and AA); this may help to explain why they are at increased risk for developmental and health problems. Nature has provided a perfect delivery system for these fats during pregnancy through the placenta and umbilical cord. A growing fetus accumulates about sixty-seven milligrams of DHA every day through the third trimester of pregnancy.
- Fish oil has also been found to be therapeutic for people with irregular heartbeat (arrhythmia) and as a preventive against heart disease.

Chapter 7 will explain how to add fish to your diet, if you haven't already. We'll address concerns about mercury contamination and tell you how to maximize DHA-rich fish intake while minimizing mercury exposure. You will also find out how to choose a good fish oil supplement to enhance DHA levels in your milk. If you are still pregnant, taking DHA now will directly nourish your baby and will prepare your body to make milk rich in DHA when the time comes by increasing your body's stores of this fat.

Fatty Acids Are Chemical Messengers: The Role of Eicosanoids

Fats are the raw material from which many vitamins and hormones are manufactured in the body—particularly, a group of hormone-like substances called *eicosanoids* (eye-KOH-suh-noyds), chemical messengers that powerfully influence immunity, blood pressure, mood, skin health, and inflammation. In studies on animals and children, asthma, eczema, and allergies have been linked with diets too low in fats that are made into certain eicosanoids.

There is evidence that modulating your fatty acid balance in the ways we recommend will protect *you* against diseases linked

Genetics May Affect DHA in Moms' Milk

Genetics may play a role in the amount of DHA a woman absorbs from her diet and passes into her breast milk. Wake Forest University School of Medicine researchers gave 111 lactating women a meal with added DHA, then had them pump their milk once per hour for twelve hours. The milk, and the women's body tissues and blood, were analyzed to see how well they absorbed and utilized the DHA and passed it into their breast milk. The researchers also did genetic testing on the women to see whether they carried a specific variant of the ApoA4 gene (involved in the absorption of fat from foods) or the E4 variant of the gene ApoE, which is implicated in increased risk of Alzheimer's disease in old age. The results of the study were startling: the bodies of women with the ApoA4 variant were significantly better at getting DHA into their breast milk. The women with the ApoE4 gene—the Alzheimer's gene—had 40 to 75 percent less total fat in their breast milk than the women who did not have that ApoE4 gene. It is believed that about 20 percent of the American population carries this gene.

Richard B. Weinberg, the study's main author, cautions that a lot more research will be needed to assess the impact this research might have on women who wish to optimize the nutritional value of their breast milk. He does suggest that the addition of supplements to the mother's diet could end up being recommended to women with certain genetic variants. Dr. Weinberg's team is doing further research to find out whether genes affect a mother's body storage of DHA and other omega-3 fats during pregnancy, which can affect the availability of those fats once she starts to lactate.

with excessive inflammation in the body, including heart disease, cancer, asthma, allergies, and autoimmune disease. These benefits can be traced to the role of certain fatty acids in the making of eicosanoids.

Before you dive into this complex section, keep in mind that the issue of eicosanoid balance and its relationship to your diet has more to do with *your* health than with your baby's health—at least until your child is past one year of age.

How can any one nutrient class protect against so many health problems? The answer to this question has to do with its role as raw material for the eicosanoids.

Eicosanoids and Mom's Health. The word *eicosanoid* is derived from *eicos*, the Greek word for the number twenty. Eicosanoids are constructed from long-chain essential fatty acids, twenty carbons long. They first appeared in living organisms hundreds of millions of years ago. Nearly every one of our sixty trillion or so cells makes eicosanoids. They exist only briefly, dissolving within seconds of their creation. The balance of eicosanoids in your body is dictated by the balance of fats in your diet.

The eicosanoids are made from the short-chain polyunsaturated fatty acids LA and ALA, which first are converted into long-chain polyunsaturated fats by specialized enzymes.

In the body, LA is transformed into gamma-linolenic acid (GLA). GLA is acted upon by enzymes, transforming it into an intermediary substance called *dihomogammalinolenic acid* (DHGLA). There, it reaches a crossroad, where it can travel down one of two pathways, changing into either of the following:

- Arachidonic acid (AA)—and then into pro-inflammatory eicosanoids called *leukotriene B4* and *prostaglandin E2*
- An anti-inflammatory eicosanoid called prostaglandin E1

Whether DHGLA becomes prostaglandin E1 (good) or prostaglandin E2 and leukotriene B4 (not so good) is decided by the action of an enzyme called *delta-5-desaturase* (D-5-D).

"Good" and "Bad" Eicosanoids: An Explanation

Throughout this chapter, you will see references to "good" and "bad" eicosanoids. Let's clarify here that none of the eicosanoids are inherently good or bad. *These chemicals are all produced for a reason, and we couldn't survive without them. Problems arise when there are persistent imbalances—and the imbalances that are almost always found in people eating the standard American diet have to do with an overabundance of eicosanoids made from AA and a relative lack of eicosanoids made from eicosapentaenoic acid (EPA), another long-chain omega-3 fat from fish oil. Because of this imbalance, the AA-derived eicosanoids are often labeled "bad," while those from EPA are labeled "good."*

The "good" versions:

- *Soothe inflammation, working as natural anti-inflammatories*
- *Decrease blood pressure*
- *Make blood less prone to excessive clotting*
- *Ratchet down excessive immune responses*
- *Improve and/or even out mood*

The "bad" versions have opposing effects and:

- *Enhance inflammation*
- *Raise blood pressure and immune reactivity*
- *Increase the likelihood of mood swings, irritability, and depression*

Aspirin controls pain and inflammation and helps protect against heart disease by blocking the production of most of the eicosanoids, both "good" and "bad." But aspirin suppresses the production of an eicosanoid that

continued

is needed for intestinal health. Bleeding ulcers are not an uncommon side effect of aspirin use.

For simplicity's sake, we call the pro-inflammatory eicosanoids "bad" and the anti-inflammatory eicosanoids "good." But remember as you read that even the so-called "bad" eicosanoids have important jobs in the body.

For example: a fatty acid called prostacyclin is made from arachidonic acid, the source of the PGE2 series of eicosanoids—often referred to as "bad" because of their pro-inflammatory effects. Prostacyclin is critical for helping to keep blood vessels from constricting. The COX-2 inhibitor drug Vioxx, which was withdrawn from the market in 2004, ended up threatening heart health because it blocked the production of prostacyclin.

Strong research evidence has shown that aspirin, Vioxx, and other eicosanoid-modulating drugs offer protection against cancer when used long term. Unfortunately, the research into using eicosanoid-blocking drugs to prevent cancer revealed that the increase in heart disease risk (with Vioxx) and ulcers (with aspirin) outweighed the benefits for cancer prevention. It looks like maintaining a balance of eicosanoids that is anti-inflammatory could offer anticancer and anti–heart disease benefits.

Our bodies—and the system of eicosanoid communications between cells—evolved over millions of years. Through about 99 percent of those years, the diet humans lived on contained about a one-to-one to one-to-three ratio of omega-3 to omega-6 fats. In modern diets, this ratio has become skewed, and the result is overproduction of pro-inflammatory eicosanoids. The meats, eggs, dairy, and fish we ate in past centuries were naturally rich in omega-3 fats because they came from

> *animals that ate their natural omega-3 rich diets. Today, these foods are high in omega-6 fats, particularly AA, because they are fed primarily grains and soybeans.*
>
> *We also eat far more sugar and refined grains than any of our ancestors before us, further shifting enzyme function to produce more "bad" eicosanoids.*

D-5-D is controlled by levels of two hormones in your body: *insulin* and *glucagon*. When you eat sugars and other refined carbohydrates, insulin production rises, and so does the action of delta-5-desaturase, increasing in turn the production of AA and its pro-inflammatory eicosanoids. This is why sugar and refined carbs are, in the end, pro-inflammatory and a contributor to many health problems in our sugar-and-refined-carb-loving culture.

The conversion of DHGLA into arachidonic acid is only moderately active in humans. It's unlikely that this conversion will produce enough AA to cause an eicosanoid imbalance. Most of us consume a lot of preformed AA in our diets, providing a steady source of ready-to-use raw material for pro-inflammatory eicosanoids.

For what it's worth, though, eating a diet like the one we recommend instead of a diet high in refined carbohydrates causes D-5-D to lose some of its kick, shuttling more DHGLA into making PGE1. Adequate intake of magnesium, zinc, vitamin C, vitamin B_3, and vitamin B_6 will help shift DHGLA into "good" eicosanoid formation rather than "bad."

Another influential factor in the formation of eicosanoids is your consumption of the omega-3 fats. When you eat a food rich in alpha-linolenic acid (ALA), such as flaxseed, an enzyme called *delta-6-desaturase* (D-6-D) converts it into a substance called *stearidonic acid* (SDA). SDA is converted to eicosapentaenoic acid (EPA) by another enzyme, and then into prostaglandin E3, a very "good" eicosanoid. EPA can be transformed into docosahexaenoic acid (DHA), the omega-3 fat that is so important for the formation of the baby's nervous system and for Mom's emotional health.

Eating foods or taking supplements that are high in EPA will bypass the first part of this cascade, increasing the formation of PGE3 and of DHA. Adding EPA to your diet by eating fish will dramatically block the conversion of LA into AA—it reduces the activity of the enzyme that transforms DHGLA into AA and into "bad" PGE2 and leukotriene B4, enhancing the formation of anti-inflammatory PGE1.

Hydrogenated oils block the production of "good" eicosanoids by interfering with D-6-D activity, and should be avoided.

Does eicosanoid imbalance in Mom affect baby's health? Little research has been published specifically about the effects of over-production of "bad" eicosanoids in nursing infants—or in formula-fed infants, for that matter. But we have reason to believe that this imbalance could make a major contribution to the growing problems of eczema, asthma, chronic ear and respiratory infections, depression, anxiety, and attention and learning problems in kids over the age of one. A growing number of studies show that omega-3 fatty acid supplements can help to alleviate these conditions.

One omega-6 fatty acid, gamma-linoleic acid (GLA), is highly beneficial for preventing (or at least reducing the severity of) asthma, nasal allergy, and eczema. In the body, GLA is made into a highly anti-inflammatory substance that soothes the slow-burning inflammation that underlies eczema, asthma, and allergic rhinitis (nasal allergies). These complaints form the triad of *atopic disease.*

Atopic disease is *inflammatory*, meaning that it is caused by an out-of-balance or "overshooting" immune system response. Also, there is a genetic factor in atopic disease. If one child in a family has infant eczema, other children in the family have a 25 percent risk of developing it. Children who have two eczematous parents have a 40 percent risk of having it themselves, and children with eczema usually also have asthma and allergic rhinitis.

But could there also be an influence of breast milk fatty acid composition? And could manipulating breast milk fatty acids have a protective effect against the development of atopic disease in children who are predisposed to it?

At physician D. J. P. Barker's lab, researchers looked at fatty acid levels and markers of immune activity in breast milk samples and found that moms who were *not* atopic had more of a substance called *transforming growth factor beta* (TGF-B) in their breast milk. TGF-B is known to have anti-inflammatory effects in the body. Lack of TGF-B in the atopic moms' milk could represent a way of transferring atopy from mother to child.

These studies also found that breast milk inflammatory factors and fatty acid composition were related. There was a relationship between TGF-B and proportions of total polyunsaturated fats and omega-6 fatty acids in the breast milk samples.

Research suggests it is possible to alter maternal diet in ways that will reinforce the immunity-balancing qualities of breast milk. Much evidence points to DHA as the secret ingredient. So far, using modest amounts of DHA in nursing women (300 to 600 mg per day) hasn't proven to raise levels of immune factors known to reduce allergic diseases, but a study where fish oil supplements were started during pregnancy did lead to desirable changes in immune factors in breast milk. Research in this area is continuing.

The results of the research to date imply that fatty acid balance, eicosanoids, and immune system activity are connected in ways that could lead us to ways of preventing or controlling these common illnesses in ourselves and in our children.

As it stands, improving breast milk's fatty acid profile through the mother's diet may help and is unlikely to hurt. One 2003 study found that supplementing GLA to formula-fed infants with high risk of developing atopic disease helps reduce the severity of outbreaks of eczema. We'll give recommendations for supplements of omega-3 fats later on. If you have eczema, or your nursling is showing signs of eczema, try a supplement from borage oil or evening primrose oil that contains 200 to 1,000 mg of GLA per day.

Exclusive breastfeeding, without any introduction of solid foods, for the first six months of life protects against atopic disease. Studies have found that the longer an atopic woman continues to breastfeed, the more protected her child. Formula feeding and mixed feeding (formula and breast milk) increase a child's risk of atopic disease. Probiotics—the "friendly bacteria" found in yogurt—are also a promising nutritional intervention for atopic infants (see Chapter 10).

Lauric and Capric Acids in Breast Milk: Nice Pair of . . . Coconuts!

Lauric and capric acids are saturated fatty acids. They are found most abundantly in coconut and coconut oil. They are also made in a nursing mother's milk ducts, providing powerful defenses against infection.

Lauric and capric acids protect against microbes (HIV, herpes, chlamydia, *H. pylori*, and protozoa) that can cause infection in a baby with an immature immune system. In parts of the world where coconut is a regular part of the diet, women's milk concentrations of lauric acid can be as high as 21 percent of total saturated fat, and capric acid as high as 6 percent. Coconut oil's fatty acids have been found to promote brain development. Mouse experiments in the 1970s found that mice fed coconut oil had better, faster brain development than mice fed unsaturated vegetable oils.

Coconut oil appears to promote weight loss. In the 1940s, where farmers attempted to find ever cheaper ways to fatten cattle, they found that coconut oil had the opposite effect: the cattle got leaner and more energetic. They theorized that this was due, at least in part, to the oil's effects on the animals' thyroid glands. Feeding animals corn and soy, both of which slow the thyroid down, had the opposite effect—and this is what cattle are fattened on to this day.

Studies comparing coconut-eating populations in Mexico with Americans showed that the Mexicans had a 25 percent faster metabolic rate on average, despite the warmer climate of their Yucatan home (which usually causes metabolism to slow down).

These fats offer great protection to nursing babies. At this writing, many concerned scientists advocate the addition of lauric and capric acid to infant formulas. Nursing mothers can simply add coconut and coconut oil to their diets to increase these fats two- to threefold in their milk. You will find recipes that include coconut in Chapter 9.

What It All Means: The Skinny on Fats

To summarize our discussion of fats:

- Nursing mothers can increase their milk's content of omega-3 fats—particularly DHA—by consuming more of them through food and supplements. This will enhance the building of baby's nervous system and promote Mom's own emotional and psychological well-being.
- Avoiding hydrogenated oils and sugars and refined carbohydrates will improve fatty acid balance in a manner that will promote improved balance of eicosanoids in the body of the mother. Although the jury is still out on whether this may help to improve the health of the nursing baby, some evidence says it will.
- Adding coconut and coconut oil to a nursing mom's diet increases her milk's content of lauric and capric acids, which are antibacterial, antiviral, and brain-building, and may help to promote postpartum weight loss.

3

Vitamins: Does Your Breast Milk Have Enough?

A baby girl born to a couple in a southeastern state was not doing well. She had been breastfed through much of her first year and was given whole-grain, organic cereals and fruit shakes from eight months of age forward. Still, her growth was slow. A pediatrician diagnosed her with failure to thrive at fifteen months of age. She was severely anemic and lethargic. Her appetite was poor. She vomited often.

A series of tests determined that she didn't have any genetic problems that could explain her difficulties. She was hospitalized and given extra food through a nasogastric tube, along with high-calorie, nutrient-dense meals. More tests revealed the source of her problem: a severe deficiency of a nutrient called cobalamin, also known as vitamin B_{12}. Her blood B_{12} levels were measured at 100 picograms per milliliter (pg/mL), with normal levels between 210 and 911 pg/mL.

Restoring her to health involved intensive supplementation of this nutrient at doses of 5 milligrams per day by injection. Unfortunately, a good deal of damage had already been done. An MRI showed that her brain was smaller than normal, and at the age of twenty-eight months, her development was far behind that of her peers. Her fine motor skills were at the level of a nine-month-old and her language skills at a ten-month-old level. At thirty-two months she still had major developmental delays, especially with speech and language, despite taking daily B_{12} supplements.

This is a true story, one of two cases from a single state that were reported in the *Journal of the American Medical Association* in 2003. How could a child be so malnourished on what would seem to be an optimal infant diet?

The baby's mother had followed a vegan diet for seven years prior to the birth of her baby. She had taken nutritional supplements, but the writers of the article in *JAMA* didn't know the composition of those supplements. The mother's B_{12} stores were probably depleted well before she became pregnant. Even if her supplements had contained B_{12}, the nutrient hadn't gotten into her body or milk in amounts adequate to sustain her baby.

It's amazing that a single nutrient—or lack of it—could have such enormous effects on the well-being of a child. A nursing mother's vitamin and mineral nutrition does double duty, because it also affects her own well-being. Her own stores of a vitamin or mineral have to be quite drained for her milk to become frankly depleted; lactation is designed to give the nursling adequate nutrition even when it means taking needed nutrients from the mother.

A Short Course on Vitamin and Mineral Nutrition

Even if you had never taken vitamins before, you probably were strongly advised to do so during your pregnancy. Prenatal vitamin use cuts the risk of spina bifida and other neural tube defects by almost half when started three months before conception.

Use of a multivitamin just before and during pregnancy reduces the occurrence of heart and urinary tract defects, helps prevent cleft palate, and reduces risk of brain tumor in children. Some studies show that the best preventive measure is to start the prenatals before conception, but most indicate that starting them during pregnancy helps—and it certainly won't hurt.

You're probably familiar with the government's guidelines for minimum intakes of the various vitamins and minerals. Over the years, they've been referred to as the *Recommended Daily Allowance* (RDA), *Recommended Daily Intake* (RDI), and other collections of capital letters.

What you need to know about those guidelines is that they are neither optimal nor universal. Different bodies have different requirements for nutrients, and over a lifetime, each person's nutrient needs vary. Stressful times—including pregnancy, illness, or staying up all night with a new baby—increases need for certain nutrients. Genetics make a difference, too. Ensuring vitamin and mineral adequacy with diet and supplements will ensure that you have nutrient stores adequate for both you and your nursling.

Try to get as many of the needed vitamins, minerals, and accessory nutrients into your body and your baby's body via carefully chosen, nutrient-dense foods. On top of those foods, a multivitamin and mineral supplement and a few other supplements are smart insurance against deficiencies, but they're just that—*supplements* to a health-promoting diet. Chasing your maple pecan scone and giant decaf mochaccino with a multivitamin isn't going to keep you in top form or your breast milk optimally nutritious.

Research into the effectiveness of vitamin and mineral supplements at preventing or reversing disease processes is a mixed bag. Some studies show that vitamin C supplements help to reduce the duration of cold symptoms; other studies show that they don't. Some studies of vitamin E suggest that supplements of this nutrient protect against heart disease, while others suggest that high doses of this nutrient could actually increase risk of certain cardiovascular conditions. Large-scale studies of various populations have shown us that higher intake of these vitamins—and many other vitamins, minerals, and other kinds of nutrients—is linked with longer life and better health. Why the discrepancies?

The most likely explanation here is that nutrients are designed to work in teams, in the context of actual food. A piece of spinach is a synergistic dance of vitamins, minerals, fiber, fatty acids, proteins, water, accessory nutrients, and a lot of things we haven't discovered yet. It has evolved over billions of years to become what it is today. The same goes for a piece of meat, a fish filet, or even a slice of cheese.

A vitamin made from lab-created, isolated vitamins and minerals doesn't match up, any more than formula matches up with the

A Note About the RDA (Recommended Daily Allowance)

The RDA is the recommended dietary allowance. *It describes, according to Linda Meyers, director of the Food and Nutrition Board, "the average daily level of nutrients necessary for us to meet our nutrition requirements." Meyers says that of all the acronyms, the RDA is the one to refer to when deducing a food's nutritional value.*

The DV is the daily value, *created in 1990 by the FDA. It is meant to show label-readers how much of their daily requirement for a specific nutrient is being met by the food they're considering tossing into their shopping cart (or putting in their mouth). There are DVs for vitamins, minerals, fats, carbohydrates, and protein.*

The UL is the upper intake level. *ULs were developed as nutrition scientists culled data about possible toxicity with high doses of single nutrients. Consider the UL to be a guideline to attend to, but also keep in mind that the ULs for most nutrients are conservative— i.e., playing it safe. Even at doses above the UL for nutrients like vitamin C, vitamin D, and vitamin E, the hazards of these nutrients are completely dwarfed by those posed by many commonly prescribed, wholeheartedly FDA-sanctioned medications. (Toxic reactions to prescribed drugs are the sixth leading cause of death in the United States, while vitamin and mineral supplements have not been linked with a single death.)*

The DRI is the dietary reference intake. *When nutritionists talk about the DRI, they are referring to all the other acronyms tossed around in conversations about the nutrient content of foods: RDA, UL, DV, and others you don't need to know about unless you, too, are a nutritionist.*

The RDA, DV, and DRI are useful as broad recommendations, but incomplete. You can get adequate nutrition from a diet and supplement program tailored to meet these recommendations, but you can also fine-tune and "amp up" your program in certain areas that can safely enhance your health and the nutritive value of your breast milk.

fresh dairy made in a lactating woman's breasts. This is not to discourage you from taking supplements—we will make detailed recommendations about that—but to drive home the message that a well-designed diet provides a necessary foundation.

Some less-than-forthright purveyors of vitamins, minerals, and herbs will sometimes try to sell products by describing them in the same terms as the mainstream medical magic bullets of drugs and surgery. Instead of antidepressant drugs, they recommend "herbal Prozac" (Saint-John's-wort) or "herbal antibiotics" (goldenseal or echinacea). This is deceptive advertising. Don't believe it.

When you use nutritional supplements, the emphasis should be on three key factors:

- Enhancing overall health
- Balancing immune function
- Supporting metabolism and detoxification

Nutritional and herbal supplements aren't drugs. They have diverse effects that promote improved health and energy in a variety of ways, enabling the body to heal itself.

Macronutrients and Micronutrients

When you eat food, your digestive tract breaks it down into its most basic components: fats, carbohydrates, and proteins, otherwise known as *macronutrients*; and vitamins, minerals, and accessory nutrients, which are called *micronutrients*.

Generally, modern people in Westernized countries consume an abundance of macronutrients—we eat some three hundred calories more per day than people did in the 1970s—but those macronutrients tend to come in forms that aren't married to the micronutrients. Calorie-dense, highly processed foods made from sugar, flour, other grains (like corn), and oil are mainstays of our modern diets. These foods give us plenty of energy, much of which ends up stored as fat, but they don't offer high concentrations of the micronutrients we require.

Changing the way we eat requires motivation, which in turn requires education about why the good choices are good (and the bad choices bad).

Vitamins to Include in Your Diet

If you're nursing, think twice about putting those prenatal vitamins away. Your body has a lot of recovering to do and a lot of milk to produce. Even if you are not nursing, you need vitamins: you've used a lot of your body's nutrient stores to build a baby.

Vitamins act as catalysts in the chemical reactions that go on within each of our body cells, making these reactions go smoothly and maintaining normal growth, development, immunity, and day-to-day physiological function.

Vitamins are required in minuscule amounts by the body, but we can't live without most of them. Vitamin D and vitamin K can be made in the body, but most vitamins have to be consumed in the foods we eat. Even nutrients made in the body can be needed in the diet under more stressful circumstances or when needed dietary factors for making them are missing.

Vitamins work at the level of individual cells. Each of our body cells is its own tiny factory, making energy out of calories and using that energy to drive a wildly diverse and complex group of physiological activities, including the building of new, healthy cells. This process is running like gangbusters in the body of your new bundle of joy.

Each of our organs is made up of different kinds of cells, each of them with specialized functions. All cells require vitamins to drive the processes that create energy and get rid of the waste prod-

Choosing Quality Supplements: What to Look for

The market for supplements has exploded, and it's not easy to know what you're getting. Here are some points to consider as you make your choices about vitamins, minerals, herbs, or some other natural supplement.

- *Reputation and longevity of the company. Talk to the employees at the health food store about supplement companies. A few stand out for their longevity and for having higher standards.*
- *Willingness of the company to disclose source products, harvesting and extraction methods, choice of ingredients. Call or visit company websites to see whether they openly share this information.*
- *Standardization of ingredients. Many products contain herbal extracts that are standardized to contain a certain amount of a well-researched "active constituent." These products are generally of higher quality.*

Independent comparison of different supplement brands can be found at consumerlab.com. Subscribers have access to detailed comparative information on a variety of supplements. Some material is available free on the site.

ucts created by cellular activities. When you consider that typical cells are only twenty micrometers across—a human hair is ten times as wide—their diversity of function and the variety of the materials they need to perform these functions is astonishing.

Many processed foods have vitamins added back in after they've been stripped out by processing. But these foods are lacking in many other ways: they are low in fiber, high in sugar, or loaded with unhealthy oils. There are better sources for the vitamins you need for yourself and for your nursing baby.

Vitamin B_{12}

This nutrient is also called *cobalamin*, because it contains an ion of the metal cobalt. Cyanocobalamin is a form of the nutrient that easily converts to active forms in the body.

Vitamin B_{12} is needed to transform one amino acid, homocysteine, into another, methionine. In turn, methionine is required for reactions in the body that are important for the creation and maintenance of DNA and RNA, the genetic templates from which our cells—and, ultimately, our bodies—are made. A growing infant's body is making new cells like mad, and when B_{12} isn't available in adequate supply, growth and development suffer. It converts folic acid (discussed in the next section) into its active form; plays a pivotal role in the synthesis of DNA and RNA, cells' genetic material; is needed to make myelin, the fatty sheath that rapidly conducts nerve impulses; maintains optimum fat metabolism; and promotes better antioxidant function in the body.

In one interesting study, researchers found that breastfed babies had gradual increases in homocysteine levels as their mothers' B vitamin status gradually declined. The implications of elevated homocysteine levels in babies aren't yet known.

What's the RDA? The RDA for B_{12} is 2.4 micrograms (mcg) a day.

Best food sources. Three ounces of the following foods have the specified amount of vitamin B_{12}: clams (84 mcg), mussels (20.4 mcg), crab (8.8 mcg), salmon (2.4 mcg), beef (2.1 mcg).

Risks of not getting enough. Shortage of B_{12} in adults can potentially lead to increased risk of cancer (because DNA methylation is believed to help prevent cancer) and heart disease (because homocysteine accumulates and has damaging effects on blood vessel walls). B_{12} is also needed for the proper formation and activity of the nervous system. Deficiency of B_{12} can lead to a specific type of anemia—pernicious anemia—as this nutrient is crucial for the proper formation of red blood cells. Adequate vitamin B_{12} is also necessary for the proper activity of another B vitamin, folate, in the human body.

B_{12} lack has also been linked with depression and foggy thinking. Methylation reactions help to make the neurotransmitters that can make or break our moods. Studies have found that 30 percent of people hospitalized for depression are deficient in vitamin B_{12}; also, that B_{12}-deficient women over the age of sixty-five were two times more likely to suffer from severe depression than women who were not deficient. Vitamin B_{12} is a commonly recommended natural therapy for low energy.

According to the Centers for Disease Control, it is difficult to diagnose vitamin B_{12} deficiency in babies because the symptoms can be so varied and are also characteristic of other health problems.

When you are pregnant or nursing, you are at higher risk of depletion, and it's worthwhile to use supplements or eat foods rich in B_{12} often. Breastfed babies have been found to have B_{12} levels lower than those of babies fed formula.

Who's at risk for deficiency? Most at risk for B_{12} deficiency are vegetarians—especially vegans, who avoid all animal products, including meat, dairy, and eggs. Veg-friendly websites and books may claim that seaweed, tempeh, and miso are good sources of B_{12}, but research shows that they are unreliably absorbed by the body. The science on this is conclusive: plant foods that are not fortified are not adequate sources of B_{12}. There is an inarguable link between vegan or almost-vegan diets and B_{12} deficiency, particularly in breastfed babies of vegan or nearly vegan mothers. Any woman who is wholeheartedly committed to vegetarianism should take special care to use a B_{12} supplement that fulfills her needs and enriches her milk.

Ensuring adequacy for mom and baby. Vegetarianism expert Reed Mangels advises vegans to use a brand of nutritional yeast called Red Star T-6635 (may be labeled Vegetarian Support Formula), which contains active, bioavailable vitamin B_{12}. Some soy and rice milks, vegetarian "meats" made from soy protein, and some cereals (not all) are fortified with this vitamin. (Fortified cereals alone are not, according to the *Physicians' Desk Reference*, adequate sources of B_{12}.) Supplements labeled as having vitamin B_{12} may or may not contain a form that is bioavailable. The only truly reliable food sources of vitamin B_{12} are animal products, including meat, dairy products, and eggs.

Even if you take many times the dose we are recommending, B_{12} poses no danger to you, or to your baby when she gets more through your milk. All commercially available formulas include bioavailable forms of this nutrient.

Supplements: what kind, how much. Typical prenatal and postpartum supplements contain 10 to 12 micrograms of B_{12}. Take B_{12} one or two times weekly—500 to 1,000 micrograms is the usual dosage range. Or, if you prefer to take it daily, use 100 micrograms per day. Sublingual (under-the-tongue) or intranasal supplements are more effectively absorbed. If you have had a gastric bypass operation, or if you have Crohn's disease or celiac disease (extreme sensitivity to wheat, causing damage to the inner lining of the intestines), you will need a sublingual or intranasal supplement to ensure absorption.

Potential risks and interactions. None reported.

Folic Acid/Folate

Increased need for folic acid during pregnancy and breastfeeding is well established. Amounts in mothers' milk do not vary much in women who, overall, have adequate nutrition, but it deserves a mention here anyhow.

This B vitamin is well known for its role in preventing neural tube defects when taken during pregnancy. Deficiency during pregnancy is associated with low birth weight. Recent studies find that prenatal supplements of folic acid may help to prevent neuroblastoma and acute lymphoblastic leukemia—both deadly cancers—in children. Deficiency can cause anemia. Folic acid is protective of heart health, helping to keep levels of homocysteine, a substance that damages blood vessels, low in the body. It is believed to protect adults against several cancers, including colon and breast cancers. Much of folic acid's benefit arises from its role in producing and maintaining new cells—specifically, the DNA and RNA that are cells' genetic material.

Folic acid is the natural form of the vitamin found in food; the synthetic version used to supplement processed foods and in vitamins is folate. In your multivitamin supplement, you should get at least 500 to 600 micrograms of folic acid (the folate form is fine). Eat plenty of green vegetables, whole grains, beans, and brown rice, and make fortified processed grain-based foods a minor source of this nutrient.

Vitamin B_6 (Pyridoxine)

This vitamin plays an integral role in the functioning of the nervous and immune systems, in the making of new cells, and for the making of the neurotransmitters that conduct the symphony of your moods. It also is needed for the maintenance of steady blood sugar levels: when you go without food for a few hours, B_6 is part of the system your body uses to access stored carbohydrates and fats, transforming them into glucose (sugars) that can be used by your cells for energy.

What's the RDA? The RDA for B_6 in lactating or pregnant women is 2 mg per day.

Risks of not getting enough. Severe deficiency of pyridoxine is rare in developed nations like the United States. With mild to moderate lack of B_6, you may have what's known as a subclinical deficiency—not enough to be characterized as deficient, but enough to cause relatively mild alterations in the way your body and mind function. This is true of most vitamins.

If a mother had low B_6 reserves during pregnancy, her baby may not have put away enough of this nutrient to last through an extended period of exclusive breastfeeding. The risk of B_6 deficiency is higher in babies who are exclusively breastfed beyond six months of age. Moms whose nurslings show little to no interest in solid foods even after the first six months can help ensure that adequate amounts of B_6 go into their breast milk by eating foods rich in B_6 and by continuing with a high-potency prenatal supplement for as long as baby nurses.

Research shows us that when a mother does not take in enough B_6, this is reflected in her breast milk. A study published in the *Journal of the American Dietetic Association* in 2002 found that scores on tests of habituation (a measurement of learning where the child stops reacting to the environment in ways that aren't needed) and autonomic stability (maintenance of stable breathing and heart rate in response to changes in the child's environment— a good measurement of nervous system development) were higher in infants whose mothers had higher B_6 levels in their milk.

Researchers at the University of Helsinki in Finland monitored forty-four infants for both their B_6 status and their growth. The infants who had low B_6 status between the ages of four and six months grew more slowly and had a greater decline in growth in length for age at ages six to nine months compared to those with higher B_6 levels.

Best food sources. A serving of the following foods has the specified amount of vitamin B_6: ½ cup fortified, ready-to-eat cereal (2.00 mg—check the label of your cereal to be sure it contains B_{12}), a baked potato with skin (.70 mg), a banana (.68 mg), ½ cup garbanzo beans (.57 mg), a chicken breast (.52 mg), 1 cup fortified oatmeal (.42 mg), 3 oz. pork loin (.42 mg).

Who's at risk for deficiency? Ironically, a woman who eats lots of processed, vitamin-enriched cereals and breads—which are not exactly health-promoting foods—is likely to get more B_6 than a woman who subsists mostly on vegetables and fruit.

Ensuring adequacy for mom and baby. A woman with access to a varied diet will be able to get the RDA, no problem. Because this nutrient is so important for development, and because studies demonstrate that good development is promoted when breast milk B_6 levels are higher, supplements seem like a good idea. Most prenatal/postpartum multivitamin supplements contain 25 to 50 mg of B_6.

Potential risks and interactions. Some research has looked into a relationship between low B$_6$ levels, premenstrual syndrome (PMS), and depression. So far, supplementing B$_6$ in women with either set of symptoms hasn't yielded significant benefits—in fact, high-dose B$_6$ (100 or more milligrams per day) in women with PMS has been found to *cause* neurological symptoms, and we don't recommend it.

Vitamin D

Vitamin D is made in the skin from the combination of cholesterol and ultraviolet rays from the sun and is transformed into a hormone-like substance in the body. This hormone-like substance communicates to the intestines that it's time to increase absorption of the bone-building minerals calcium and phosphorus.

Vitamin D is also found in some foods—most notably, fish, egg yolks, and fortified dairy products. Cod liver oil, which some older folks might have been forced to take as kids to prevent the vitamin D deficiency disease rickets, is a common supplemental source of this vitamin. But the best place to get enough—and not too much—is from the sun.

Sunshine is nature's plan for supplying adequate vitamin D to the human body. In one half-hour sunbathing session, under direct sun in the middle of the day, Caucasian skin can make 10,000 to 12,000 IU of vitamin D. Darker-skinned people need more time: a very dark-skinned person requires 120 minutes of sun exposure to make this much vitamin D. Depending on your level of brownness, you'll need something in between. It's the UV rays that make vitamin D production happen; sunscreen and glass windows block UV rays, and so they block vitamin D production.

Vitamin D is a fat-soluble vitamin that can be stored in the body for leaner times. A few sessions of sunbathing in the direct sun of summer can fulfill vitamin D requirements for months following. But people who live in areas where sunshine is scarce may have trouble fulfilling their requirements for vitamin D. Smog and industrial pollution, far-out geographic latitude, and cloud cover can get in the way of the UV light needed to make vitamin D.

Every mother knows how important it is to protect her children against overexposure to the sun. Every mother knows that too much sun on her own skin will lead to wrinkles, brown spots, even skin cancer. But a child who is exclusively breastfed, not supplemented, and kept completely out of the sun can end up not getting enough of this vitamin.

What's the RDA? The RDA for pregnant and lactating women is 400 IU per day. For babies, the recommendation is 200 IU per day.

Risks of not getting enough. A child who fits the preceding description has a good chance of developing rickets, a disfiguring bone disease that is a direct result of vitamin D deficiency. Rickets deforms the legs, arms, spine, skull, and chest, and may cause fractures, seizures, dental deformities, and pain.

As levels of vitamin D rise in the body, calcium absorption increases. Intake of 3,000 IU a day was found in one study to boost calcium absorption by 65 percent. In adults, vitamin D deficiency can lead to a weakening and softening of the bones called *osteomalacia*.

Vitamin D is involved in immune system function and in helping to prevent the abnormal cellular reproduction that yields cancerous cells. Inadequate intake of this nutrient has been linked to many health problems: increased cancer risk, depression, seasonal affective disorder, bipolar disorder, even schizophrenia.

The number of depressed people in the United States rose dramatically in the years following World War II—years during which Americans spent more and more time indoors, out of the sun. Children born in the winter or spring, when sunlight is scarce, have slightly higher risk of schizophrenia, bipolar disorder, autism, and depression. Studies show that people with depression and schizophrenia have lower levels of vitamin D; other research suggests that in healthy men, there are strong correlations between the amount of sunshine exposure and the production of the "feel-good" neurochemical serotonin in the brain. It's just a theory, but a link between inadequate vitamin D and psychological complaints is far from improbable.

Research shows that people who get more sunshine are protected against cancers of the breast, colon, and prostate, and they are less likely to become depressed. Sun-worshippers can even relieve symptoms of psoriasis, multiple sclerosis (MS), and tuber-culosis by taking a sun-splashed constitutional.

Who's at risk of deficiency? With parents keeping children out of the sun, and the rising number of women exclusively breastfeeding for the first six months, the incidence of rickets—a disease once thought to have been eradicated—is rising. Many women's milk is too low in this vitamin to be the baby's only source.

A survey of American adults from various locations across the United States found that 42.4 percent of African-American women and 4.2 percent of Caucasian women had low levels of vitamin D in their bloodstreams.

A recent study from the University of Manitoba, Canada, found that half of mothers and a third of infants tested were defi-cient in vitamin D. Deficient infants weighed more and were longer than the nondeficient infants, but they had lower bone mass rela-tive to their body weight.

Children who are not given any dairy products because of lac-tose intolerance or who are from vegan families, and breastfed babies with lactose intolerant moms, are at heightened risk of vita-min D deficiency. Women who wear head coverings and clothing that covers most of their skin are also at risk of vitamin D lack, and so is their breast milk.

Food consumption records from the Institute of Medicine (IOM) show that the intakes of vitamin D in pregnant and lactat-ing women are below the current recommendations of 400 IU per day. Breast milk averages about 25 IU per liter.

Ensuring adequacy for mom and baby. The American Academy of Pediatrics recommends that infants be kept out of direct sunlight and be slathered with sunscreen and/or covered with protective clothing, and that they be given 200 IU of vitamin D a day start-ing at age two months—unless they are weaned to two cups per day of vitamin D–fortified formula. But vitamin D adequacy for a nursing baby can be achieved without supplements if both nursing mom and baby get fifteen to twenty minutes of sunshine two or three days a week.

We don't wish to discourage the use of sunscreens, but we do feel we should point out that widespread use of sunscreens has not yet been found to protect against melanoma (the deadliest form of skin cancer) or basal cell skin cancers (the most common form). In fact, sunscreen has been linked with *higher* incidence of melanoma and basal cell skin cancers—not in all studies, but in some.

Best sources. You and your baby can make plenty of vitamin D in a fifteen- to twenty-minute period of sun exposure twice weekly. As soon as you begin to burn even slightly, you've gotten as much vitamin D as you'll get from this sunbathing session. If you're going to stay out longer, use a sunscreen that's SPF 15 or greater, reapplying it to your skin and baby's skin every two hours and after swimming. And if you'd rather avoid the sun, you can still get more vitamin D into your body and your breast milk through supplementation. Vitamin D supplements for infants two months of age and older are also available. There is no risk in giving these supplements to your baby—and they can protect her against rickets now and osteomalacia and osteoporosis later.

If you would like to try to add more UVB to your life to boost your body's production of vitamin D and improve winter blahs, commercially available UVB lamps can be used for both purposes.

Supplements: what kind, how much. At this writing, vitamin D supplementation—200 IU per day—is recommended for all breastfed babies by the American Academy of Pediatrics and others. Keep in mind, however, that if the mother's levels are adequate or better than adequate, the amount of vitamin D in her milk will increase.

A study by research team Bruce Hollis and Carol Wagner examined the effects of either 2,000 or 5,000 IU of vitamin D per day in lactating women—five and ten times the RDA. After three months of breastfeeding, the babies' vitamin D levels were within optimum ranges. Earlier studies found that 1,000 IU for Mom didn't do the trick; 2,000 IU was the minimum dose for moving adequate vitamin D into breast milk.

Potential risks and interactions. Toxic accumulation of vitamin D has been reported, especially when coupled with high intake of foods fortified with vitamin D. Symptoms of toxicity include heightened blood calcium levels, which in turn can cause confusion, irregular heartbeat, and deposits of calcium and phosphate in soft tissues such as the kidneys. You cannot get too much vitamin D from the sun. Any excess made during a sunbathing session is destroyed.

Supplements containing anywhere from 800 to 2,000 IU are safe to use daily. Studies have shown that doses as high as 4,000 IU per day are safe, and that *hypercalcemia*—heightened levels of calcium in the blood, which can be very dangerous—fails to develop at daily doses below 40,000 IU per day. Vitamin D toxicity is a rare condition.

Remember that the 2,000 IU intake is the one that has been demonstrated to reliably increase milk levels of this vitamin. There's no need to go beyond this dosage level without physician guidance.

If you are using cod liver oil as a DHA and EPA supplement, it may contain all the vitamin D you need, unless it's a brand with reduced vitamin D.

Vitamin C

Vitamin C is important for good immune system function. It is an antioxidant, which means that it helps to prevent damage done by free radicals in the body (as explained in the sidebar "Antioxidants and Free Radicals Explained"). Vitamin C also plays a central role in the building and maintenance of connective tissue—the stuff that holds your skin, tendons, muscles, gums, and organs together.

Vitamin C is so important that most animals make their own. Humans and guinea pigs are among the only animals that don't make abundant vitamin C in their own bodies. It is water soluble, like the B vitamins, which means that it cannot be stored in the body. Whatever you take in that you don't need is eliminated through the urine.

What's the RDA? According to government guidelines, women aged nineteen and older are advised to get 75 mg of vitamin C per day. The RDA for pregnant women is 80 mg a day, and for lactating women, the requirement is 120 mg a day. Infants from birth to

Antioxidants and Free Radicals Explained

The process of cellular metabolism—where energy is made out of the foods we eat—creates renegade electrons called free radicals. *Electrons, which like to travel in pairs, are split off singly, and they tear about looking for a new electron partner. They'll try to take it from proteins, DNA, or fats, causing damage that is believed—over time—to increase risk of cancer, heart disease, and premature aging.*

When free radicals attack DNA, they can cause genetic mutations that increase risk of cancer. When free radicals attack fats or cholesterol, they create oxidized versions of these fats. Oxidized fats and cholesterol are believed to be damaging to blood vessels, speeding up the progression of heart disease.

When free radicals attack proteins, they can change their configuration, making them unsuitable for their roles as building materials in the body. Exposure to pollutants and toxins increases free radical production in the body, raising requirements for antioxidant nutrients.

Polyunsaturated fats like EPA, DHA, and AA are especially vulnerable to damage by free radicals, so it's important to get plenty of antioxidant nutrients in the diet and in supplement form if you eat a lot of these fats or take them as supplements. Evidence from hundreds of studies implicates free radical overload as an underlying cause of many diseases. Fortunately, we have a natural defense: antioxidants.

Right where energy is produced in the cells, antioxidant substances that are made in the body hang out, waiting to donate electrons to "quench" free radicals. The raw materials found in a health-promoting diet help to ensure that your body cells can make adequate amounts of these endogenous antioxidants. Staying fit and well-rested will also support better production of these substances.

Certain vitamins found in healthy diets—including vitamin E, vitamin C, and carotenes—perform the same job. Substances found in culinary and medicinal herbs, tea, coffee, and even chocolate have proven to have powerful antioxidant activity.

The research on the potential health benefits of single antioxidants in higher doses—especially vitamin C— is still not conclusive. The safest route at this writing is to try to maintain balance and not rely upon any one nutrient to pave the way to better breast milk or better health for you.

Free radicals can do good in the body and in breast milk. They are used as weapons against bacteria, viruses, and other infectious agents. Breast milk has naturally high levels of certain free radicals that team up with nutrients to knock out bacteria. Formula has no such free radical activity. Maintaining health is not about eradicating free radicals altogether, but about establishing a balance that is similar to what humans evolved on over the millennia. However, with free radical sources—namely, pollutants in our foods and environment—on the rise, and with food sources of antioxidants on the decline, it stands to reason that some extra antioxidants will work to our advantage.

Total antioxidant capacity of breast milk is higher in moms who consume more antioxidants in food and as supplements. Take in a wide variety of antioxidant-rich foods and supplements like leafy green vegetables, chlorella, green tea, berries, and purple grape juice (more on these in later chapters); don't rely on high-dose supplements of single antioxidants like C or E.

six months of age are said to require 40 mg per day; from seven to twelve months of age, 50 mg per day; and from ages one to three, they should get at least 15 mg per day.

Risks of not getting enough. Extreme vitamin C deficiency causes scurvy, a disease virtually unknown today. Scurvy causes easy bleeding and bruising, hair and tooth loss, and joint pain and swelling. You only need to consume 5 to 7 mg of vitamin C each day to prevent scurvy.

Research dating back to the 1960s strongly suggests that taking a little more vitamin C is supportive of improved immunity and antioxidant protection. A lot of energy has gone toward figuring out whether high-dose vitamin C helps prevent or shorten the duration of colds, flus, and other contagious illnesses and whether high-dose vitamin C given intravenously is a useful tool in helping people recover from cancer. Lower blood levels of vitamin C (and of alpha-carotene, beta-carotene, and beta-cryptoxanthin, described in a section to come) in children have been linked with significantly increased risk of developing asthma.

Who's at risk for deficiency? The risk of vitamin C deficiency isn't high, even in mothers who are pregnant or breastfeeding. But it has been established that women who consume more vitamin C from food and supplements will make milk richer in this nutrient. A study of European and African lactating women found that supplementing 1,000 mg per day of vitamin C tripled the content of this vitamin in the African mothers' milk (the vitamin C content of their milk was, on average, 50 percent lower than that of the European moms to start with). Three to five daily servings of orange juice doubled their milk's vitamin C content.

There is considerable evidence that more vitamin C is better for both halves of the mother-infant dyad. This may be particularly true for premature babies. Health problems that often threaten the lives of preemies—including necrotizing enterocolitis, lung disease, retinopathy of prematurity, and intraventricular hemorrhage—can be traced back, at least in part, to excessive oxidative stress (free radical production). One study showed lower levels of a marker of oxidative stress in breastfed than formula-fed premature babies during the first two weeks of life. While formulas do contain many antioxidant nutrients, breast milk contains several antioxidant enzymes that can't be added to formulas.

Even full-term newborns have been found to be under a lot of oxidative stress. It appears that this is just a fact of early life. Not coincidentally, the highest antioxidant levels in human milk appear in colostrum.

Researchers have begun to investigate whether supplemental antioxidants could help newborns to move through this early time. The best way to achieve this end is to get extra antioxidants into Mom—who probably could use them herself—and into her milk.

Some research points to a role of supplemental vitamin C in helping to reduce levels of lead in nursing moms and in their breast milk. Studies show that elevated blood lead levels tend to be associated with low blood vitamin C levels. A study of dairy cows found that injecting vitamin C into their udders helped them to resist mastitis caused by *E. coli*.

Greater concentrations of vitamin C in breast milk have been found to reduce a child's chances of developing atopic disease (eczema, allergy, and asthma). A research team from the University of Turku in Finland found that the greater an atopic mother's intake of vitamin C from foods, the more went into her milk; and the more C went into her milk, the less risk her infant had of developing atopic disease.

Ensuring adequacy for mom and baby. A vitamin C–rich diet contains lots of citrus fruit, citrus juices, strawberries, tomatoes, sweet red peppers, and broccoli. Some of these foods don't agree with mom or baby; some moms will find that if they consume these foods, their nursling develops mild allergic reactions or gas. Any nursing mother who can't or won't eat vitamin C–rich foods on a daily basis should supplement with this nutrient.

Supplements: what kind, how much. The recommended upper intake limit for adults nineteen and older is 2,000 mg per day. Taking 1,000 mg of supplemental vitamin C per day will put more of this vitamin into your breast milk. You can take C in powdered, chewable, or pill form; if the acidity of ascorbic acid, the most commonly used form of this nutrient, irritates your stomach, try buffered calcium or sodium ascorbate. If your supplement does not contain citrus bioflavonoids, take them separately; flavonoids are necessary for proper vitamin C absorption and utilization.

Potential risks/interactions. Taking more than 10,000 mg of vitamin C a day can cause diarrhea. There's no reason for a nursing woman to take this much vitamin C.

The antioxidant vitamins work together with your body's natural antioxidants in a cooperative way. In test tube studies, most antioxidants have been found to become oxidized—in other words, they become free radicals—when they donate electrons to "quench" other free radicals. Ideally, plenty of other antioxidants are around to reactivate that spent antioxidant.

Studies where subjects take high doses of single antioxidant nutrients, such as vitamin C, E, or beta-carotene, often report less than exciting findings with regards to prevention of disease. This is most likely due to the interactive nature of the antioxidants. They have to work together in a balanced fashion, or you could end up with more free radicals than you started with.

Vitamin A

While labels and nutrition experts tend to refer to vitamin A and beta-carotene as one and the same, they are, in fact, quite different. There are hundreds of carotenoids found in plants, and about 10 percent of them—including beta-carotene—can be transformed into vitamin A, also known as retinol. We'll address carotenes in the next section.

Retinol is, as the name suggests, important in the formation of the retina, the part of the eye that transforms light into nerve impulses that zip into the appropriate place in the brain for translation into images.

One form of vitamin A—made in the body from vitamin A found in foods or made from carotenes—is called *retinoic acid*.

Storage of Breast Milk Reduces Its Vitamin C Content

For moms who pump and store breast milk: keep in mind that after twenty-four hours in the refrigerator, human milk has lost, on average, a third of its vitamin C. A month in the freezer has the same effect. The range of vitamin C loss varies between 6 and 76 percent in the fridge and 3 to 100 percent in the freezer.

Avoid storing milk for more than a few hours in the fridge if you want to ensure optimal nutritional value. If you won't be using it within a few hours, freeze it and use it within a week or two. If you have to use milk stored for long periods, consider adding 20 to 40 mg of powdered vitamin C in the ascorbate form (it's buffered so that it is not acidic; most vitamin C supplements are in the form of ascorbic acid) to the bottle before feeding.

This form of vitamin A plays a pivotal role in the way that genetic material in DNA is translated into the synthesis of proteins.

Vitamin A enhances immune function and maintains the integrity of the skin and the cells that line the respiratory, urinary, and digestive tracts, boosting their resistance against becoming infected by bacteria or other invading pathogens. It also helps to make the white blood cells that are one of the body's first-line defenses against infection, and to make the red blood cells that carry oxygen around in the bloodstream.

What's the RDA? Infants aged zero to six months: 1,333 IU (400 micrograms) a day; infants aged seven to twelve months: 1,667 IU (500 mcg) a day; children one to three years old: 1,000 IU (300 mcg) a day.

In pregnancy, a woman over nineteen needs 2,567 IU (770 mcg) a day; under nineteen the recommended dose is 20 IU lower.

For breastfeeding women: 4,000 IU (1,200 mcg) a day for women nineteen and under; 4,333 IU (1,200 mcg) a day for women over nineteen.

Risks of not getting enough. Vitamin A adequacy is a major hurdle for most of the babies born worldwide. Insufficient dietary supplies of this vitamin are the leading preventable cause of blindness in developing nations. Children who are even mildly deficient in vitamin A are more at risk for respiratory diseases, diarrhea, blindness, and death from infectious disease.

During a baby's development in the mother's belly, vitamin A deficiency—and excess—can cause birth defects. Inadequate vitamin A can hamper proper development of baby's arms and legs, eyes, heart, and ears, while too much of this fat-soluble vitamin during pregnancy has been indisputably linked with birth defects.

Who's at risk for deficiency? Outright vitamin A deficiency is rare in developed countries. A lactating mother who is consuming preformed vitamin A and/or foods rich in carotenes that are transformed into vitamin A passes that bounty along to her nursling.

Best food sources. Cod liver oil (4,500 IU per teaspoon), fortified breakfast cereal (500 to 770 IU; check label), eggs (296 IU per one large), butter (317 IU per tablespoon), whole milk (227 IU per eight ounces), two percent milk (447 IU per eight ounces), nonfat milk (500 IU per eight ounces).

Ensuring adequacy for mom and baby. A Brazilian research group found that vitamin A levels were higher in hindmilk than in foremilk. If a baby isn't allowed to nurse long enough to get to the richer hindmilk, she may not get all the vitamin A she would if allowed to nurse as long as she likes on the first side before shifting to the second.

Supplements: what kind, how much. A single teaspoon of cod liver oil contains 4,500 IU of preformed vitamin A. Because of concerns over vitamin A toxicity during pregnancy and nursing, we do not recommend cod liver oil as a daily supplement for women in the thick of either of these wonderful transformations.

Use a prenatal multiple vitamin that supplies no more than 3,000 IU of preformed vitamin A (retinol) per day. Many contain 5,000 IU of vitamin A plus carotenes, with 50 percent as beta-carotene.

Check labels on packaged foods to see whether preformed vitamin A has been added. It's conceivable that you could get into dangerous levels of vitamin A consumption with a 5,000 IU-per-day supplement program plus a lot of vitamin A–enriched food.

Potential risks/interactions. Prescription medicines with vitamin A activity—tretinoin (Retin-A) and isotretinoin (Accutane) are two examples—are highly potent medicines that should not be used even within months of pregnancy, and certainly not during breast-feeding. Women who take retinoid drugs to treat severe acne or psoriasis (which can be treated with etretinate or acitretin) should take extreme care to avoid pregnancy, and they should not breastfeed.

Symptoms of vitamin A toxicity—also known as *hypervitaminosis A*—include nausea, headache, fatigue, poor appetite, dizziness, and dry skin.

Carotenes/Carotenoids

A *carotenoid* is a yellow, orange, or red pigment made in a plant, lending it brilliant color—unless that color is masked by the more overpowering green of chlorophyll. Some six hundred carotenoids exist in nature, but beta-carotene, alpha-carotene, lutein, lycopene, beta-cryptoxanthin, and zeaxanthin are the most abundant carotenoids in our food supply. Of these, only alpha- and beta-carotene and beta-cryptoxanthin can be transformed into retinol (vitamin A) in the body. Another way of putting this is that they have "vitamin A activity."

The official biological function of carotenoids is their role in ensuring adequate vitamin A. But these pigments have other salutary effects on the body as well. They work as antioxidants. In fact, this is the role they play in plants: quenching the abundant free radicals that form while plants soak up UV rays from the sun.

What's the RDA? No RDA has been established.

Risks of not getting enough. In a multinational study of well-nourished mothers in Australia, Chile, Canada, China, Japan, Mexico, the Philippines, England, and the United States, University of Arizona researchers found sizeable differences in the concentration of breast milk carotenoids. Japanese mothers' milk had the highest concentration of carotenoids, and Philippine mothers the lowest. Beta-cryptoxanthin levels varied up to ninefold between these populations, with others varying between ninefold and threefold. The research team proposed that infants getting less carotenoid nutrition might be compromised in terms of their immunity and vitamin A status.

Who's at risk for deficiency? A nursing mom who doesn't eat a diet containing five or more servings of colorful vegetables and fruit each day is probably not getting enough carotenoids or getting optimal amounts of these nutrients into her milk.

The price of a low-carotene diet isn't known for sure, but diets high in the carotenoids have been associated with decreased risk of heart disease and some cancers. Lutein and zeaxanthin are especially good for the eyes, protecting the retinas against free radical damage from highly energized blue light wavelengths present in sunlight that can, over years, cause cataract or macular degeneration (a blinding eye disease).

Carotenes have been found to help preserve the *differentiation* of cells: healthy cells in various organs are adapted to function as part of those organs, while cancer cells are undifferentiated and can't do much besides grow, multiply, spread, and suck up energy. This could explain why these nutrients aid in the prevention of some types of cancer.

Ensuring adequacy for mom and baby. A University of Arizona study found that supplementing beta-carotene to mothers with poor vitamin A status markedly enhanced blood beta-carotene levels in the moms and in their breast milk—by seven to nine times!— and raised vitamin A levels in their nurslings.

Best food sources. Foods rich in carotenes: vegetables and fruits that are orange (pumpkin, carrots, sweet potatoes, cantaloupe, orange, papaya, tangerine), red (tomato, tomato paste, sweet red pepper), green (spinach, broccoli, kale, brussels sprouts, collards, turnip greens, dandelion greens), or yellow (plantain, yellow corn, winter squash) are good sources of the various carotenes.

Lycopene, found abundantly in tomatoes, is concentrated by cooking and is especially good at neutralizing free radicals, carcinogens, and other toxins. It may be the most biologically potent of all the carotenes.

Carotenes are best absorbed into the body if they are eaten with fat. Try tomatoes, olive oil, and basil; green salads with oil and vinegar dressing; marinara sauce; or pureed pumpkin or baked sweet potato with butter.

Supplements: what kind, how much? Your multivitamin/mineral supplement likely contains one or more of the carotenoid nutrients—usually, those that have vitamin A activity. Lutein, lycopene, and zeaxanthin may also be included. Combination green drinks like Greens First (greensfirst.com) are an excellent quick source of a wide range of carotenes.

Current evidence doesn't support high doses of these nutrients in supplement form for pregnant or lactating moms who eat a healthful diet. In third-world countries, carotenoid supplements may be helpful to promote better vitamin A levels in pregnancy and during breastfeeding, but if you have access to foods rich in these nutrients, eating those foods is your best bet. We'll give you some ideas about how to do so in Chapter 9.

Potential risks/interactions. None known.

Vitamin K

Vitamin K is a building block for clotting factors in the blood. It also plays a part in bone mineralization—the maintenance of healthy bone through the adding of new minerals.

One of the first things to happen to a baby born in an American hospital is an injection of vitamin K. While the notion of stabbing one's brand-new babe with a needle seems barbaric, this little injection provides insurance against bleeding into the brain or elsewhere in the body (hemorrhagic disease of the newborn), which used to affect about 1 percent of newborns.

Vitamin K is, like vitamin D, made in the body as a matter of course—but not in the skin. It is made by the friendly probiotic bacteria that live in the intestines and is then absorbed into the circulatory system through the intestinal wall. Vitamin K doesn't move well through the placenta during pregnancy, and newborns' GI tracts need a few days' worth of feedings to develop the intestinal bacteria that make vitamin K. Formulas contain vitamin K.

There are two naturally occurring forms of vitamin K: K_1 (*phylloquinone*), which is found in green plants, and K_2 (*menaquinone*), found in animal foods (the form made by intestinal bacteria). Some supplements contain a third form, called K_3 (*menadione*), which can do the job as well.

The production of K_2 by intestinal bacteria fulfills a significant part of the body's need for vitamin K. Disruption of this intestinal "ecosystem"—usually, through the use of antibiotic drugs and/or a diet made up mostly of processed foods—will compromise vitamin K production in the body.

What's the RDA? Adult females are recommended to get 65 micrograms of vitamin K per day. Infants aged zero to six months: 5.0 mcg per day; seven to twelve months, 10 mcg; and aged one to three, 15 mcg.

Risks of not getting enough. It appears that during the six months following birth, breastfed infants may be lacking in this nutrient. Lack of vitamin K in adults has been linked with higher risk of developing osteoporosis in the later years of life. Some research has drawn a tenuous link between vitamin K lack and elevated heart disease risk.

Who's at risk for deficiency? A study by researchers at the University of Wisconsin's Department of Pediatrics found that 119 exclusively breastfed infants who received the requisite one milligram of vitamin K at birth had low blood levels of the nutrient through twenty-six weeks of age. The mothers' breast milk vitamin K was also low, and the author suggests that higher intake of vitamin K–rich foods, along with vitamin K supplements for exclusively breastfed infants, may be a good idea.

Some women who have heavy periods (menorrhagia) have been found to benefit from vitamin K supplementation. People who frequently get nosebleeds may be deficient in this vitamin. Elderly women with osteoporosis have low vitamin K levels.

Ensuring adequacy for mom and baby. Although some moms question the need for the vitamin K injection at birth, it has been proven to do no harm and has helped to prevent many newborn deaths from hemorrhage. Then breastfeeding will help to establish normal colonies of probiotic bacteria in your baby's GI tract, and vitamin K production will proceed apace.

You can raise your breast milk vitamin K levels by eating plenty of green vegetables—the richest sources are turnip greens, broccoli, lettuce, spinach, asparagus, watercress, and cabbage—and using a multinutrient supplement that supplies this vitamin. A half-cup serving of broccoli or a mixed-green salad will supply your body with 250 mcg of vitamin K. Multinutrient formulations usually include some vitamin K.

Risks/interactions. Two studies suggested a link between vitamin K injections and childhood leukemia; these studies have since been refuted. The use of the anticlotting drug coumadin (Warfarin) counteracts vitamin K action in the body.

Summing Up Vitamins

Table 3.1 gives a summary of the vitamins reviewed in this chapter. Your requirements for B_6, vitamin A, and carotenes can probably be met with a good multivitamin; for B_{12}, vitamin D, and vitamin C, an additional supplement may be needed.

Table 3.1 Vitamin Sources

Vitamin	RDA	Good Food Sources	Supplements
B_{12}	2.4 mcg	Shellfish, fish, beef, eggs	500–1,000 mcg/day intranasal or sublingual
B_6	2.0 mg	Cereals, baked potato, banana	25–50 mg
Vitamin D	200 IU	Fish, egg yolk, fortified dairy	15–20 minutes of direct sun twice weekly or 200 IU a day for breastfed babies and 2,000 IU a day for nursing moms; try a calcium/vitamin D supplement to meet needs for both nutrients.
Vitamin C	80 mg (pregnancy) 120 mg (nursing)	Citrus fruit, strawberries, tomatoes, sweet red peppers, broccoli	1,000 mg/day
Vitamin A (retinol)	2,567 IU (pregnancy) 4,000 IU (nursing)	Fortified breakfast cereals, eggs, butter, milk (more in whole)	3,000 IU retinol or 5,000 IU vitamin A with half as beta-carotene
Vitamin K	65 mcg	Leafy greens	The RDA can usually be found in a good multivitamin.
Carotenes	None	Colorful fruits and vegetables	None needed—best to get from diet; can get some to fulfill needs for vitamin A.

4

Minerals: Does Your Breast Milk Have Enough?

Like vitamins, minerals work as catalysts in biochemical reactions within our sixty trillion body cells. They set up the electrochemical gradients across cell membranes that shoot nerve impulses from one neuron to the next and orchestrate the contraction and relaxation of muscle fibers. Minerals are the stuff from which bones are made. They are used to build hormones; even some of the active forms of vitamins in the body include minerals. Minerals play a role in immunity and in the systems that rid the body of waste.

Minerals are classified as *major*—those that are required in amounts greater than 100 milligrams per day; and *minor*—those required in much smaller microgram amounts.

Minerals to Include in Your Diet

Not many minerals vary in breast milk according to the mother's diet. These nutrient compounds are so crucial for development and survival that our milk-making machinery has developed systems for ensuring that the nursling gets a steady supply. A few exceptions to this rule exist, however. Levels of some minerals in your milk can rise or fall, depending on your intake.

Iron

This minor mineral is important for building hemoglobin, the molecule that transports oxygen in the bloodstream. Lack of iron is known to cause anemia, a common complaint during pregnancy. Low energy and chronic infection can also be traced back to depletion of iron. On the other hand, an excess of iron can increase free radical production in the body, as it catalyzes the reactions that create these renegade electrons.

What's the RDA? The RDA for iron for nonpregnant, nonlactating women aged eleven to fifty is 15 mg per day; for pregnant or lactating women, 30 mg; for children from ages one to ten,10 mg. Iron should be supplemented in breastfed infants only with a recommendation from your pediatrician. Formula-fed infants on iron-fortified formulas will get an adequate amount of iron.

Risks of not getting enough. Insufficient iron in a growing infant has been linked to language and motor skill delays, poor coordination, even fatigue and shortened attention span. But supplementation of iron to deficient children with iron-fortified formula has not always been found to yield improvements in these areas.

Iron deficiency anemia is not uncommon in babies and toddlers. If a child has behavioral problems, lacks appetite, is lethargic, has strange food cravings (for example, wants to eat dirt, not just put it in her mouth), or is growing slowly, suspect deficiency of iron.

On the other hand, iron can interact with bacteria in a fashion that encourages bacterial growth—more so with gram-negative bacteria such as *Campylobacter*, *Escherichia*, *Hemophilus*, *Klebsiella*, *Pseudomonas*, and *Salmonella* strains. Babies are particularly vulnerable to meningitis and gastrointestinal infections from these types of bacteria. It has been postulated that low iron during the breastfeeding period is actually part of nature's design for protecting suckling babies against these sorts of bugs.

Lactoferrin, an ingredient of mother's milk that doesn't change with her diet, is an iron *chelator*. This means that lactoferrin binds with iron in the baby's body and causes it to exit, via dirty diapers. During the first two months of the baby's life, his body contains plenty of iron (as long as there was adequacy when he was in utero); during the first few weeks of life, breastfed babies excrete some ten times more iron than they absorb. (This is not the case in formula-fed babies.) By the seventh month of life, the baby's body is able to better manage iron levels, excreting what isn't needed.

Some research suggests that the decline in iron levels in newborns are part of nature's plan for defending against infection. Does the formula-fed baby's increased risk of infection have something to do with their higher iron levels? At this writing, we don't know, but it's certainly possible.

Also, keep in mind that taking too much iron can unbalance zinc, another mineral needed for good immune function. Women in Spain who took in 200 percent of the daily requirement for iron had lowered zinc levels during pregnancy and in their milk. In the study, 29.8 percent of the women were using iron supplements.

Who's at risk for deficiency? Premature or low birth weight babies; babies who are exclusively breastfed beyond the age of six months; babies or toddlers who drink a lot of cow's milk or other nonhuman, nonformula milks before twelve months of age; babies or toddlers who consume little to no meat; or children with gastrointestinal illnesses.

Babies store up iron in utero, particularly during the last few months of pregnancy. This is why it's so essential for Mom to get adequate iron while pregnant. Babies who get adequate iron while inside Mom's belly have enough stored away to last them through the period of exclusive breastfeeding, as long as it doesn't go much past six months. If you engage in extended breastfeeding—past one year of age—be sure that your child also eats food that serves as a good source of iron. Some young children would rather drink cow's milk than eat, and these children are at higher risk of iron deficiency.

Ensuring adequacy for mom and baby. Table 4.1 contains a list of dos and don'ts for avoiding iron deficiency in your nursling. This is not going to be a concern for moms who formula-feed, as long as they use an iron-fortified formula.

Best food sources. Kelp, wheat bran, pumpkin and squash seeds, almonds, beef liver, millet, lean beef, poultry, fish, deep green leafy vegetables, pork, and eggs.

Supplements: what kind, how much? Consult with your pediatrician, midwife, or other health-care practitioner before choosing an iron supplement—especially if you are still pregnant. It's easy to take too much, and this can cause constipation. Ditto for finding an iron supplement for a baby or young child.

Risks/interactions. Never use children's or adult iron supplements for a toddler or baby or leave your iron supplements anywhere your toddler might get at them; *iron overdose of only six grams can be FATAL in children younger than six years old* and is one of the most prevalent causes of poisonings in young children.

Table 4.1 Dos and Don'ts for Avoiding Iron Deficiency

Do	Don't
Breastfeed for the first six months.	Don't give cow's milk, goat's milk, or soy or rice milks—all low in iron—to a child younger than one year of age.
Give your child iron-fortified cereal and/or pureed fish or meat (a tablespoon a day) after six months of age; if your child doesn't like meat or cereal, try eggs, peas, beans, or fortified grains.	Don't delay introducing solid foods any more than six months; you can start a little sooner if your child seems interested.
Have tests for anemia during pregnancy, and take iron supplements if directed to do so by your doctor.	Don't try to put a young child on a vegetarian diet; if you are vegetarian during pregnancy and nursing, an iron supplement is a good idea for you.
Encourage baby (and yourself) to eat a lot of vitamin C–rich foods, which help the body to absorb more iron.	Don't give a child juices, cow's milk, or sodas instead of food; stick with water to encourage the child to eat.

Calcium

We all know that calcium is a major building material for bone. The human body contains more calcium than any other mineral. Most of it—about 99 percent—is tied up in the making of bones and teeth, while the other 1 percent or so helps to control muscle contraction and relaxation, transmission of impulses along nerves, and the proper clotting of blood.

What's the RDA? For children aged one to three, 500 mg a day; for pregnant and lactating women under nineteen years of age, 1,300 mg; pregnant and lactating women over the age of nineteen require 1,000 mg a day.

Who's at risk for deficiency? With all the calcium a woman gives up during pregnancy and breastfeeding—first making her baby's skeleton, then continuing to give over calcium in her milk at a rate of about 200 mg per day—it seems like a no-brainer that she'd need extra calcium. But most evidence runs contrary to the notion that pregnant and nursing women who eat a decent diet need extra calcium beyond what other women require. In fact, much of the research strongly suggests that women who breastfeed end up with stronger skeletons than women who formula-feed.

What isn't known is whether women who breastfeed for extended periods—over a year, and perhaps with more than one child—have compromised bone mineral density when it's all over. Studies of less well-nourished populations suggest that several pregnancies and years of lactation could weaken the mother's bones. This is most likely to be the case in women who are also lacking vitamin D, which promotes calcium absorption into the body from the gastrointestinal tract. Overall, the evidence shows that calcium balance is adjusted for during both pregnancy and nursing so that Mom's bones stay strong throughout.

In a British study, investigators gave two groups of women 1,000 mg of calcium a day: nursing mothers for six full months of breastfeeding and during weaning, and another group of moms who were not lactating but had recently given birth. In the end, the calcium supplement improved bone mineral density in the spines of both groups of women. It had no effect on breast milk calcium content.

Another study involving what in medicine is known as *grand multiparas*—women who bear at least six children—further shows that bones stay strong even with multiple pregnancies and almost continuous breastfeeding. Researchers from the University of Michigan gathered thirty grand multiparas from a community of Finnish American women who were members of the Laestadian church in Washington state. (Laestadians do not use contraception or bottle-feed.) The bone mineral density of these women was compared with that of other premenopausal women in the same community who had borne no children. On average, the women who had had children were eight years older than the women who had no children, but their bone density was the same. Constantly being pregnant or lactating, with no recovery period in between pregnancies, had no adverse effect on calcium content of their bones.

You do need to get *enough* calcium—1,000 to 1,300 or so mg per day. Calcium deficiency in Mom during pregnancy is directly linked to lower bone content in her newborn, particularly if the baby is born prematurely. Formula-fed babies have faster increases in bone density postpartum than do breastfed babies.

Some research shows a link between inadequacy of dietary calcium and higher blood lead levels during lactation; enhanced bone turnover seen in breastfeeding women may free up lead that has been stored away in the bones. Blood lead levels in a breastfeeding woman are reflected in lead levels in her milk. Women with adequate intakes of calcium have been shown to have less dramatic increases in lead release from their bones during lactation, compared with women who don't get enough of this mineral.

Ensuring adequacy for mom and baby. In a popularity contest between calcium-rich foods, dairy would win, hands down. Products made from milk have the extra benefit of added vitamin D.

Now that you know how much the food you eat affects your milk, keep this in mind when choosing dairy products. Nonorganic dairy products may have been fed a lot of stuff you wouldn't want to eat yourself, including antibiotics, hormones, blood, tallow (that's beef fat), cottonseed (a pesticide-intensive crop), and corn

silage. Dairy cows living at factory farms are genetically manipu-
lated, fed, repeatedly impregnated, and given hormones to artificially increase their milk production well beyond what they would
naturally give if raised in a pasture and allowed to nurse their
calves. For the cows' sake, and for your own, we recommend
organic dairy from pasture-raised, grass-fed cows.

The alternative is to buy dairy products raised locally, where
you can actually meet the animals that are giving the milk. The
same goes for eggs, even meat—if you can get it locally raised with
love, you and your nursling will be better for it.

If you are limited to run-of-the-mill dairy products by financial
constraints or availability in the area where you live, try to get calcium from other food sources, or take a calcium/vitamin D supplement that gives you 1,000 to 1,500 mg of calcium per day.

Best food sources (aside from dairy). Calcium-rich alternatives to
conventionally raised dairy products are green, leafy vegetables
such as bok choy and kale; sardines (with bones in); broccoli; and
orange juice fortified with calcium. Some brands of tofu contain
calcium; check labels. Cereals fortified with calcium are also widely
available.

Supplements: what kind, how much? Use of calcium supplements
has been found to protect against osteoporosis and colon cancer.
Inexpensive calcium supplements are easy to find. Choose brands
that either have the United States Pharmacopeia (USP) symbol on
the label or state on their labeling that they are purified. Calcium
carbonate, calcium phosphate, calcium citrate, calcium lactate, or
calcium Krebs cycle chelates are all bioavailable sources of calcium.
Many brands of coral calcium, which has made headlines because
of outrageous claims for its bioavailability and its curative effects
against cancer and other serious diseases, are overpriced, trendy
rip-offs; others are perfectly adequate supplemental sources of calcium but are usually more costly than other forms of calcium.

Avoid calcium supplements made from unrefined oyster shells,
bone meals, or dolomite (they are refined if they carry the USP
symbol). Unrefined versions may be contaminated with lead or
other toxic heavy metals.

Calcium supplements are best used by the body when taken in divided doses—for example, if you are taking 1,500 mg a day, take one 500 mg tablet with each meal. Calcium carbonate is better absorbed with food.

Risks/interactions. There aren't any known risks of taking calcium in the recommended dosages. Doses of calcium above 2,000 mg a day have been linked with decreased absorption of zinc, magnesium, and iron and could boost your risk of developing a kidney stone.

If you have to take a medicine that needs to be taken on an empty stomach, don't take that medicine with calcium supplements, either.

Selenium

Selenium is a trace mineral—a minor mineral, needed by the body in miniscule microgram concentrations. In the body, it is used to make antioxidant enzymes called selenoproteins, which protect cells against free radicals, help to regulate the function of the thyroid gland, and support immune system function. Concentrations of selenium in breast milk vary widely in different parts of the world. Soils contain varying amounts of this mineral, and the foods grown in soils absorb it in varying concentrations.

Magnesium

This mineral does not vary much in milk according to Mom's diet, but it's as important as calcium for human health. Adequate magnesium intake strongly impacts Mom's health and well-being, affecting energy levels, cellular energy production, bone health, and the action of the hormone insulin. Try supplementing at 300 to 500 mg per day with a mineral supplement that contains calcium, magnesium, and vitamin D.

What's the RDA? So far, there is no infant RDA for selenium, but an Adequate Intake (AI)—based on the average intake of healthy breastfed infants—has been established: 15 micrograms (mcg) per day for infants zero to six months old and 20 mcg per day for infants seven to twelve months old. The RDA for children aged one to three is 20 mcg a day, and for women who are pregnant it's 60 mcg. During lactation, needs rise to 70 mcg.

Risks of not getting enough. The thyroid gland makes hormones that control your metabolic rate—the rate at which your body burns fuel for energy. Hypothyroidism can reduce your metabolic rate by 40 percent, and hyperthyroidism can cause resting metabolic rate to double.

Selenium is needed to transform one form of thyroid hormone into another, more active form in the cells of the body. If this transformation doesn't happen, thyroid hormone levels can measure normal on a blood test, but because an active form of the hormone is low in body cells, the body will behave as though it is *hypothyroid* (low thyroid). The high prevalence of fatigue, overweight, and thyroid disease (some estimates show that 25 percent of people have some form of thyroid imbalance) in the United States suggests a role for selenium in solving these health problems.

Most thyroid problems are *autoimmune* in nature, meaning that the immune system mounts an attack on the gland, causing damage that makes it either overproduce or underproduce thyroid hormones. Some women swing back and forth between hyper- and hypothyroidism during the postpartum period. Thyroid dysfunction can sometimes be traced back to deficiencies in selenium and/or iodine. (See sidebar, "A Simple Test of Thyroid Function.")

An underappreciated but common trigger for autoimmune thyroiditis is gluten sensitivity, also known as *celiac disease*—a sensitivity to proteins found in wheat, oats, barley, and other grains. Anyone diagnosed with autoimmune thyroiditis should get a blood test for celiac disease.

Symptoms of *hypothyroidism* include low energy, rapid weight gain, aches and pains, constipation, brittle hair, cold hands and feet, severe depression, feeling mentally "slow," dry skin, hair loss, goiter (swollen thyroid gland, in the front of the neck), loss of libido.

Symptoms of *hyperthyroidism* include hyperactivity, feeling hot/shaky/sweaty, rapid heart rate, feeling overwrought/upset, rapid weight loss, goiter (yes, hyperthyroidism can cause goiter too), sudden increase in libido, and protrusion of the eyes.

If you have any of these symptoms, talk to your health-care provider about having your thyroid function tested.

A great book for women who suspect they have thyroid dysfunction is Ridha Arem's *The Thyroid Solution: A Mind-Body Program for Beating Depression and Regaining Your Emotional and Physical Health* (New York: Ballantine Books, 1999). This endocrinologist's thorough book talks in detail about the potential emotional and psychological consequences of thyroid disease, how it can be brought on and worsened by stress, and how it is often misdiagnosed or completely overlooked. *Feeling Fat, Fuzzy or Frazzled? A 3-Step Program to Beat Hormone Havoc, Restore Thyroid, Adrenal and Reproductive Balance, and Feel Better Fast!* by Karilee and Richard Shames is a great book that addresses the connection between environmental toxins and endocrine diseases.

Tenuous links have also been drawn between selenium and iodine depletion and increased risk of sudden infant death syndrome (SIDS). The connection here, again, is thyroid health in both mother and baby.

Who's at risk for deficiency? People who don't eat a diet that includes foods rich in selenium are at risk. People with Crohn's disease or who have had gastric bypass surgery may not absorb enough selenium from the foods they eat. In one review of studies on selenium in breast milk, breast milk levels of selenium were below desirable ranges in 30 percent of samples.

Best food sources. Tuna, wheat germ, Brazil nuts, smelt, herring, beef, turkey, lobster, apple cider vinegar, scallops, barley, shrimp, red Swiss chard, oats, clams, crab, oysters, milk, cod, and brown rice all contain generous amounts of selenium.

Ensuring adequacy for mom and baby. The exact content of these foods is hard to pinpoint, because they will vary depending on how much selenium was in the soil in which they were grown or in the foods they ate. Some data show that organic foods are much richer in selenium than nonorganic.

Supplements: what kind, how much? A supplement that contains between 70 and 200 micrograms per day of selenium is good insurance in the face of uncertain selenium concentrations in our food supply.

Selenium supplements given to nursing mothers have been found to improve milk's selenium content and babies' selenium levels. The supplements also increased the activity of glutathione, a powerful antioxidant, in breast milk and in the bodies of the nursing babies.

Research has shown that the kind of selenium a lactating mother takes will make a difference in how much of it passes into her milk. Organic forms (selenomethionine) are passed more readily into milk than inorganic forms (selenite, sodium selenite) of the mineral. High selenium yeasts may contain a combination of organic and inorganic forms. At this writing, it appears that your best bet is selenomethionine.

Risks/interactions. The National Academy of Sciences has set an upper tolerable intake level (UL) for selenium at 400 mcg a day. Too much selenium in supplement form can cause selenosis; symptoms include garlic breath odor, fatigue, gastrointestinal discomforts, blotchy nails, irritability, and possible mild damage to the nervous system.

Iodine

This trace mineral is used by the body to make thyroid hormones. In most developed nations, it is added to table salt in amounts that ensure that virtually every person gets more than the RDA.

Iodine concentration in mothers' milk varies widely according to the intake of the mother. Mean breast milk iodine concentrations range from 5.4 to 2,170 micrograms per liter!

What's the RDA? In adults, the RDA is 150 mcg a day. Pregnant and nursing women are recommended to consume 220 mcg a day, and children one to three years old need 70 mcg a day.

A Simple Test of Thyroid Function

A simple self-test of thyroid function is measuring basal body temperature—your temperature as soon as you wake in the morning, before rising. Place a thermometer on your night table before going to sleep, then put it in your armpit for a full ten minutes as soon as you awaken in the morning, moving around as little as you can. Repeat the test for three mornings in a row. (If your periods have returned, do the test on the second, third, and fourth days of your period.) If your temperature is below 97.2 on all three days, you may be hypothyroid; if it is above 98.6 (and you don't have a feverish illness), you may be hyperthyroid.

This is only a screening test. A lot of other conditions besides thyroid disease can cause body temperature to fall or rise. Results need to be confirmed with a blood test.

Risks of not getting enough. Most Americans get 300 to 700 mcg a day from their diets. Iodized salt supplies enough to have made iodine deficiency virtually unheard of in the United States.

Who's at risk for deficiency? In parts of Europe and in less developed parts of the world, iodine deficiency is a common problem, causing tragic cases of hypothyroidism in pregnant mothers that can handicap—even kill—their babies. As you know from the earlier section on thyroid problems, anything that compromises the function of this gland can have powerful impact on health and well-being.

Some interesting research suggests that iodine supplements could help to protect the body against the thyroid-damaging effects of perchlorate. Pernendu Dasgupta of Texas Tech University found alarmingly high levels of this chemical—which is naturally occurring in very small amounts, but that is also created during the burning of rocket fuel—in samples of breast milk. Dr. Dasgupta found, on average, 10.5 micrograms per liter of perchlorate in the women's milk samples, which came from eighteen different women, each residing in a different state. This was about five times the levels found in cow's milk. If an eight-pound baby drinks seven-tenths of a liter of milk with this concentration of perchlorate in it, that baby will have consumed twice the EPA's recommended threshold for this chemical.

Dr. Dasgupta's team also found that levels of iodine in breast milk have declined dramatically since the 1980s. He hypothesized that perchlorate may block the passage of iodine into breast milk because of its structural similarity to iodine. He suggests that women may be lacking in iodine because they are getting less than ever from fresh foods.

Further research suggests that selenium lack and organochlorine pollutants could be working against proper thyroid function in breastfed babies. Fire retardants (PDBE), have also been implicated in the disruption of thyroid function.

Ensuring adequacy for mom and baby. One way a modern American who gets plenty of iodine in the diet may become deficient, leading to hypothyroidism, is to eat lots and lots of raw cabbage, cauliflower, broccoli, turnip, rutabaga, mustard greens, radishes, horseradish, cassava root, soybeans, peanuts, pine nuts, or millet. In their raw form, these foods are *goitrogenic*. Goitrogens bind to iodine and prevent it from being used by the thyroid gland. They cause the thyroid gland to swell up in an effort to make more thyroid hormones. So, if you like to eat raw cruciferous vegetables, limit your consumption to three or four times weekly. Cooking goitrogenic foods neutralizes most of the iodine-blocking substances they contain.

Best food sources. The best food sources of iodine are seafood. The following foods have the specified amount of iodine per 3.5

ounce serving: clams (90 mcg), shrimp (65 mcg), haddock (62 mg), halibut (46 mcg), oysters (50 mcg), salmon (50 mcg), and sardines (37 mcg). Pineapple, eggs, pork, spinach, and butter also contain iodine in smaller quantities.

Supplements: what kind, how much? The dosage of iodine in a typical multivitamin—usually 150 mcg—is safe and adequate for pregnant and nursing mothers.

Risks/interactions. Getting too much iodine can be dangerous to thyroid health. Dr. Arem writes that "too much iodine in your diet will cause iodine to be trapped by a large protein found in the thyroid gland called thyroglobulin . . . . High amounts of iodinated thyroglobulin prompt the immune system to react and to cause an inflammation in the thyroid that is characteristic of autoimmune hypothyroidism." Worldwide, the overconsumption of iodine has been linked with increased risk of hypothyroidism and thyroid cancer.

Summary: Minerals for Mom and Baby

Table 4.2 gives a summary of the minerals reviewed in this chapter. Your needs for supplemental iron and iodine can most likely be met with a high-quality multivitamin. An additional calcium supplement might be necessary to meet these requirements; look for one that supplies some of the vitamin D dose recommended in Chapter 3.

Table 4.2 Mineral Sources

Mineral	RDA	Good Food Sources	Supplements
Iron	30 mg	Kelp, wheat bran, pumpkin seeds, almonds, millet, lean beef, poultry, fish, deep green leafy vegetables, pork, and eggs	Consult with your health care practitioner to see whether they are needed and how much you should take
Calcium	1,000– 1,300 mg	Dairy products, green leafy vegetables, sardines (with bones), tofu, broccoli, calcium-fortified orange juice	1,000–1,500 mg a day in divided doses
Selenium	60 mcg (pregnant) 70 mcg (nursing)	Beef, turkey, seafood, wheat germ, Brazil nuts, barley, red chard, brown rice	70–200 mcg selenomethionine
Iodine	220 mcg	Seafoods, seaweed	150 mcg

5

The Toxin Conundrum: Defining the Problem

"Those of us who are advocates for women and children and those of us who are parents of any kind need to become advocates for uncontaminated breast milk. A woman's body is the first environment. If there are toxic materials . . . in the breasts of women, then it becomes our moral imperative to solve the problem."

—SANDRA STEINGRABER, "WHY THE PRECAUTIONARY PRINCIPLE?
A MEDITATION ON POLYVINYL CHLORIDE (PVC) AND THE
BREASTS OF MOTHERS" (RAFFENSPERGER, CAROLYN, AND JOEL A.
TICKNER, EDS., PROTECTING PUBLIC HEALTH AND THE
ENVIRONMENT: IMPLEMENTING THE PRECAUTIONARY
PRINCIPLE, WASHINGTON, DC: ISLAND PRESS, 1999)

The precautionary principle states that if the consequences of an action are unknown, but can reasonably be expected to have major or irreversible consequences, it's better to avoid that action. In other words: *Better safe than sorry. First, do no harm.* By taking action in advance of solid scientific proof of harm, when we know enough to make an educated guess about the likelihood of that harm, we avoid costly damage to ourselves or the environment.

Following the dictates of the precautionary principle has become increasingly difficult as scientific progress and the riches it makes possible have swept the civilized world. Taking precautions often entails hard work, delayed gratification, and significant financial losses. It may entail derailing ways of doing things that earn a livelihood for hundreds, thousands, even millions of people. Because corporate interests are so powerful in the modern world, and because virtually every person's life is affected when their interests are threatened, the precautionary principle is a difficult road to travel these days.

This is particularly true in an area that urgently needs our attention: high levels of toxic contaminants that have been found in three places where those kinds of things do not belong: umbilical cord blood, newborn babies, and breast milk.

Removing these chemicals from our environment means changing the way whole industries operate. Unless there is significant evidence of harm—and a lot of clamoring from the people who *could* be harmed—things will change at a snail's pace, if at all. Not surprisingly, the chemical industry and others insist there isn't adequate proof of harm to change their procedures or materials or to stop producing and selling the chemicals that are turning up in women's breast milk. If ever there was a place to apply the precautionary principle, however, it's here.

In this chapter, you will read about the major classes of chemicals found in breast milk and the harm they may do, according to the current research. You'll also find ways you may be able to remediate that harm in yourself, your nursling, and any other babies that enter this plane through the haven of your body.

The Detoxification Question

Is there anything you can do to protect your child? Will any action you take now only serve to protect your grandchildren, or your grandchildren's grandchildren? The research on the subject is far from conclusive.

Detoxification is a big selling point in the natural products industry. Ads promoting colon cleanses, liver flushes, fasts, and other draconian-sounding measures for eliminating toxins are abundant. For a pregnant or nursing mother, these options aren't even worth discussing. It would be unwise to put your body through an aggressive cleansing regimen during this time.

Engaging in a series of cleanses in the year or so before conceiving, with the guidance of a skilled health-care practitioner, is a positive step (see sidebar, "Preconception Detox Programs"). But once you're pregnant, you need to take an entirely different approach to detoxifying your body. You need to keep the flow of nutrients at optimal levels, while gently empowering the natural pathways of detoxification and digestion to move as many toxins out of your body as possible through routes other than breast milk.

Although the concentrations of toxins in our fat are only in the parts per billion (ppb), or even parts per trillion—an amount comparable to a few drops in several hundred to thousands of swimming pools' worth of water—the nature of these substances is such that they are highly potent. Animal research has repeatedly demonstrated that even these tiny amounts can have dramatic effects on living things. The adverse effects of chemical toxins on our children arise largely from the way they interact with the developing hormonal and nervous systems of babies while they are still in utero. Continued exposure through breast milk could have additional problematic effects. At this writing, no one is sure what the consequences of that exposure might be.

Biomonitoring of breast milk shows that even women who are careful to eat well and who try to avoid toxins in their everyday life have these substances in their milk. These pollutants are pervasive and persistent: they are everywhere on the planet, and they do not break down or flush out of the body easily. But when you hold your baby and nurse him with your rich, sweet milk, know that current evidence shouts that the benefits of that milk are helping far more than the chemicals in it are hurting.

Preconception Detox Programs

Fasting and detoxification are both age-old methods for maintaining or regaining good health. Most of the world's religions recommend periodic fasting as a purifying, centering act. Traditional medical practices—particularly Ayurveda, the form of medicine that developed in India centuries ago—center around practices that help the body unburden itself of toxic substances and dead tissue. These practices may include changes in diet, use of herbs and other supplements, hydrotherapy (hot and cold contrast showers and saunas, for example), colon hydrotherapy (where the colon is flushed with water), breath work, and special exercises. Many of these practices are too intense for a pregnant or breast-feeding woman, but many of them can be used in a much less extreme form during this period.

Resources we recommend for information on fasting and detoxification with diet and nutrients include the following:

- The New Detox Diet: The Complete Guide for Lifelong Vitality with Recipes, Menus, and Detox Plans, *by Elson Haas and Daniella Chace (Berkeley, Calif.: Celestial Arts, 2004), a mild but effective approach from a well-respected complementary/alternative medicine physician*
- The Detox Revolution: A Powerful Program for Boosting Your Body's Ability to Fight Cancer and Other Diseases, *by Thomas J. Slaga and Robin Keuneke (Chicago: McGraw-Hill, 2004), a book that gives detailed, research-based information on the use of specific nutrients for detoxification*

Intensive detox and fasting will free up toxins in your body, increasing the burden on your eliminative systems and possibly leading to some uncomfortable side effects. A health practitioner can guide you in making a fast or detox regimen less traumatic. (See the Resources section for contact information for the Institute for Functional Medicine, an organization that can help you find a doctor to guide you in a safe, gentle, but effective detox program.)

Do Not Let Toxins Dissuade You from Breastfeeding!

La Leche League and other breastfeeding advocacy groups are against the biomonitoring of toxins in breast milk and the publicizing of the results of those studies in the media. They are certain that it will convince women not to breastfeed. The idea that women should not be troubled with the facts about the toxins that their bodies and milk may contain, and that their growing babies may have been exposed to before birth, is unconscionable and more than a little condescending.

Women who never knew their bodies and breasts were serving as junkyards for cast-off vinyl siding; incinerated medical equipment; methylmercury from coal-fired power plants; or innumerable other chemicals from pesticides, solvents, and building materials deserve to be fully informed. *What they don't know won't hurt them* sounds alarmingly patriarchal and disrespectful—mainly because it *can* hurt them. Pregnant and nursing women shouldn't be treated as though they can't be told the truth because they might not be able to deal with or understand the information.

Stay Informed—but Unafraid

The unprecedented prosperity we enjoy has its roots in industries that have done enormous damage to the natural world—and have left a legacy of toxic chemicals in the bodies of virtually every creature that swims, crawls, or walks on the face of the Earth. Depending on which source you consult, there are between seventy-five thousand and over eighty-five thousand synthetic chemicals currently registered for use in the United States. Fewer than 50 percent have been tested for safety. If we invoke the precautionary principle, we certainly have enough evidence to incriminate many of the most pervasive chemical threats. On the other hand, there isn't enough evidence for immediate, outright bans of many of these chemicals, either. There is a need for concerted action, but not for panic.

The small amount of toxicity research that has been done up to this point has mostly looked at whether chemicals cause death, obvious birth defects, immediate poisoning, or cancer. It's much less well known whether the chemicals that are produced in the billions of pounds per year in the United States—that are found in the environments, foods, and products our bodies come into contact with each day—cause more subtle problems that will, in the long run, damage our health and the health of our children. The regulatory laws governing the production and use of these chemicals is a scenario that recalls the old tale of the fox guarding the henhouse: thorough toxicological testing to gauge the safety of these chemicals is not required by the government. Only when significant proof of harm has been established can the government require testing and restrict the chemicals' use. It's the precautionary principle in reverse: assume that it's safe until overwhelming evidence proves otherwise.

With so many chemicals commonly produced and used, it's an impossible task to thoroughly test them all. It's even more impossible to imagine testing all the potential effects of every combination of those chemicals on living things. But there is strong evidence that these chemicals have played a role in the rise in chronic diseases over the past fifty years—the period during which most of these chemicals were created and entered into widespread use. Recent research from England and elsewhere shows that in combination, some chemicals are potent disruptors of hormone function even in concentrations well below previously established toxicity thresholds.

Persistent Organic Pollutants

Most of the toxins we discuss here are *persistent organic pollutants*, or POPs. (In this context, *organic* means simply that it contains carbon.) The Stockholm Convention defines POPs as "chemicals that remain intact in the environment for long periods, become widely distributed geographically, accumulate in the fatty tissue of living organisms and are toxic to humans and wildlife." POPs are endocrine (hormone) disruptors at extremely low concentrations. Endocrine disruptors mimic, amplify, block, or otherwise tweak the production and/or effects of natural hormones in the body.

Hormones create a delicate balance in the body that affects development of the reproductive, nervous, and immune systems, and if their action is disrupted—especially during infancy and fetal development—the resulting effects on health can be far-reaching. Hormone-altering chemicals can alter the production and activity of estrogens, androgens (male hormones, especially testosterone), and thyroid hormones. All of these hormones are enormously important for proper sexual development and healthy pregnancy. Alterations in estrogen and androgen activity are also implicated in increased risk of cancer in adults and in defects of the reproductive system in infants. These chemicals are *lipophilic*—fat loving—and are absorbed readily into the fats in food and breast milk and in the bodies of animals and humans, where they remain for decades without being broken down. Thyroid hormones play a major role in the developing nervous system of a fetus, and disruption by chemicals could help to explain the skyrocketing incidence of learning disability, behavioral problems, and autism in today's children. (This is only speculation at this point, but makes sense in the big picture.)

How POPs Bioaccumulate to Toxic Levels

POPs do a fascinating thing when released into nature: they *bioaccumulate* in the fatty tissues of plants, land and sea animals, and humans. Once there, they don't break down, but take up residence throughout the fat in the creature's body. Because our bodies are made up largely of fat molecules—not just the deposits used to store energy, but also the membranes around our cells, many of our hormones, and much of the nervous system—these toxins find many a safe haven.

As POPs in the oceans move up the marine food chain, they collect in toxic concentrations in larger predatory fish, polar bears, and birds of prey. Animals at the top of the food chain begin to develop bizarre diseases and deformations. Epidemics of strange viruses kill off large numbers of these animals because their natural immune defenses are handicapped.

In humans, who are at the top of the food chain, bioaccumulation—sometimes referred to as *biomagnification*—has not yet been found to take as much of a toll. Unless we've been doing the Atkins diet to the extreme for an extended period of time, we don't subsist entirely on the flesh of animals that have already biomagnified POPs to potentially dangerous levels. By maintaining a varied diet, humans have stayed beneath the threshold of broadscale, life-threatening toxicity. We aren't seeing deformations of children or deaths directly attributable to high body concentrations of POPs, except in places where chemical contamination at high levels has been found.

Nourishing food contains natural chemicals that help protect us against the damaging effects of environmental toxins. As synthetic chemical use has soared, there has been a dramatic *decrease* in humans' consumption of nourishing, natural foods, and this has probably had some effect on our health and the health of our children.

Are POPs Bad for Moms and Babies?

The toxic effects of these chemicals are probably greater in babies in utero than in babies who are nursing, and the effects of these chemicals are likely to extend throughout the lifespan of the baby who is exposed to too many or the wrong combination. Also keep in mind that we don't have control over past exposures, or even present exposures, and we don't have complete information about the harm that can be done by the chemicals found in breast milk. This could mean that some of the chemicals we think might be harmful could turn out to be less so. This section is designed not to scare the heck out of you, but to give you information that will help you understand the recommendations we make later for gently cleansing foods, herbs, and nutrients.

Environmental toxins disrupt the fundamental signals of life critical to specific organ systems in the body. Organ systems that appear to be most affected when a baby is exposed in utero or early in life include the following:

- **Endocrine system.** Effects can lead to disruption of organ function, particularly the reproductive organs. Evidence links synthetic chemicals with early puberty, diabetes, lowered sperm count, hypospadias (a deformity of the penis where the opening of the urethra is in the wrong place), diabetes, infertility, and thyroid hormone function.
- **Central nervous system (brain and nerves).** Signal disruption can lead to both chronic behavioral problems, learning disability, ADHD, depression, and aggression.
- **Immune system.** Disruption can lead to cancer, autoimmune disease (where the immune system goes turncoat, attacking the body's own tissues; for example, rheumatoid arthritis, lupus, multiple sclerosis), allergy, and chronic infection.

We know from test-tube and animal studies that these possibilities exist, and that they are likely to some degree. A lot more investigation is needed into these diverse effects.

Man-Made Environmental Toxins: Understanding the Seven Ps

Dr. Rountree refers to the "seven Ps" in lectures and conversations about chemical toxins. This approach allows for a quick—if not entirely comprehensive—overview of man-made environmental toxins.

Petrochemicals

Petrochemicals are fuels—including perchlorate from rocket fuel—and solvents like benzene and perchloroethylenes used in dry cleaning. For example, *perchlorate* widely contaminates drinking water supplies. A 2001 report from the Environmental Working Group found perchlorate in fifty-eight California water systems and in the water or soil of seventeen other states. A small study performed by University of Texas researchers found perchlorate in human breast milk in alarmingly high concentrations. The fuel contaminates the soil and water during testing of missiles and rockets, and is found in most areas where this fuel is made or used. It is toxic to developing thyroid glands and nervous systems.

Pesticides

Pesticides are organochlorines and organophosphates used on crops and elsewhere to kill bugs and other pests. Banned pesticides including dieldrin and toxaphene; the herbicide trifluralin; DDT and its metabolite, DDE; and several widely used insecticides—including endosulfan, malathion, methoxychlor, and kepone—all work in the body as hormone disruptors and nervous system toxins.

Plasticizers

Plasticizers are chemicals used to improve the texture, function, or appearance of plastics. Some examples include bisphenol A and phthalates. Bisphenol A is found in polycarbonate plastic bottles, tin can linings, and dental sealants. A recent review of the research on this chemical revealed "overwhelming evidence that bisphenol A alters cellular signaling, fetal development and adult physiology and reproduction in animals at doses far beneath the current 'safe exposure' level established by the U.S." This chemical has been found to alter the development of the prostate gland and other reproductive organs (both male and female) in ways that make it more vulnerable to overgrowth or cancer later on.

Phthalates are a class of industrial chemicals widely used in plastics, hair sprays, cosmetics, safety glass, wood finishers, resins, and perfumes. The coveted "new car smell" is the smell of phthalates outgassing from the car's plastic parts. A billion pounds per year are produced worldwide. Animal studies link phthalates, which are found in the bodies of every person in which the chemical is measured, with birth defects in lab animals, including hypospadias, atrophy of the testicles, and low sperm count.

Research has demonstrated a link between fetal exposure to phthalates and adverse effects on the formation of the genitals in male babies. A study from the Federal Centers for Disease Control and Prevention found that almost 75 percent of twenty-five thousand people analyzed for phthalate exposure had some in their urine.

Preservatives/Preparation of Foods

Preservatives are found in foods (for example, nitrates), in cosmetics, and in building materials (for example, formaldehyde). Preparing foods by heating them to very high temperatures—such as charbroiling or deep-frying—creates toxins through chemical reactions. Most commercially available brands of lotion, hair products and dyes, deodorants, cosmetics, skin cleansers, and perfumes contain one or more questionable chemical ingredients. Find suggestions for nontoxic cosmetics and body care products at the Environmental Working Group's Skin Deep website, which rates brand-name cosmetics and other beauty products for content of potentially toxic chemicals: ewg.org/reports/skindeep2. Another good site is safecosmetics.org.

Some examples of preservatives include the following:

- **Formaldehyde.** This substance—found in many cosmetics, building materials (pressed wood, fiberboard, particleboard, plywood), glues, adhesives, permanent press fabrics, adhesives, and household products—is classified as a probable human carcinogen. Formaldehyde outgasses into the air, and some people are more sensitive to it than others.
- **Acrylamide.** This class of chemicals—used in cosmetics as stabilizers, binders, foam-builders, antistatic agents, and hair fixatives—is also formed when carbohydrate-rich foods are heated to high temperatures. Potato chips, french fries, even breakfast cereals are common sources. Exposure to acrylamide over a lifetime is believed to pose significant increases in risk of cancer.
- **Parabens and methylparabens.** These are preservatives used in personal care products that lab studies have found to be potential endocrine disruptors and carcinogens.

- **Fluorinated compounds from Teflon.** Nonstick coatings on pans release nonchlorinated perfluorooctanoic acid (PFOA) into the air when heated. According to a study done in 2001 by chemical maker 3M, PFOA was found in the blood of 96 percent of 598 children from twenty-three states and the District of Columbia. Animal studies show developmental toxicity and other effects. DuPont's website warns that pet birds kept in rooms where Teflon pans are heated can die from inhaling the fumes—but their effects on humans have not yet been elucidated.

Pigments (from Paints and Dyes)

Volatile organic compounds (VOCs) are toxic substances used to make paints, stains, sealants, solvents, and dyes. VOCs evaporate into the air we breathe, and in some people they cause dizziness, headache, nausea, even damage to the heart and lungs. These chemicals have been found to sensitize breast cells to the growth-promoting effects of estrogens, increasing breast cancer risk. They also react in the air with ultraviolet rays to produce smog. Many paints and stains also contain toxic bug and mold/mildew killers (fungicides). Fortunately, non-VOC, nontoxic alternatives are becoming ever more available; you can find a multitude of brands and options by searching the Web for "nontoxic paint."

Lead was long an important pigment ingredient in paints. Studies of formula-fed and breastfed babies suggest that formula-fed babies tend to have higher levels of lead, possibly due to contamination of water supplies or from formula cans. Lead does move into breast milk as it is released from where it is stored in the mother's skeleton into her bloodstream. Consuming adequate calcium (1,000 to 1,300 mg per day) helps to reduce this release of lead during pregnancy and breastfeeding. No evidence currently shows that a woman should avoid breastfeeding because of lead in her milk unless she herself has signs of lead poisoning.

Lead is neurotoxic, and in high levels or during pivotal points of development can adversely affect children's hearing, growth, and behavior. Seek out and remediate potential sources of lead in your home, including the following:

- A job for yourself or your spouse that involves lead, including the building trades, trades having to do with car repair or building, ceramics, the chemical or petroleum industries, smelting, or making jewelry
- Paint in houses built before the 1970s (Older homes and the soil around them are more likely to be contaminated with lead.)
- Unwashed or unpeeled vegetables grown in city soils

Pollutants (Industrial)

Breast milk is not a major source of potentially toxic heavy metals in babies. Heavy metals bind to protein in the body, not fat. The movement of these metals from the mother's body into the baby's during pregnancy is a greater concern. Although much of the news about mercury in fish and breast milk is alarming, this heavy metal is not likely to be much of a threat during breastfeeding in women who consume moderate amounts of low-mercury fish. Other types of these pollutants include dioxins and furans, PCBs, polyaromatic hydrocarbons (PAHs), heterocyclic amines, alkylphenols, and heavy metals such as mercury, arsenic, lead and cadmium.

- **Polycyclic aromatic hydrocarbons (PAHs).** PAHs are air pollutants from car exhaust, residential heating systems, and the wastes from power generation. Any time organic materials combust, they create PAHs; tobacco smoke and charbroiled meats are other sources. These pollutants have been linked with reductions in birth weight and head circumference in newborns, and with future risk of cancer and developmental problems in children.
- **Alkyl phenols.** This class of chemicals, which includes nonylphenol and octylphenol, are used in the making of detergents and plastics, and in many industrial processes. Spermicides contain them in the form of nonoxynol-9. These persistent chemicals are found in the air and in water pipes, and are absorbed through the skin when we use personal care products that contain them. Animal research has showed these chemicals to have estrogenic effects.

- **Polybrominated dibenzodioxins (PBDDs) and furans (collectively known as dioxins).** These contaminants are found in brominated flame retardants and pollutants created during the incineration and production of plastics, the bleaching of paper pulp, production of dyes, pigments, and some pesticides, metal production, and the burning of wood, hospital wastes, and sewage sludge. Breast milk is ten to one hundred times more contaminated with dioxins than the flesh foods we eat (eggs, meat, and fish). Dioxins have been strongly linked with rising rates of endometriosis, a disease that causes a great deal of pain and infertility among women today. They are also believed to contribute to a woman's lifetime risk of breast cancer.

  PCBs and dioxins have been found to have potentially damaging effects on the thyroid gland of a growing fetus. This, in turn, can affect the baby's growth and the development of her nervous system. It's not much of a leap to guess that thyroid-disrupting chemicals—especially in concert with other chemicals that directly damage the nervous system—could set the physiological stage for ADHD, autism and related disorders, learning disability, and other psychological difficulties that are being seen in children with unprecedented frequency.

- **Polybrominated diphenyl ethers (PBDEs).** Used primarily as flame retardants, these chemicals are found in furniture foam, computers, and televisions. Animal studies show disruption of spontaneous behavior, learning, memory, and the activity of certain neurotransmitters. The author of one study states that PBDEs "appear to be as potent as the PCBs"—which have been banned because of their dangers to humans, animals, and the environment.

- **Polychlorinated biphenyls (PCBs).** Probably the best-known endocrine-disrupting chemical, and probably the most ubiquitous. PCBs are in every person's body, despite the fact that their production was banned in the United States in 1976. PCBs were used as industrial insulators, coolants, and lubricants, and were used for a time as paint and adhesive additives. Once they are freed up into the environment, PCBs persist for decades, bioaccumulating. High concentrations of this chemical damage the nervous, hormonal, and immune systems.

- **Mercury.** Formed during the production of power in coal-fired power plants and industrial processes, mercury ends up accumulating in seafood. Mercury's damaging effects on the brain and nerves are well documented, and may be especially problematic in a growing infant or young child. Levels of mercury in the mother are approximately three times the level in her milk.

Pharmaceuticals

Yes, pharmaceuticals are also toxins, particularly in light of the fact that they have contaminated the water supply and the food supply. Prescription and over-the-counter drugs are, believe it or not, the sixth leading cause of death in the United States. They are far more dangerous than any vitamin or herb.

Drugs find their way into our bodies even when we don't swallow them on purpose. Antibiotics given to livestock end up in their meat and milk. Trace amounts of breakdown products from drugs commonly taken by humans, including cholesterol-reducing medicines, birth control pills, and painkillers, have been found in water supplies in the United States and Europe—water supplies that are considered drinkable.

General Tips for the Nontoxic Life

There are a few simple, safe steps you can take now that we believe will help reduce the burden of chemicals in your breast milk. While there is not conclusive research on the role of nutrients and herbs in aiding detoxification—or in "cleaning up" breast milk—we do know a lot about the human body's toxin-removal systems. The trick during preconception, pregnancy, and breastfeeding is not to do anything that could threaten your health or the health of your baby, but to use gentle nutritional methods and avoidance of toxins wherever possible.

Toxins from Indoor Air

"Sick of Dust: Chemicals in Common Products a Needless Health Threat in Our Homes" was the publication that came from a study that sampled indoor dust samples from seventy homes across the United States. All of the samples contained every chemical class analyzed for alkylphenols, brominated flame retardants, phthalates, pesticides, and perfluorinated chemicals. Most of the chemicals found in household dust in this study have been found in humans through testing of blood, urine, and breast milk. (The study in its entirety can be found at ecocenter.org/releases/dust_rpt/Dust-Report.pdf)

A HEPA filtration system, a HEPA-filtering vacuum cleaner, hardwood or other hard floors, allergen-proof mattress and pillow covers, and good ventilation— including electrostatic furnace filters—will do a lot to keep dust and the toxins it contains to a minimum. Many of these items can be purchased online from National Allergy Supply Incorporated: natlallergy.com. If you prefer, get specific guidance and order by phone, call (800) 522-1448.

Avoiding toxins *now* won't make much difference in the amount that goes into your breast milk. Still, every little bit helps, and these tips certainly won't hurt you or your nursling.

- Choose meat or dairy lower in fat, which will contain fewer toxins. (However, organic, whole-milk dairy is the best choice for children under the age of two, as explained in Chapter 6.)
- Drink two to three eight-ounce glasses of clean, pure water before each meal and before going to bed at night.

- Avoid drinking liquids from plastic bottles. The older the bottle, the more it breaks down and leaches out the phthalates—especially if bottles are washed in high heat in the dishwasher.
- Eat frequent, small meals to help reduce absorption of lead and mercury in the gastrointestinal tract.
- Do not cook in Teflon pans. Use glass, stainless steel, or cast iron instead, and use healthful oils (coconut, olive, small amounts of butter) to prevent sticking.
- Seek out natural, organic alternatives to pesticides and herbicides. Flea dips, treatments, powders, and collars are an important source of pesticide exposure.
- Do not heat foods in plastic or Styrofoam containers.
- Ensure that your home is well ventilated. Remove carpeting and replace with hardwood, bamboo, tile, polished or painted concrete, or nontoxic linoleum.
- Find nontoxic alternatives to new, outgassing mattresses, rugs, and paint (ditto for personal care products).
- Avoid walking near heavy traffic.
- Don't have mercury amalgam dental fillings put in or taken out while pregnant or nursing.
- Avoid solvents such as glues, nail polishes, nail polish removers, paints (unless nontoxic), varnishes, fiberboard, processed woods, and room deodorizers.
- Use nontoxic cleaning products.

In the Resources section (Appendix B), we'll give you some great resources for nontoxic alternatives to chemicals commonly used in the home and for personal care. But first, take a look at the next chapter for more advice on reducing breast milk toxins.

6

Proactive Steps for Reducing Toxins

Now that your head is spinning with long chemical names and lists of dreadful diseases, let's look at ways you can support your body's natural detoxification processes so that fewer toxins go into your body and breast milk while you are pregnant or nursing.

Your body has five major pathways for getting rid of toxins:

- Urine: kidneys, bladder, and urethra
- Feces: small and large intestines
- Breath: lungs, throat, sinuses, nose, and bronchial tubes
- Skin: sweat, sebaceous (oil) glands, tears
- Breast milk

Our goal, then, is to move as many toxins as possible out of the body through the first four, theoretically minimizing their release into breast milk. This is a largely unresearched area. We are basing our advice here on our knowledge of how the body's cleansing organs and systems work and how to safely, gently use nutrients and traditional cleansing practices to encourage their activity.

There are few studies that investigate the use of nutrients and internal cleansing to clean up or otherwise reduce breast milk toxins. Here, we attempt to give you safe advice based on what is currently known.

If you would like professional guidance on this front, you can contact organizations that train doctors in a grounded, level-headed, science-based approach to detoxification. Refer to the Resources section in Appendix B for two such organizations (the Institute for Functional Medicine and Xymogen Professional Products), both of which Dr. Rountree has worked with closely. They can be contacted for lists of doctors in your area who have this training.

The Nontoxic Diet: Is Organic Really Worth It?

Before focusing on the specific areas of the body, in general, eating organic foods can broadly reduce your current exposure to toxic chemicals. An organic diet may also help your body's toxin-eliminating systems work better, but so will a nonorganic but healthful diet that contains a lot of vegetables, fruits, and whole grains. Some critics say that organic food isn't much of an improvement over nonorganic versions. Studies analyzing toxin levels find that organics aren't exactly free from toxins, although they are much less contaminant-dense than conventionally grown foods. Changes in organic standards—pushed by food producers who want the sales power of that label but don't want to jump through all of the USDA's hoops to get it—increase suspicion that buying organic isn't worth the considerable extra expense. Here's a short tutorial on why buying organic is, indeed, better.

Organic plant foods are raised or grown naturally, without the aid of chemical pesticides, herbicides, hormones, and other man-made toxins. The health of organic crops is reliant on the health of the soil in which they are grown.

Organics do not include genetically modified organisms (GMOs), are not irradiated, and cannot be fertilized with sewage sludge. Where conventional farmers use insecticides and herbicides to deal with pests, weeds, and plant diseases, organic farmers use natural fertilizers, insect predators, and physical barriers. Organic farmers also use traditional methods such as crop rotation, hand-weeding, growing more than one crop in combination, and mulching to enhance the health of their crops. A farmer wishing to shift over to an organic operation has to plant in soil that has been pesticide- and herbicide-free for at least four years.

Animals that yield organic and free-range eggs, dairy, and meats are spared the antibiotics and growth hormones that are pumped into conventionally raised animals. Until 2002, U.S. federal regulations demanded that animals yielding organic meat,

What About Genetically Modified Organisms (GMOs)?

Genetically modified foods are a major area of research and discussion at this writing. While some fears about GMOs have to do with their "Frankenfood" nature— the fact that we're consuming foods that have been tinkered with and could have untoward effects on our health—most pressing is the way in which agribusiness is using gene-tweaking technologies to control the worldwide seed market.

By creating seeds that cannot be gathered and planted again the next season, GMO seed producers force farmers to purchase new seed every year—a potentially disastrous circumstance for small third-world farmers. Not coincidentally, the agricultural practices that revolve around GMO seeds promote dependency on pesticides, another cash cow for companies that make GMO seeds. A documentary film called The Future of Food *explains the situation well. Visit the film's website, futureoffood.org, for more information.*

dairy, and eggs could only be fed organic feed. After that time, the regulations were loosened: a loophole buried in the middle of the lengthy new set of regulations allowed organic farmers to use conventional feed if organic feed cost more than twice as much. Until 2005, regulations stipulated that nonorganic ingredients cannot be used at any point in the production of organic foods. At the end of October of that year, this stipulation was overridden.

It's likely that the trend toward loosening organic standards will continue—particularly in light of the fact that government officials are careful not to state, implicitly or explicitly, that organic foods are in any way more healthful than conventionally grown foods. They call the organic label a marketing tactic rather than an issue of health. With that kind of attitude, it's no surprise when the guidelines change to please those who wish to continue with pesticide- and herbicide-intensive farming techniques. If it's just a matter of marketing, it doesn't matter what the guidelines are, as long as the market competition is fair.

Those who have tried to add organic foods to their lives know that they are considerably more costly than nonorganic foods. Current estimates show that they are 57 percent more costly than conventional foods, on average.

If you can afford it, and if it's available to you, buy as much organic as you can. The more people buy organic, the more farmers will turn to organic methods, and the more widely available and cheaper it will become. Be an aware consumer of organic foods; keep up-to-date on the debate and make your voice heard, as some 275,000 Americans did after the initial creation and publication of organic guidelines in 1999.

Already, at this writing, organic food production is increasing at a rate of 20 percent per year. If your food budget doesn't allow you to buy as much organic as you'd like, you're better off eating conventional vegetables and fruits than you are not eating these foods at all. If you can buy some organic vegetables and fruits, choose those with the highest levels of pesticide and herbicide contamination in conventional versions. (Table 6.1 shows the foods found to have the highest and least levels of pesticides and overall residues according to data from the Environmental Working Group.) Buy organic versions of the most contaminated vegetables

Table 6.1 Most- and Least-Contaminated Fruits and Vegetables

Most Contaminated	Least Contaminated
Spinach	Asparagus
Bell peppers	Broccoli
Hot peppers	Cauliflower
Celery	Sweet corn
Potatoes	Onion
Peaches	Sweet peas
Apples	Banana
Nectarines	Kiwi
Strawberries	Avocado
Pears	Mango
Cherries	Papaya
Red raspberries	Pineapple
Imported grapes	

and fruits whenever you can, and if you can't, wash them very thoroughly and peel them if they can be peeled.

Any vegetable or fruit, organic or not, that is eaten peel and all should be washed carefully with a scrub brush and rinsed well. When eating lettuce or cabbage, discard the outer leaves, then rinse what's left before using it. Some sources recommend that you find out from your market which days organics are delivered—this will help you to get the fresh stuff that hasn't wilted because of its lack of waxes and other preservatives. Peel any produce that has been waxed. Wax holds in pesticide residues.

Where Best to Spend Your Organic Food Dollars

Although vegetarianism can fall short in supplying needed nutrients to pregnant mother and nursing baby, it also is the least toxic diet, because vegetarian foods are lower in fat overall. Choose organic when you are buying dairy, meat, cheese, butter, and poultry, and save money by buying conventional lower-fat foods like vegetables or canned beans.

Whether you choose organic or not, keep portion sizes to a minimum when you are eating meat, poultry, pork, or fish. Don't eat portions any larger than a deck of cards at a sitting. Use meats and dairy products as condiments and flavorings rather than main dishes.

When buying fish, you can choose between farm-raised and wild-caught. A sizeable body of research shows that wild-caught fish is severalfold less contaminated with PCBs and dioxins. Farmed fish are fed ground-up fishmeal instead of their natural diets, accelerating the bioaccumulation of toxins. Some fish farms are located in less than pristine waters. Wild-caught is also more flavorful. (See Chapter 7 for more detailed information on how to shop for fish that's safe to eat.)

Lamb is one meat that is raised by standards that are almost as good as organic. It isn't a very popular food, so the farmers haven't had reason to shift to the production methods that have contaminated most of the other kinds of meat available.

If they are available to you, try wild game (rabbit, venison, or buffalo). They are higher in omega-3s and lower in overall fat than conventionally raised beef. Check around to see whether anyone in your area has chickens, goats, and/or cows and whether they might be able to sell you fresh eggs, poultry, beef, cheese, or milk.

Consumer-Supported Agriculture

Consumer-supported agriculture (CSA) is a growing trend where farmers—usually organic, or nearly so—sell shares of their crops to consumers. For your share, you pick up or receive a box of whatever's in season, once a week or thereabouts. Many CSAs also ask that members volunteer their labor at the farm on a regular basis.

Go to nal.usda.gov/afsic/csa, the website of the Alternative Farming Systems Information Center, to find a state-by-state listing of CSAs. Or, if you don't have Internet access, call them at (301) 504-6559 and ask them to help you find one near you.

Deep Organic: Local, Seasonal Produce

A "shallow organic" operation will do the minimum necessary to meet government standards for organics, mainly so that it can slap the organic buzzword on its packaging as a marketing tool. "Deep organic" operations meet and exceed organic regulations, doing their best to grow and process food in ways that are inspired by and in tune with the natural world. Much of the deep organic focus is on creating and maintaining optimal soil conditions, using deep-rooting legumes, crop rotation, proper drainage, manure, and compost. Deep organic farmers recognize that pests will rarely decimate a healthy crop that is balanced nutritionally and in tune with the seasons.

Local, seasonal, organically grown foods usually qualify as deep organic. There is no certification for deep organic; it's tied up with the farmer's creativity and knowledge of how to work the land, and so varies in its characteristics. Local game is probably safe to eat, but if you want to eat locally caught fish, check for any advisories for your area about potential toxicity.

Nowadays, there are more online sources for organic, free-range, and wild-caught foods than ever before (see Resources in Appendix B). However, in the end, whether you buy organic or not, you'll be better off if you eat plenty of vegetables and whole grains and otherwise follow a healthful diet.

Toxins in Your Body: Fat-Soluble Versus Water-Soluble

Once a toxic substance enters your body—which it can do through your skin, your respiratory system (lungs), or through the gastrointestinal system via food, drugs, or liquids—its fate depends on whether it is fat-soluble or water-soluble.

Fat-soluble (*lipophilic*) chemicals are stored in fats in the body, especially fat cells and cell membranes. Fat acts as a reservoir that continually releases traces of toxin into the bloodstream. Toxins stored in fat trigger inflammatory signaling pathways within those cells, contributing to the overall "fire" of inflammation throughout your body—a fire that has been causally linked with chronic diseases such as asthma, allergy, autoimmune diseases, heart disease, and cancer. When you lose weight or breastfeed, these toxins are more rapidly freed into the body, where they are processed and made water-soluble. Then, they can be excreted through urine, feces, sweat, breath, or breast milk.

Water-soluble toxins, including heavy metals, end up in bone or in other protein-rich tissues of the body. Those not stored in bone are easier to get rid of than the fat-soluble toxins; the simple act of drinking extra water can help escort these substances out of your body through sweat or urine. One of the more important jobs of the liver is to transform fat-soluble toxins into water-soluble versions that are easier to dispose of through these routes.

Fat-soluble toxins must go through a complex biotransformation in order to become water-soluble—a process that is one of the most energy-consuming processes in the body. Intensive fasting is not recommended for this reason: the body requires high-quality, nutrient-dense food and adequate calories in order to safely and thoroughly detoxify.

Before reading about some real-world solutions for promoting the movement of toxins out of your body through routes other than breast milk, take a look at the sidebar, "Unrealistic Solutions for the Toxin-Averse Lactating Mother." If you're thinking about any of these ideas, just put them out of your head right now. Near the end of this chapter, you'll find options for avoiding exposure to additional toxins where possible, because every little bit is likely to help.

Taking Care of Your Liver: The Phases of Liver Detoxification

Your liver, a football-sized organ that lies across your trunk just below your ribcage, does the lion's share of the work of detoxifying chemicals and sending them out of your body through the urinary and intestinal tracts. A diet that is truly nontoxic will not only contain minimal toxins; it will also include foods that promote good liver function.

Some two quarts of blood pass through your liver each day to be detoxified. This blood flows right from the vessels that surround the small intestine, where nutrients—and toxins that enter through the GI tract—are first absorbed into the circulatory system. Cells called Kupffer cells grab up toxins from this river of blood and go to work on them as the newly cleansed, nutrient-filled blood flows back out into the circulation.

Unrealistic Solutions for the Toxin-Averse Lactating Mother

The following solutions are theoretically possible but highly impractical, extreme, or impossible to actually do in real life.

- **Pump and discard milk before beginning to breastfeed and/or between feedings.** *The first milk—the* colostrum—*which contains the most concentrated dose of toxins, also contains the immunoglobulins and growth factors that are known to be so beneficial.*
- **Be a strict vegetarian (vegan).** *Shifting to a vegan diet during pregnancy and/or breastfeeding will decrease the nutritional value of your milk. It has not been shown to reduce the amount of fat-soluble toxins going into that milk. A lacto-ovo vegetarian diet (one that includes eggs and dairy), on the other hand, can produce the NBD's version of Grade A dairy, as long as fish oil supplements are used.*
- **Don't lose weight while breastfeeding.** *If you are eating a low-toxin diet and nursing, it's hard to keep the weight on. (Seriously!)*
- **Breastfeed for only a couple of months and then switch to formula before the baby's toxin levels get too high.** *Breast milk toxin levels are highest in the first months of nursing.*
- **Have babies early in life, have lots of them, and have them one right after another.** *Ridiculous for any mother who is already past that "early in life" stage, or who doesn't want to contribute to the population explosion.*
- **Avoid toxins altogether.** *Impossible. Besides, you already harbor a wide array of toxins in your body.*

Liver detoxification occurs in two phases. When toxins are filtered out of the bloodstream as it passes through the liver, the enzymes of phase 1 detox begin to act on them. Of this group of roughly fifty to one hundred enzymes—collectively known as the *cytochrome P450* enzymes—each specializes in detoxifying specific kinds of chemicals. Considerable overlap between the enzymes exists, providing us with a fail-safe mechanism.

The P450 enzymes transform toxins in one of three ways:

- They turn the toxin into a less toxic version.
- They make the toxin water-soluble so that it can be flushed out through the urine.
- They convert the toxin into an even more toxic form, called an *intermediate*, which then has to be handled by phase 2 detox or can end up doing more damage than the original form of the toxin.

The enzymes of phase 1 detoxification work by oxidizing the toxins, producing abundant free radicals in the process. Fortunately, the liver makes generous amounts of antioxidant substances, including *glutathione*, one of the highest-powered antioxidants made in the body. Glutathione is rich in the mineral sulfur. Eating foods rich in sulfur, such as garlic, onions, shallots, leeks, eggs, and brassica vegetables (broccoli, cauliflower, brussels sprouts, cabbage) will promote glutathione protection in the liver.

Other antioxidants from food help protect your liver against the free radicals that are formed during phase 1. Vitamins C and E, beta-carotene, and *bioflavonoid* nutrients like quercetin (found abundantly in onions and apples) and *epigallocatechin-3-gallate* (EGCG; found in green tea) fit the bill here. Later in this chapter, when we talk about supplements for detoxification, we'll tell you about some "super antioxidants" that can be safely added to your program while you are breastfeeding to support optimal liver function.

A substance found in broccoli and broccoli sprouts, *indole-3-carbinol* (I-3-C), has been found to block the binding of xeno-estrogens DDT and dioxin to estrogen receptor sites. This could help these xenoestrogens go straight to detox and out of the body. I-3-C has also been found to cut the rate of chemically induced DNA damage in breast tissue by a whopping 92 percent. Breast cancer risk is strongly associated with exposure to organochlorine pesticides, and I-3-C has shown significant promise as a preventative against breast cancer. Because of contradictory evidence that suggests possible cancer-promoting effects of I-3-C in concentrated supplement form, Dr. Rountree does not recommend it. He does, however, recommend another nutrient found in broccoli called *sulforaphane*, which can safely be taken in supplement form. To get both of these nutrients from food, eat lots of broccoli and/or broccoli sprouts.

A diet low in protein can slow down phase 1 detox. Using a rice or whey protein powder to make smoothies or as an addition to yogurt or hot cereal can help you maintain adequate protein for good phase 1 enzyme activity.

Drugs (antihistamines, benzodiazepine tranquilizers, cimetidine and other acid-blocking drugs) and grapefruit juice reduce the activity of phase 1 enzymes. Some toxins, such as dioxins and PAHs, have phase 1–inducing effects. The toxins are then turned into even more toxic intermediates that need quick handling by phase 2. In other words, environmental toxins may induce the very enzymes that make them more toxic.

Once phase 1 has worked on the toxins in question, phase 2 enzymes further alter them by the attachment of another substance—for example, glutathione, sulfur, or the amino acids glycine, taurine, or cysteine—to them. This further transforms the toxins into forms that are readily and harmlessly excreted through urine or feces. To help promote phase 2 detoxification, get plenty of the following:

- Brassica foods (broccoli, cauliflower, brussels sprouts, cabbage)
- Foods rich in sulfur (brassica, eggs, garlic, onion)
- Foods rich in vitamin C (sweet peppers, citrus fruit)
- Fish (fish oil supplements have the same effect)
- Foods rich in B_{12} and folic acid (whole grains, vegetables); deficiency of B_{12} and folic acid has been found to inhibit phase 2 detox
- Green tea (EGCG activates phase 2 enzymes)

A large percentage of prescription and over-the-counter drugs increase the burden on the detoxification enzymes of the liver. Use them only when absolutely necessary.

As mentioned earlier, it's also important to take the best of the vegetarian diet—fresh vegetables and fruit, greens, whole grains, beans, nuts, and seeds—and add small helpings of meat, fish, poultry, and some dairy here and there. Think of meat and poultry as condiments rather than main dishes, and use dairy in small amounts as a taste and texture accent rather than piling it on. Make a variety of vegetables and whole grains like brown rice your main dishes.

If you're the kind of mom who just loves a big, juicy burger, you can reduce the formation of some carcinogens in cooked meat to almost zero by mixing antioxidant-rich food—like blueberries, cranberries, cherries, and rosemary—into ground meats prior to cooking. If steaks are more your speed, marinades made with turmeric (the bright yellow spice found in curry powder) and garlic, and even standard store-offered teriyaki sauces, have been found to reduce carcinogen formation in cooked meat.

Bile, Bile, Toil and Trouble: A Cautionary Tale for Fiberphobes

As if it didn't have enough to do already, your liver also is responsible for making a fatty substance called bile—a quart per day. Bile soaks up fat-soluble toxins in the liver, then is stored in the gallbladder to be excreted into the GI tract. Bile also is used by the body to break down fats and aid in the digestion of the fat-soluble

Ensuring That the Water You Drink Is Pure

Unfortunately, water from your tap probably contains several—or several dozen—chemical contaminants. Bottled water isn't subject to stringent regulations for quality or purity; some is nothing more than tap water poured into a bottle with a fancy label. Most tap and bottled water contains chlorine, which can combine with naturally occurring organic substances to form carcinogenic compounds called trihalomethanes. If you shower or bathe in chlorinated water—and you do, if you do not filter it with a special filter—you breathe and soak in these compounds every time you bathe.

The first step to purifying your water completely is to find out what contaminants might be in it. If you get your water from a public source, call the provider and ask for the Annual Consumer Confidence Report. If your water comes from a well, you will need to buy a test kit, which should be available at your local hardware or home supply store or online. (Or call a local expert to do it for you.) Send water samples to a reputable testing service such as Heart Spring (heartspring .net/home_water_testing.html); Doctors Data (only tests for metals; doctorsdata.com/ docs/pdf/water.pdf, or call 800-323-2784); or James McMahon, an ecologist who specializes in helping people to choose the right water treatment systems (sweetwater.biz, or call 866-691-4214).

Once you know what is in your water, you can choose the right system for cleaning it up. A simple carbon-block filter may be all that's needed—to remove chlorine—for city water supplies that are pretty clean. Other choices include distillation (not recommended because it removes the minerals from the water); reverse osmosis (cleans some contaminants from drinking water); activated carbon filters (absorb chlorine, volatile organic compounds, herbicides, and pesticides, but are vulnerable to contamination with bacteria); ultraviolet light (for killing bacteria and other organisms); and KDF treatment (oxidation and ionization processes that remove metals, pesticides, herbicides, and chemicals).

Use a system that combines these methods to remove whatever toxins you find in your water supply without removing the water's natural mineral content. If you do not use a whole-house system that removes chlorine, look also into filters for your showers.

nutrients they contain. It can continue to soak up toxins in the intestines as it moves down the line.

When bile is released into the intestines with a load of toxins from the liver, the hope is that the next meal that comes down will be rich in fiber, particularly soluble fiber like that found in apples, grapes, broccoli, oats, carrots, seaweed (which contains a soluble fiber called algin), or fiber supplements made from apple pectin. A fiber-rich meal will bind up fat-soluble toxins in bile and quickly move them out of the body through your next bowel movement. Pectin and algin are also effective at detoxifying mercury in the body and in preventing its absorption into the body through the intestinal wall.

If fiber intake is inadequate, fat-soluble toxins move more slowly down the GI tract (fiber increases *gastrointestinal motility*, the speed with which a meal moves through your body and out as waste). Bacteria hanging around in your intestines then have more time to transform these toxins into even more toxic versions that can then be reabsorbed. Toxins can recirculate from bowel to body and back again several times in this way.

Vegetables and fruit are the best way to get fiber into your body. Drinking adequate water will decrease transit time, too, as will maintaining a healthy balance between good and bad intestinal bacteria (probiotics; more on this in a bit). If you want to use a fiber supplement, try apple pectin, oat bran, or ground flaxseed, or a combination. Or try prunes, prune juice, or figs.

Promoting the flow of bile can aid in toxin removal through bowel movements—and in lowering cholesterol. Artichokes contain *caffeoylquinic acids*, compounds that increase bile flow. Beets, dandelion root (taken as an herbal extract or tea), dandelion greens, and the spice turmeric (a main ingredient in curry powder) also improve the flow of bile from the liver. A diet high in fat and low in fiber can cause gallstones. Roughly a half-million gallbladders are removed each year because of these stones.

Promoting Good Liver Function: Chlorella and Liquid Chlorophyll

Chlorella is a species of algae with a thick, tough cell wall. It is the richest natural source of *chlorophyll*, the plant chemical that makes plants green and that transforms energy from the sun into fuel for the plant. It isn't well known in the United States, but chlorella is an enormously popular supplement in Japan. The research community there is leaps and bounds ahead of the rest of the world in studying chlorella as a detoxifying agent, and their studies so far are encouraging.

In one study, researchers enrolled forty-four pregnant women and measured levels of dioxins in their blood, fat stores, breast milk, placenta, and cord blood. Roughly half of the women were instructed to take chlorella supplements throughout the study. Total dioxin equivalents in the breast milk of the women taking chlorella were 30 percent less than in those who did not use chlorella!

Other research suggests that chlorella helps to pull mercury and other toxic heavy metals out of the body. Its fibrous cell wall—which has to be broken or crushed through special processes in order to make its contents available for digestion—binds to toxins and sends them out with bowel movements. Chlorophyll, too, has antitoxin effects, helping to balance the action of phase 1 and phase 2 detox enzymes so that toxic intermediates do not build up in the liver. This green plant chemical forms tight molecular complexes with a variety of chemicals, facilitating their removal from the body. Chlorella supplements are safe during pregnancy and breastfeeding. Every pregnant and lactating woman should use chlorella every day.

Spirulina, another form of algae, is another excellent green supplement for breastfeeding women. It is nutrient-dense and chlorophyll-rich. Liquid chlorophyll can be used, too, but it doesn't have the tough, fibrous cell wall that contributes to your daily intake of fiber. Chlorella has other benefits over chlorophyll alone: it has been found to stimulate immunity against disease and contains enzymes that can aid in digestion. Both chlorella and liquid chlorophyll are internal "deodorants" that have long been used as natural therapies for bad breath, body odor, and foul-smelling intestinal gas or stools.

Since chlorella binds to heavy metals in the environment, it is important to use a supplement that has been grown in pristine conditions and is certified to be low in contaminants. We recommend Prime Chlorella because it is especially pure and reasonably priced; it can be purchased at primechlorella.com. If you are interested in trying spirulina as well, we recommend Earthrise Spirulina (earth-rise.com/home.asp).

Detox Enhancers and Powerful Protectors

Derived from broccoli, *sulforaphane* appears to be one of the most potent of all the phase 2 enhancers. This nutrient is particularly effective at upregulating glucuronidation, the liver detox process that aids in eliminating estrogenic hormone–disrupting chemicals. Sick of broccoli and broccoli sprouts? Try a tea that contains sulforaphane glucosinolate (SGS™), a trademarked form of this nutrient. Made by Brassica Products (brassicatea.com), the tea is sold in black, green, and rooibos varieties, and can be found on the Web and in health food stores. These teas are highly recommended for lactating mothers. Drink one to two cups a day.

Ellagic acid (found in raspberries, pomegranates, walnuts, and muscadine grapes) is another powerful phase 2 enhancer. Most of the research on ellagic acid has been performed on raspberry concentrates, so at this writing, it's best to obtain ellagic acid from foods instead of pills. Try pomegranate or raspberry juices, or dried fruit when fresh isn't available. When raspberries are in season, stock up and keep them in the freezer.

Garlic aids in liver detoxification by improving the action of phase 2 enzymes. The sulfur it contains helps to promote glutathione production. It also has potent antimicrobial properties, which means that it helps the body to resist illness caused by viruses, bacteria, and yeasts. In a study of pregnant rats exposed to methylmercury, animals given garlic juice before a single high dose of the toxin had lower maternal death rate, better increases in body weight (both mom and baby rats), and greatly improved survival of the offspring. The garlic appeared to move significantly more of the mercury out of the rats' bodies in comparison to rats who got mercury but no garlic juice. Garlic has been found to help thin the blood, lower blood pressure, and may even help to prevent cancer. If you don't like to eat garlic, or if it doesn't seem to agree with your nursling, try a freeze-dried garlic supplement, 500 to 1,500 mg a day. If you or baby cannot tolerate the odor or residual taste of the whole garlic supplement, use three to four grams per day of odorless garlic, like Kyolic. One study found that breast-fed babies nursed longer when their mothers had eaten garlic recently!

Grape seed extract (GSE) is another helpful supplement, as grapes have been considered health food for more than six thousand years. Today, there's some debate over whether their considerable benefits to our health come from the skins, the seeds, the juice, or the wine made from them. The current research strongly points to a substance found in the seeds of grapes and in red wine: *oligomeric proanthocyanidins*, or *OPCs* for short. OPCs are enormously effective antioxidants that also promote improved function of the body's naturally made antioxidant enzymes. Animal research finds that they protect the liver against damage done by acetaminophen (Tylenol) when given for a seven-day period before the drug is given. OPCs have blood vessel–strengthening effects, making them helpful for varicose veins and postpartum hemorrhoids. Eat organic seeded red, purple, or black organic grapes (just chew the seeds and swallow them); or sip a glass of red wine each day. You can also take a supplement that supplies 100 to 300 mg per day of OPCs—preferably combined with other antioxidants such as vitamin C, alpha lipoic acid (discussed later in this section), and green tea.

Green tea is an ancient beverage that has performed splendidly in tests of its protective properties against cancer and heart disease. It contains EGCG, one of the most powerful antioxidants yet discovered. Green tea extracts have repeatedly been found to prevent carcinogen-induced DNA damage in test-tube studies; and green tea is one of the better established inducers of phase 2 detoxification, which moves toxins out of the body through urine or stool. Sip up to four cups of green tea daily. The caffeinated versions are fine; in green tea, caffeine's stimulatory properties are counteracted by another substance called L-theanine. Or use a multivitamin/mineral or individual supplement that includes 100 to 300 mg of green tea extract.

N-acetylcysteine (N-AC) is an amino acid that is the first-line medical therapy for patients who come to the emergency room with acetaminophen poisoning. It is used to thin mucous secretions in cystic fibrosis and chronic bronchitis patients, and it has antiviral effects. N-AC is used to treat acute heavy metal poisoning from mercury, lead, and arsenic and exposure to high concentrations of some pesticides and herbicides. It works because it dramatically increases the liver's ability to produce the all-important antioxidant glutathione. Take 250 to 1,000 mg a day of N-acetylcysteine in supplement form, in divided doses. You may find it in combination with alpha lipoic acid and other antioxidants.

Methylsulfonylmethane (MSM) is a supplemental form of organic sulfur that donates sulfur molecules to make amino acid precursors to glutathione (cysteine, methionine). If you would rather not take N-acetylcysteine, try 500 to 1,000 mg per day of MSM instead—but note that MSM is nowhere near as effective as N-AC at raising glutathione levels.

Curcumin is an extract of the yellow spice turmeric and a potent antioxidant, detoxifier, and phase 2 upregulator. Include it by taking lots of curry, or with a supplement of 300 to 500 mg per day. (Use a supplement that contains Bioperine, a black pepper extract that enhances absorption of curcumin; otherwise, it is poorly absorbed.)

Alpha lipoic acid (ALA) is made in the body in small amounts to help run the metabolic machinery of cells. ALA has antioxidant activity when taken as a supplement. It is fat- and water-soluble; most antioxidants only do their thing in one medium or the other. In animal studies, it protects against arsenic, cadmium, and mercury accumulation by *chelating* these heavy metals—binding to them so that they can be harmlessly excreted. ALA, like milk thistle (see next paragraph), is an effective treatment for death cap (*Amanita phalloides*) mushroom poisoning, which causes extreme formation of free radicals in the liver, often leading to liver failure. While only 10 to 50 percent of those who unwittingly eat death cap mushrooms survive without treatment, one study found that sixty-seven of seventy-five people (89 percent) survived following an intravenous infusion of ALA. Supplemental ALA is short-lived in the body, so use a supplement that will give you 100 mg twice a day, or a timed-release form.

Milk thistle is an herb that is a well-known *lactagogue* (herb or food used to promote increased breast milk production) among herbalists and midwives. In ancient Greece, this plant was used to treat diseases of the liver and gallbladder. Modern science shows that this herb has amazing regenerative effects on liver cells—due, at least partly, to the boosting of glutathione levels in that organ. It is recommended as a natural therapy for hepatitis and cirrhosis. Studies show that it is protective against liver damage caused by the air pollutant carbon tetrachloride and against kidney damage caused by acetaminophen and chemotherapy drugs. Milk thistle is a natural anti-inflammatory and antioxidant that decreases the oxidation of fats in the body. Its active constituent, *silymarin*, is reabsorbed through the intestinal wall after being released into the GI tract, effectively being recycled. Adverse reactions to milk thistle are virtually unheard of; the worst are some gastrointestinal discomfort with high doses. It doesn't interact with any drug. Try capsules of the herb, 150 to 175 mg three times a day, with an extract standardized to 80 percent silymarin.

Selenium is a mineral that helps to detoxify the body of lead and mercury and promotes glutathione production. Follow the guidelines we gave in Chapter 4 for daily selenium intake.

Rosemary is another very powerful antioxidant and detox enhancer. Supplements are hard to find; use fresh or dried rosemary in cooking whenever suitable.

Kidney Detoxification

One kidney cleanse we found on the Internet suggested that we buy twenty to one hundred pounds of watermelon, fill up a warm tub, and sit in the tub eating the watermelon all day, urinating into the water. We're not sure what value sitting in a tub full of one's own watermelon pee might have, from a medical standpoint. Anyhow, you don't need to go to such extremes to promote kidney health!

Your kidneys are responsible for maintaining the right balance of fluid, electrolytes (minerals like calcium, sodium, magnesium, and potassium), and the proper acidity of the body. They don't do much direct detoxifying of chemicals, but a lot of chemicals in the process of detoxification pass through them on their way out in the urine. To keep kidneys clean and functioning well, drink plenty of pure water and herbal teas. Eat foods like watermelon, cantaloupe, oranges, and grapes, all rich in water, and sip broths and soups. Sea vegetables also have toxin-fighting properties.

Aiding Detoxification Through the Digestive Tract

Your digestive tract—mouth, throat, esophagus, stomach, small intestine, and large intestine (colon)—is an important way out for toxins. Extra fiber and water reduce transit time, giving your system fewer opportunities to absorb or reabsorb toxins from food.

Sea Vegetables Reduce Toxicity

Sea vegetables—including kelp, wakame, kombu, hijiki, sea lettuce, and nori—are rich sources of vitamins, minerals, and healing plant chemicals. They contain algin, a type of soluble fiber that helps to bind lead and other heavy metals in the intestinal tract, helping to move them out of the body before they can be absorbed. Sea vegetables are used to make stabilizers that are widely used in the making of processed foods.

Most westerners don't know how to incorporate sea vegetables into their diets. Asian cuisines use them to make soup bases, wrap sushi rolls, and as part of stir-fries. Dulse and wakame are also commonly cooked with beans to help reduce their gas-producing quality. Dulse has a salty flavor and can be used to replace salt in recipes or eaten raw like beef jerky!

We will offer further suggestions for incorporating these foods into your meals in Chapter 9, and in the Resources section (Appendix B) you'll find mail-order sources for dried sea vegetables.

Once your meal has traveled along the digestive tract far enough to pick up bile expelled from the liver through the gallbladder, moving it out of the body quickly is even more essential for preventing toxin reabsorption.

Although it's hard not to wolf down your food when you're saddled with the care of a nursling, chewing food thoroughly until it is liquid in your mouth will prepare that food to be better absorbed once it reaches the small intestine. Here are some additional tips for reducing toxin absorption from food and for getting toxins out of your body once they've been processed by the liver.

Try a Digestive Enzyme Supplement

Your pancreas and stomach make some digestive enzymes to finish the job of turning your meal into a soup from which nutrients are easily absorbed through the intestinal wall, but the system is designed to work cooperatively with enzymes naturally present in raw food. Heating food above 120 degrees permanently neutralizes enzyme activity, putting a bigger burden on the body to produce more enzymes.

When you eat a meal consisting mostly of cooked food, take a chewable or pill-form enzyme supplement that contains lactase, cellulase, protease, and lipase enzymes—they break down milk sugars, digestible fibers, protein, and fats in the digestive tract. The enzyme supplement will help to ensure that your meal is broken down into its most easily absorbable components by the time it hits the small intestine, enabling the process to go a bit faster.

Treat Reflux or Heartburn Naturally

Reflux or heartburn are common complaints in people eating diets rich in fat and grease. During pregnancy, hormones relax the muscles that keep acid down out of the esophagus. Acid-reducing drugs and antacids aren't the answer; you aren't making too much stomach acid, more likely, you are making too little.

Hypochlorhydria, or low stomach acid production, can be prevented by drinking a glass of room-temperature water a half-hour before a meal. (Cold water decreases stomach acid production.)

Add a tablespoon of apple cider vinegar (a good source of selenium) if water alone doesn't do the trick. Don't eat too much food at a sitting; don't lie down just after eating; and avoid fried foods. Enzymes from raw food or supplements will also help to prevent heartburn. A supplement called *betaine hydrochloride* can be taken with meals to enhance digestion in the stomach; follow the directions on the bottle.

Maintain Good Probiotic Balance

In the large intestine (colon) lives an entire ecosystem of friendly bacteria that help you to digest food. They also produce important nutrients (vitamin K), help with detoxification, keep the "bad guys"—yeasts and unfriendly bacteria—in check, and aid in preventing constipation and reabsorption of toxins. These *probiotic* bacteria are found in foods—notably live-culture yogurt, but also in sauerkraut (fermented cabbage) and miso (fermented soybean paste).

Numerous studies show that probiotics are the single best supplement—especially for children—for the prevention of respiratory and gastrointestinal infections. Probiotics naturally maintain their own populations in your GI tract (and in other parts of your body, including your vagina) as long as they're well-fed with fiber-rich whole foods and not killed off by antibiotics. A processed-food diet can lead to an imbalance that increases your chance of overgrowth of yeasts and unfriendly "bugs" in the colon.

Bad bacteria and yeasts can transform toxins that are being excreted into more harmful versions. They also putrefy undigested food in waste, leading to foul-smelling stools and gas. This is one of the reasons why formula-fed babies' diapers have such an unpleasant odor, while the exclusively breastfed babe's diaper smells like warm yogurt: breast milk supplies everything the baby's system needs to establish and maintain healthy probiotic populations. Your breast milk contains probiotics and *prebiotics*—carbohydrates that are probiotics' favorite foods.

Using a living probiotic supplement once or twice a day with meals is a good fail-safe measure for keeping your colon in great working order. You can find them in your health food store in the refrigerated section. Some versions do not need refrigeration. An adult probiotic may contain strains of bifidobacterium and lactobacillus bacteria; a probiotic yeast called *Saccharomyces boulardii*; or other friendly bacteria, including *Streptococcus thermophilus* and *Enterococcus faecium*. A good dose of probiotics should provide at least 10 billion viable bacteria per day for adults, and one to five billion for children, including infants.

Probiotic supplements may contain prebiotics, too—also called *fructooligosaccharides (FOS)*. You can get FOS from foods like garlic, leeks, onions, bananas, asparagus, and artichokes. Another good source of FOS is arabinogalactan, also called Larix, from western larch. It has immune-boosting properties, too. Larix can be dissolved in water or juice; it's easier to digest than FOS (causes less gas) and is inexpensive. Try up to one tablespoon per day.

Is "Colon Cleansing" Necessary?

Never do any kind of colon cleansing with herbs or undergo a "high colonic" (given by a specialized colon hydrotherapist) while pregnant. It could induce premature labor or cause dehydration. Nursing mothers need to be cautious about taking the powerful herbs usually prescribed for colon cleansing.

Your best bet while pregnant or nursing is to keep the bowels clean and moving along briskly with the right diet, supplements, and plenty of water. Once you are done nursing, you can look into a more intensive colon-cleansing program, if you feel it is appropriate for you. One good bowel movement a day is enough; two is better. Stools should be soft and easy to pass. If you have to strain, if your bowel movements have a very bad odor, or you have gastrointestinal distress on a regular basis (excessive, malodorous flatulence or gas pains, for example), you may want to increase your fiber and water intake. Some additional tips for enhancing bowel function:

- First thing in the morning, have a large glass of warm water with half a lemon squeezed into it. Squat down on the floor with your toes folded underneath you and alternately drop each knee toward the floor to help move the warm water through your system.

- Try the occasional store-bought saline enema, or use an enema bag with a solution made from two tablespoons of salt or Epsom salts (magnesium sulfate) per gallon of distilled or purified water. You can also use brewed chamomile tea. Some commercially available solutions also include castile soap, which is gentle enough to use while nursing. Drink plenty of water following any enema. Do not use enemas daily, or any more than a few times a month.
- Prunes and prune juice work as well as any laxative. (Organic, please!)

Helping Toxins Move Out Through the Skin

Some toxins can be expelled through the skin. Here are a few ways you can encourage this process:

- Get regular and sweaty exercise. Drink water before and during your workouts as needed. If you are still pregnant, observe the guidelines laid out by your doctor or midwife about exercise.
- Take hot baths, contrast showers (hot/cold/hot again), and saunas. These are age-old natural therapies for getting toxins out through the skin.
- Dry-brush your skin before bathing. Using a soft-bristled skin brush (see Resources in Appendix B for merchants who carry them), brush your skin all over, starting at the extremities and brushing toward your heart.
- Don't use heavy cosmetics or skin lotions that contain pore-clogging mineral oil. If your skin needs extra moisture, try sweet almond oil (has no scent)—an oil commonly used for massage—or olive or coconut oils.
- Have a professional massage periodically.
- Drink adequate water. This will aid in toxin removal through the skin.
- If you develop a rash, don't immediately try to suppress it with steroid cream or other medicine. Naturopathic

medicine states that a rash is your body's attempt to get rid of something toxic through the skin. Let it run its course if you can.

Moving Toxins Out Through the Nose and Mouth

Some practitioners of macrobiotics, an ancient Eastern way of eating and living that has helped many people improve their health, state that when mucus is abundant, this is an indication that the other avenues for cleansing—liver, kidneys, intestinal tract—are overworked or depleted. A person who shifts to a macrobiotic diet, which consists mostly of specially cooked grains and vegetables (including sea vegetables), detoxifies quickly, and this is believed to cause excess mucus to be formed in the nose, throat, and sinuses as toxins are driven out of the body through every possible avenue. A lot of mucus in your sinuses, throat, and nose might not be from allergies, but toxic overload.

While no study has shown the presence of chemical toxins in mucus, the rationale for expelling mucus instead of suppressing it is sound. To help release toxins through mucus, don't take drugs to suppress its formation. Instead, use the following natural therapies that thin the body's secretions and help move the stuff out to where it can be eliminated.

- Make a nasal/sinus wash. You can do this with one-quarter teaspoon salt, one-eighth to one-quarter teaspoon baking soda, and eight ounces of warm water. Pour the solution in your palm, hold one nostril closed with your other hand, and snort the solution up into your nose. Let it drain, then repeat with the other nostril. Or use a bulb syringe, a neti pot (a small ceramic pot specifically made for this purpose), or a newer device Dr. Rountree likes: the Nasaline irrigator, a simple and inexpensive syringe adapter. Check Whole Foods, Wild Oats, or go to camexco-inc.com to buy one.
- Brew ginger, peppermint, or cinnamon tea. These herbs are expectorants, which means that they help thin mucus

secretions and open up the respiratory passages. Deeply inhale the steam from the tea as you drink it. Fenugreek, a traditional lactagogue, is also an expectorant; teas for nursing moms often contain it.

- Try eucalyptus or juniper extract, sold as an alcohol tincture. Boil a pot of water, add a couple of droppers full of the tincture, and then tent your head above the steam and breathe it in. (Do not take these internally.)
- Gargle warm tea or salt water solution if you have throat congestion.

Summing Up Detoxification Tools

Following the guidelines in this chapter (summed up for you in Table 6.2) will help you to minimize the impact of past and future misjudgments about the safety of synthetic chemicals in our food, water, air, and in the products we use at home and elsewhere. You don't have complete control over your exposure, but you do have some, and we hope we've given you some useful tools for exercising that control.

Table 6.2 Detoxification Supplements Safe for Nursing Moms

Supplement	Dosage
Cracked- or crushed-cell-wall chlorella	Follow instructions on container
Grape seed extract	100–300 mg/day OPCs
Green tea extract	100–300 mg/day green tea polyphenols
Sulforaphane	Brassica tea, one to two cups per day
N-acetylcysteine	250–1,000 mg/day (N-AC)
or methylsulfonylmethane (MSM)	500–1,000 mg/day (MSM)
Curcumin	300–500 mg/day
Alpha lipoic acid	100 mg twice a day or 200 mg once daily of timed-release form
Milk thistle (80% silymarin)	150–175 mg three times a day
Digestive enzymes	With meals; follow instructions on container
Probiotics/fructooligosaccharides (FOS)	With meals; with Larix, take a tablespoon per
or arabinogalactan (Larix)	day, dissolved in water or juice
Garlic	500–1,500 mg/day freeze-dried or 3–4 grams/day odorless

As you take steps to reduce the output of toxic chemicals into your milk, keep in mind that this is not the real answer to the problem. As Sandra Steingraber and other very bright people have said, it is imperative that the world does what is necessary to make breast milk clean again. It may take a couple of generations of concerted effort, and each of us can play a valuable role as educators and advocates for a cleaner world.

7

Choosing Fish and Fish Oil Supplements

Yου know fish is an important part of the pregnancy and postpartum diet. You know that it's rich in DHA, which you and your baby need. But you're concerned about mercury and other toxins in the fish you eat. And if they're in fish, what about fish oil supplements? Before you spend fifteen minutes in front of the fish counter at the market—or the fish oil shelf at the health food store—scratching your head, and walk away with nothing, read this chapter. Here's the basic plan:

- Eat a total of up to twelve ounces of low-mercury fish a week. Your servings can be from three to six ounces.
- Try to vary which fish you eat. Salmon is the best alternative. It is the least toxic and highest in the fatty acids you need in your breast milk.

Mercury in Fish: Not an Exact Science

The EPA's safe limit for mercury contamination in fish is one part per million (1.0 ppm). We won't include in our list of fish possibilities the four fish that have been called "off-limits" for pregnant or nursing women: king mackerel, shark, swordfish, and tilefish. Those fish have been found to contain up to 4.54 parts per million (ppm) mercury.

Tuna steaks should not be eaten more than once a month because their mercury content can rise above EPA limits. In addition, you should avoid any fish that has been caught anywhere in or near the Great Lakes.

The averages of mercury concentration reflect a broad range of concentrations found in different samples. It's hard to know what you're getting in an individual portion of fish because the ranges can be so broad. But the ranges will give you an idea of which fish are safest and most healthful. In Table 7.1 we have supplied a range of mercury concentrations for fish that may have mercury concentrations above the EPA's safe limit; for the others, we've supplied the average concentration found in many samples.

If you have a fisherman in your family or you like to eat locally caught fish, check local advisories about fish safety before eating them. You can go to the Environmental Protection Agency's site for local fish advisories: http://epa.gov/waterscience/fish/states.htm. In addition, at oceansalive.org/eat.cfm, you will find the EDF's healthy seafood selector. Dr. Rountree has been referring patients to this site for years and finds that it continually improves on its content and scope. They provide a handy "Eco-list" that can be downloaded and printed out for trips to the market, and a list of low-contaminant fish oil supplements by brand name.

Salmon: Wild-Caught or Farmed?

Generally, nutrition experts recommend that you eat wild-caught salmon rather than farmed salmon because of concerns about tests that showed high levels of PCBs, dioxins, and pesticides in farmed salmon.

A report published in 2003 by the Environmental Working Group (EWG) found that farmed salmon purchased in the United States contained the highest level of dioxin-like PCBs found in any

Table 7.1 Commonly Eaten Fish: DHA/EPA and Mercury Content

Fish	DHA and EPA (per 3–ounce serving)	Mercury Content (average in ppm) and Other Toxins/Comments
Blue crab	351 mg	Crab, overall, averaged
Dungeness crab	335 mg	0.06
Shrimp	268 mg	None detected
Lobster	71 mg	0.05–1.31 (Atlantic), 0.09 (Spiny)
Anchovies, canned in oil	1,747 mg	0.04
Freshwater bass	649 mg	0.36–0.43
Striped bass	822 mg	0.06–0.96 (PCBs, pesticides)
Bluefish	840 mg	0.31 (PCBs)
Turbot	181 mg	None detected
Catfish	150 mg	0.05
Clams	284 mg	None detected
Atlantic cod	134 mg	Cod, overall, averaged 0.11
Pacific cod	182 mg	
Flounder/sole	426 mg	0.05
Grouper	211 mg	0.00–1.21
Haddock	202 mg	0.03
Atlantic or Pacific halibut	395 mg	0.26–1.52
Greenland halibut	1,001 mg	No data available
Herring	1,712 mg	0.04
Atlantic kippered herring	1,827 mg	0.04
Atlantic mackerel	1,023 mg	0.18
Spanish mackerel	1,059 mg	(Mackerel is a larger predatory fish—higher levels of of mercury are more likely than in smaller fish.)
Ocean perch	318 mg	Low
Perch	275 mg	Low
Pollock	461 mg	0.06
Rockfish	377 mg	No data available
Orange roughy	1 mg	Low
Atlantic salmon, farmed	1,825 mg	None detected (The clear
Atlantic salmon, wild	1,564 mg	winner for low mercury
Coho salmon, canned, with bones	999 mg	and high DHA/EPA levels;
Coho salmon, wild	900 mg	concerns have been raised
Sockeye salmon	1,046 mg	about PCBs in farmed salmon.)

Table 7.1 Commonly Eaten Fish: DHA/EPA and Mercury Content (continued)

Fish	DHA and EPA (per 3–ounce serving)	Mercury Content (average in ppm) and Other Toxins/Comments
Atlantic sardines, canned in oil, with bones	835 mg	0.02 (another good choice—low in toxins, high in omega-3s)
Sea bass	648 mg	0.27
Sea trout	405 mg	0.08–0.74 (Oceans Alive recommends avoiding this fish because of PCBs.)
Snapper	273 mg	No data available
Rainbow trout, wild	840 mg	0.11
Rainbow trout, farmed	981 mg	Slightly higher than wild (likely safer because wild is caught in landlocked waters)
Rainbow trout, wild	840 mg	0.11
Light tuna, canned in water	230 mg	0–0.85 (Eat no more than six ounces of canned tuna per week.)
Yellowfin tuna, fresh	733 mg	0.38–1.30 (Eat Yellowfin no more than once a month.)
Whitefish	1,370 mg	0.07
Mussels	665 mg	None detected
Eastern oysters, farmed	468 mg	None detected
Pacific oysters	1,170 mg	None detected

Sources: Addendum A, "EPA and DHA Content of Fish Species"; data from NDB SR 16-1, "EPA and DHA Content of Fish Species," health.gov/dietaryguidelines/dga2005/report/html, accessed October 3, 2005. FDA Surveys, 1990–2003, "National Marine Fisheries Service Survey of Trace Elements in the Fishery Resource." Ache, B. W., F. C. Kopfler, "The Occurrence of Mercury in the Fishery Resources of the Gulf of Mexico," Bldg. 1103, Room 202, Stennis Space Center, MS 39529, 2001.

food: some sixteen times that found in wild salmon and just under three and a half times that found in other seafood. The EWG recommended eating no more than one eight-ounce serving of farmed salmon once a month. Fish feed is believed to be the toxic culprit, along with the more sedentary lifestyle of farmed fish, which lets them put on extra weight as fat.

A larger survey of seven hundred fish, sponsored by the Pew Charitable Trust and published in the journal *Science*, also showed much higher levels of PCBs and dioxins in farmed salmon than in wild-caught salmon. Researchers from the University of Illinois deduced that the risk-to-benefit ratio of farmed salmon consumption—based on the benefits of the omega-3 fats they contain versus any increase in cancer risk from toxicity—suggests that exposure to contaminants in farmed salmon are partially offset by the benefits of the fatty acids. But they give this caveat: "Young women, women of child-bearing age, pregnant women, and nursing mothers not at significant risk for sudden cardiac death associated with coronary heart disease but concerned with health impairments such as reduction in IQ and other cognitive and behavioral effects, can minimize contaminant exposure by choosing the least contaminated wild salmon or by selecting other sources of omega-3 fatty acids" (Foran JA, et al., "Quantitative Analysis of the Benefits and Risks of Consuming Framed and Wild Salmon," *Journal of Nutrition* 2005 Nov 22; 135 (11): 2639–43).

Some sources of farm-raised salmon are cleaner than others. A 2004 survey from Indiana University researchers found that farm-raised salmon from Europe has higher PBDE levels than salmon raised in North America, with the European salmon having an average of ten times the toxicity level. Both European and North American farm-raised salmon has higher levels of PBDE than salmon raised in Chile.

In general, eat wild-caught whenever possible. Wild chinook salmon have been found to have higher toxicity levels than other types of wild salmon, probably because of their feeding habits and larger size. Limit consumption of farmed salmon to once or twice a month. If you don't want to pay top dollar for wild-caught, get your omega-3s from fish oil supplements.

One source of reasonably priced, clean, low-mercury canned tuna, wild king salmon, and dungeness crab that we can recommend is Carvalho Fisheries, located in McKinleyville, California. Visit carvalhofisheries.com to order their products online. With an Internet search, you can find many other companies specializing in mail-order sales of wild-caught, low-toxin fish.

Cooking Fish

Poaching, steaming, baking (at 375°F), and sautéing are best for fish. Avoid microwaving, as it has been shown to greatly reduce antioxidant content of foods (for example, some studies show a drop in flavonoid content of 97 percent). Research by Helen Vlassara at Mt. Sinai School of Medicine shows that microwaving increases formation of *advanced glycosylation endproducts* (AGEs)—very toxic inflammatory triggers. It is likely that microwaving has adverse effects on delicate long-chain omega-3 fats as well. Both authors of this book admit to occasional use of the microwave, but recommend doing so infrequently.

Grilling, barbecuing, broiling, and deep-frying are suitable only for occasional meals, as high heat creates carcinogenic chemicals called heterocyclic amines (HCAs) and benzo(a)pyrenes. Studies consistently show that people who develop cancer are likely to eat well-done or charred meat more often than those who don't develop the disease. However, fewer of these chemicals are produced in seafood than in beef or chicken cooked at similarly high temperatures. Marinating fish before cooking at high temperatures reduces HCA and benzo(a)pyrene production.

Choosing a Fish Oil Supplement

I've had patients tell me that they didn't want to take fish oil supplements because they were worried that the "acids" would hurt their stomach. However, fatty acids are not acidic. Take a fish oil supplement daily that delivers 1,100 to 2,400 mg per day of DHA. Fish oil supplements generally contain 180 mg of EPA and 120 mg of DHA per one gram of oil.

Liquid supplements usually contain between one and three grams (1,000 to 3,000 milligrams) of EPA plus DHA per teaspoon. Some higher-potency supplements contain higher concentrations of these fats—up to 400 mg EPA and 200 mg DHA per gram of fish oil. Choose a supplement with omega-3s comprised of at least ¼ DHA to ¾ EPA. During pregnancy and lactation a higher ratio of DHA to EPA—as high as 4.6:1—is believed to be more beneficial. (Once you're done nursing, you can use a supplement that contains a higher EPA to DHA ratio—and you may want to do so

if you have an allergic condition such as asthma, eczema, or psoriasis; chronic pain; or if you are interested in preventing heart disease or cancer.)

Dr. Rountree recommends High DHA Finest Pure Fish Oil, made
by a company called Pharmax (800-538-8274 or pharmaca.com).
It provides 1,200 mg DHA and 260 mg EPA per teaspoon. *This is
the single most important supplement that can be recommended
to nursing mothers*—both for neonatal brain development and prevention of postpartum depression. Do not take fish liver oils, which
have high concentrations of vitamins A and D that could build up to
toxic levels in your body.

The purity of fish oil supplements has been raised as a concern, and rightly so: since POPs concentrate in the fat of fish, concentrating this fat is also likely to concentrate those toxins even
further. To ensure purity:

- Choose oils from anchovies, sardines, or salmon.
- Check the packaging to ensure that the oil has been
  subjected to molecular distillation, which removes heavy
  metals and organochlorines. (No mercury contamination
  has been detected in commercially available fish oils;
  mercury is not a fat-soluble substance.)
- Fish oils should also contain an antioxidant to prevent
  rancidity: vitamin E and rosemary oil are commonly used
  for this purpose.

Vegetarian DHA supplements are available. These are not the
same thing as flaxseed oil, a source of the short-chain omega-3,
alpha-linolenic acid (ALA). They are derived from marine algae,
the source of DHA in the diet of salmon. Studies show that algal
DHA is well absorbed and effective at increasing body levels of
this nutrient.

Potential Side Effects from DHA/EPA Supplements

Belching, flatulence, diarrhea, bloating, and nausea have all been
reported with high doses of fish oil—higher than those we recommend here. If you do have these issues, cut down on your daily

Fish Oil for Toddlers

If your toddler is still nursing, continue taking fish oil supplements to enrich your milk with DHA. Formula-fed toddlers should either use a DHA/ARA formula or get fish oil as a chewable or liquid supplement. Liquid fish oil can be added to formula along with probiotics. Continue to use a supplement designed for children, and follow the dosage directions on the container.

Asthmatic and atopic kids may benefit most. A study from the European Respiratory Journal *found that a fish oil supplement containing 84 mg of EPA and 36 mg of DHA had significant positive effects on asthma symptoms in children, with no side effects.*

If you choose to use a cod liver oil supplement, make sure that your child is not getting too much pre-formed vitamin A (infants, more than 20,000 IU per day; older children, more than 100,000 IU per day) or vitamin D (over 2,000 IU per day over a period of years in children aged one to thirteen) in the supplement or in conjunction with a multivitamin/mineral supplement.

Why You Should Use a High-DHA Omega-3 Supplement

EPA is a great anti-inflammatory omega-3, but there is some evidence that high amounts of this oil can adversely affect a baby's ability to utilize DHA, which is far more important during infancy. Pregnant and nursing women should use an omega-3 supplement that contains mostly DHA and ALA, with a small amount of EPA.

When formula manufacturers started to add EPA to formulas along with DHA, levels of AA fell in the babies fed the formula. Other research has shown that high-EPA formulas can slow an infant's growth. Adding

> *extra AA into the formula solved the problem and didn't cause adverse effects.*
>
> *In nature, EPA and DHA exist together in about a one-to-three to one-to-six ratio. No research that we could find showed that amounts of DHA and EPA that naturally occur in mother's milk with a reasonable fish oil supplement are enough to slow growth or cause AA levels to fall. However, it seems prudent that both pregnant women and nursing mothers take an omega-3 supplement that is high in DHA. (Most fish oil supplements have slightly more EPA than DHA.)*

dose or try a different brand. One brand, Coromega, comes in a small tube and tastes like an orange Dreamsicle—it's sweet, with no fishy taste. Women who have trouble taking pills or who can't deal with "fish burps" may want to try this version of fish oil. (It's a good one for older children, too.)

If you are using fish oil while pregnant, be aware that very high doses—8,000 mg or greater—have been found to impair blood's clotting function, which could pose a threat if you require emergency C-section or bleed out after giving birth. To be on the safe side, taper off your fish oil supplements two weeks before your due date—go to the lowest dose of 200 mg a day or stop them altogether—and start taking them again the day after your baby is born. You can still eat fish during those weeks.

8

Creating the Best Possible Mother's Milk: First, Stock Your Kitchen

We know *why* we should eat better. But then there's the small matter of *how*. This matter of how to eat a healthier diet is often the worst enemy of good intentions. With the bewildering amount of dietary advice available everywhere we look, it's hard to know where to turn for reliable, simple guidelines. Most plans are ridiculously complicated, even for the person who isn't groggy from staying up half the night with a new baby. It's enough to make you want to pack the kids into the car and head for the drive-through.

Pantry and Refrigerator Staples

It helps a lot to keep certain things on hand at all times. Before we get into the specifics of recipes and daily food plans (Chapter 9), let's make sure you have these staples in your pantry (see Table 8.1), in your fridge (see Table 8.2), and in your kitchen (see Table 8.3).

Table 8.1 Pantry Staples

Canned tomatoes	Raw pumpkin seeds
Canned wild salmon	Tahini (sesame seed paste)
Canned sardines (whole fish, bones and all)	Green tea bags (try green tea flavored with orange or lemon if you don't like the taste)
Canned light tuna	Slivered almonds
Canned beans (a variety: chickpeas, black beans, pinto beans, white beans)	Whole flaxseed (for grinding and adding to dressings, hot cereal, etc.)
Chicken broth and/or vegetable broth (low-sodium, MSG-free)	Natural nut butters (try almond butter, macadamia nut butter, cashew butter)
Canned soups (MSG-free—for those times when you need something quick)	Vinegar (a couple of good types—balsamic, champagne, red or white wine)
Salsa	Raw walnuts
Brown and/or white rice	Sesame seeds
Whole-grain crackers	Oat or rice bran
Rolled oats	Extra-virgin olive oil
Corn tortillas (can freeze or refrigerate to extend shelf life)	Tamari/shoyu (naturally fermented soy sauce)
Desiccated (dried unsweetened) coconut	Canola mayonnaise
Organic dried berries	Cold-pressed canola oil*
Honey	Cold-pressed peanut oil*
Maple syrup (natural)	Coconut oil*
Condensed sweetened milk (for making coconut macaroons)	Stir-fry sauces (preferably from the health food store; refrigerate after opening)
Stevia powder and xylitol	Dried sea vegetables (wakame, nori, kelp)
Whey protein powder	Dry sherry (for stir-frying)

*Cold-pressed oils are preferable; other processing methods introduce high temperatures and/or chemicals that can make the oils less healthful.

Table 8.2 Foods to Keep in Your Fridge and Freezer

Refrigerator Staples	**Freezer Staples**
Organic omega-3 eggs	Pitted cherries
Organic whole or 2% milk	Mango or peach pieces
Purple grape juice (100% fruit; if you don't want to drink red wine)	Berries (blueberries, strawberries, blackberries, and any others you like)
Fruit-sweetened catsup	Orange juice concentrate
Organic plain yogurt (low-fat or full-fat—no sugar or high fructose corn syrup)	Variety of fresh-frozen vegetables (spinach, broccoli, peas, cauliflower, asparagus)
Apples (organic if possible; if not, peel or wash very thoroughly)	Meats—free-range boneless chicken breasts, whole chickens, pork chops, roasts, lean beef

Table 8.2 Foods to Keep in Your Fridge and Freezer (continued)

Refrigerator Staples	Freezer Staples
Organic butter	Wild-caught salmon, other fish*
Organic cheese (a variety: Parmesan, cheddar, Monterey Jack, Neufchâtel, mozzarella, feta)	Whole-grain bread, preferably made from sprouted grains**
Salad greens	
Celery	
Onions	
Minced garlic	
Minced ginger	
Lemon juice	
Lime juice	
Tofu	
Soy and/or rice milk	
Liquid chlorophyll (for adding to drinking water)	
Miso (fermented soybean paste)	

*Don't keep frozen fish or other meats in the freezer for more than one month. If you prefer to buy fresh fish and other meats, by all means do so. Having frozen versions on hand as well will help ensure that you always have what you need to make a balanced meal.

**100 percent rye is good too, but make it something you'll be willing to eat. Keeping it in the freezer ensures that you won't constantly be tossing moldy half-loaves into the trash.

Why Whey?

Curds from milk are made into cheese, and *whey* is the watery, protein-rich stuff that's left behind. Whey has had medicinal uses in many traditional cultures around the world for centuries. When dehydrated and turned into protein powder, it's an excellent source of amino acids that has low potential for allergenicity or gastrointestinal irritation. Whey protein improves the function of immune cells along the walls of the intestines. Whey protein may also help to improve mood and mental focus by boosting levels of a specific amino acid, *tryptophan*, in the body—the precursor (raw material) for the "feel-good" neurotransmitter serotonin. A rise in tryptophan levels in the brain can increase serotonin availability and can reduce levels of the stress hormone cortisol at the same time. Whey protein from cow's milk is high in beta-lactoglobulin, which effectively raises glutathione levels in the body.

Table 8.3 Helpful Spices and Cooking Tools

Spice Cabinet Staples	Kitchen Equipment
Basil	Rice cooker
Bay leaves	Salad spinner
Cinnamon	Blender
Cumin (ground)	Coffee grinder (for grinding flaxseed, other seeds, and spices)
Curry powder	Food scale (for measuring servings of fish and meat)
Garlic (dried)	Good, sharp knives
Ginger (dried)	Handheld blender (especially good for making homemade baby food!)
Onion (dried)	Glass containers with glass lids for food storage and microwaving
Pepper (white, red,	of foods*
lemon, black)	Mandoline, slicer, or Cuisinart
Parsley	Wooden spoons or spatulas
Rosemary	Ziplock bags, various sizes
Sage	Waxed paper
Thyme	
Iodized salt	
Garlic salt	
Vanilla extract	
Almond extract	

*Don't microwave anything wrapped in plastic—this releases toxic chemicals into the food.

What You Should Toss Out

In addition to stocking your pantry with the right foods, you should also be looking at what is currently in there. Get rid of any of these food items:

- Prepared foods that contain MSG—usually, most store-bought soups, sauces, and salad dressings (See Appendix A for a list of alternate names that usually mean MSG and other information on why to avoid it when possible.)
- Crisco or other hydrogenated vegetable oil shortening
- Chips, cookies, cake or cookie mixes, or other prepared foods that contain hydrogenated oil
- Liquid corn or soybean oils (These go rancid as soon as they hit the frying pan.)

- Meat substitutes made with soy (They are usually high in MSG.)
- Anything that contains cottonseed oil (It is contaminated with pesticides that aren't allowed on food crops.)
- Frozen or packaged meals that contain long lists of preservatives, hydrogenated oils, sugars, and flavorings
- Sodas and "juice beverages" that contain high fructose corn syrup or artificial sweeteners (Instead, try combining sparkling water with a small amount of grape, berry, or pomegranate juice.)
- Anything sweetened with NutraSweet, Splenda, or other chemical artificial sweeteners
- Flaxseed oil, which goes rancid very quickly; you're better off with ground flaxseed

What to Look for with Artificial Sweeteners

Artificial sweeteners don't help you to lose weight or eat more healthfully—they just whet your sweet tooth and are likely to make you crave the real thing! Aspartame has been the subject of a great many complaints to the FDA and not uncommonly has been linked with mysterious symptoms that go away when aspartame consumption stops: visual changes, confusion, dizziness, ringing in the ears, mood changes, irritability, nausea, allergic reactions, and urinary problems. Long-term use has been linked with increased risk of brain tumor. While Splenda (sucralose) is billed as safer and more "natural," there isn't enough information on it at this writing to say it's totally safe. There have been many reports of severe allergic reactions and longer-term chronic gastrointestinal problems with use of Splenda.

Two safe artificial sweeteners you can keep in your cabinets are xylitol and stevia. *Xylitol* is a sweetener derived from wood and naturally found in plums and raspberries. It poses no health risks and tastes good—and helps to prevent upper respiratory, ear, and gum infections. Because it is not completely broken down in the gastrointestinal tract, it delivers fewer sugar calories to the body. It has been used in foods since the 1960s and is a popular sweetener in foods made for diabetics. Xylitol inhibits the growth

Concerns About Canned Foods: Bisphenol A

You've probably noticed that we tell you to keep a lot of canned foods handy, and you may be concerned about the fact that the insides of many cans are coated with epoxy resins to prevent leaching of metals into the food they contain. Unfortunately, those resins contain bisphenol A (BPA), *which also can leach into the liquid or food the can contains. BPA is a xenoestrogen that has hormone-disrupting effects in the body.*

According to some sources—not surprisingly, from the makers and sellers of BPA and products that contain it—the average amount of BPA consumed per person via canned foods is 450 times less than the EPA's maximum acceptable reference dose of 0.05 milligrams per kilogram body weight per day. According to these estimates, created by the Society of the Plastics Industry, an adult would have to eat five hundred pounds of canned food a day for her whole lifespan to exceed the EPA's safe limit.

The folks at the Society of the Plastics Industry don't factor in other sources of BPA, such as polycarbonate plastics and dental sealants used in kids' mouths, or the interactive effects of this with other chemicals at levels far below the current safe limits. The safety of normal exposures to BPA are suspect enough that legislation is being batted around in some states to restrict the use of BPA-containing chemicals in any product intended for use by children under the age of three.

However, at this writing, we deduce that whatever small BPA exposure you get from canned foods is offset by the ease of using canned tomatoes, beans, and fish to whip up quick, healthful recipes. Although fresh food is always better, canned is OK in a pinch.

of the most common tooth decay–causing bacteria, *Streptococcus mutans*, and its close cousin, *Streptococcus pneumo*, a primary cause of ear infections. Mothers who chew gum that contains xylitol may help to prevent nursing caries, a form of tooth decay that strikes in toddlers and can cause considerable damage. Current theories about nursing caries (also, ironically, known as "baby bottle mouth") point to bacteria that are harbored in the mouth of the mother. When a baby's teeth start to come in, try a xylitol-sweetened, fluoride-free baby toothpaste such as the one made by Biotene. Keep in mind, however, that consuming too much xylitol can cause diarrhea.

Stevia is a sweet herb native to Paraguay. It has been used as a sweetener for at least a century. There's been some controversy over stevia with the FDA. Although it has been used safely around the world for quite some time—and although it appears to have blood pressure–lowering and blood sugar–balancing effects—the FDA has classified stevia as a food supplement. It's illegal to call it a sweetener or refer to it as "sweet" if you're selling something that contains it. This is not a reflection on stevia's safety. There's no reason why a pregnant or nursing woman shouldn't use small amounts of it to replace sugar in her diet. You can buy stevia or stevia-sweetened products in most health food stores. You can't use it for baking without adjusting for the loss of bulk and other chemical characteristics of processed sugar. It also has a more bitter taste than other sweeteners when added to tea and coffee.

Making Sense of the Soy Controversy

A handful of concerned scientists and buzz-savvy journalists are raising a stink over purported health risks of consuming too much soy. There is some concern—warranted, but still in need of investigation—about giving infants soy formula, which is estimated to deliver to their tiny bodies five times the dose of isoflavones that have been found to alter the menstrual cycle in adult women. We will cover the topic of soy formula more extensively in Chapter 10, and if you are formula-feeding, you can get all the facts there.

Soybeans contain high concentrations of hormone-like chemicals, plant estrogens (phytoestrogens) called *isoflavones*. The isoflavones genistein and daidzein are the best known and most thoroughly researched. Soy is not the only abundant source of phytoestrogens—flaxseed, alfalfa sprouts, green beans, mung bean sprouts, garbanzo beans, fenugreek, and fava beans are also rich sources. Even red wine contains phytoestrogens.

Phytoestrogens from soy readily pass into breast milk. Although theoretical adverse effects of phytoestrogens in breast milk are currently being studied, no evidence of harm to the developing reproductive system of infants has been established. Foods made from soy have been eaten by humans for centuries. Contrary to many sources, however, they have not historically been a human food staple, in Asia or anywhere else. Sources that claim that Asians are long-lived or healthy because they eat lots of soy aren't telling the whole story. Asians have a lot of other good habits, including the consumption of more fish and vegetables and few processed foods.

Soybeans contain *phytates*, which block mineral absorption in the intestines, and enzyme inhibitors that hinder protein digestion. The anti-soy camp states that phytates and enzyme inhibitors are a threat to our health, depriving us of needed nutrients by blocking their digestion, but this is not borne out in published research except in parts of the world where people are frankly mineral deficient. Preparation of these foods in traditional ways—which have been refined over centuries—and combination of soy foods with other, mineral-rich foods like seaweeds and whole grains—circumvent the potential adverse effects of chemicals in soy that could block mineral absorption.

Anti-soy crusaders make some arguments against this food that are not substantiated by published studies. One oft-cited study traces a link between soy foods during pregnancy and increased risk of hypospadias (where the opening of a male child's penis develops in the wrong place), but really, all that study tells us is that vegetarian women are more likely to have a boy child with this birth defect (which is usually fixed with surgery). Any link with soy is purely speculative.

Much good is believed to come from eating moderate amounts of soy—amounts in keeping with the recommendations from government health experts. It's a good source of low-fat vegetarian protein. A recent animal study showed that a mother rat who consumes soy isoflavones during pregnancy supports the heart health of her offspring, protecting them against cardiac failure later on. Other research suggests that girl children who eat soy may be protected against breast cancer later in life. Soy consumption has also been linked with protective effects against osteoporosis, cardiovascular diseases, prostate cancer, and thyroid cancer, and it can reduce blood cholesterol levels.

Here, as with so many other aspects of diet, it appears that moderation is key. Moderation doesn't make headlines, boost the next diet revolution, or sell books, but it's safe to consume on a daily basis while breastfeeding. Here's a quick soy primer:

- **Miso.** A paste made from fermented soybeans; it may also include small amounts of rice or barley. Use to make miso soup (see recipe in Chapter 9), flavor salad dressing, or in miso-tahini-sprout sandwiches.
- **Bean curd (tofu).** A cake made from soybeans cooked for a lengthy period with calcium salts, tofu picks up the flavors of sauces and seasonings well. Cut into triangles or cubes and stir-fry or deep-fry it; bake it in slices to eat with whole grains and vegetables; or cut tiny cubes to eat in miso soup.
- **Tamari/shoyu.** A traditionally fermented, delicious soy sauce.
- **Tempeh.** A small cake made with fermented soybeans. You can use it crumbled to replace ground beef in recipes, or pour some barbecue sauce over it and grill or bake it for eating in tacos or "sloppeh joes."
- **Edamame.** The young, green soybeans in pods that are a popular appetizer at sushi restaurants. Buy them frozen and boil for two or three minutes, then pop the beans out of the pods into your mouth with your teeth.

- **Soy milk.** Available in sweetened, unsweetened, chocolate, vanilla, and many other varieties. To be on the safe side, avoid high-isoflavone soy milk if you consume it regularly.
- **Soy protein powder and isoflavone pills.** Avoid the latter, as there is not enough evidence to support their safety for nursing mothers. Protein powders made from soy are OK every so often, but whey is probably better on a day-to-day basis.

Current recommendations call for one to four servings of soy per day. A half-cup of edamame, tempeh, or tofu, a cup of soy milk, or two tablespoons of miso is one serving.

Glycemic Index and Glycemic Load

Once you've gotten all of the recommended staples, top yourself off with some fresh produce. Choose primarily low-glycemic versions. The *glycemic index* (GI) is a measurement of how quickly and how high a food raises blood sugar levels. The glycemic index of the foods you eat won't affect the quality of your breast milk; in fact, a lot of high-glycemic foods are great sources of nutrients, like sweet potatoes, carrots, and bananas. But if you stick to lower-glycemic foods, it's going to benefit *you* by keeping your blood sugar levels steadier. You won't soar and crash and find yourself scrambling for something sugary between meals.

Generally, the more processed a food, the higher its glycemic index, but this is not always the case. For example, a boiled new potato has a glycemic index of 70, but spaghetti has a glycemic index of 50. White rice is a 72 on the glycemic index scale, and white bread is a 69; pure fructose (fruit sugar) is only a 20! (We don't recommend that you buy processed foods that are high in fructose; eating a lot of fructose causes elevations in "bad" cholesterol.)

Another term, *glycemic load* (GL), looks at the way the glycemic index and serving size of a carb-rich food interact to cause fluctuations in blood sugar. The gist of it is this: if you eat small portions of carbohydrates, the jump in insulin isn't going to be as great as if you eat large portions. You can also modulate insulin jumps by combining high-GI foods with protein, fiber, and healthy fats.

Although many diet plans designed for weight loss will tell you to completely avoid anything with a high glycemic index, we're not going to do that. Many of the fruits and vegetables that score high on the glycemic index chart are sources of highly beneficial phyochemicals that outweigh their effects on blood sugar. Just eat low–glycemic index foods often and high–glycemic index foods in moderation (see Table 8.4)—and make sure you accompany them with protein and fiber. Combining high-GI foods with protein and fiber attenuates the rise in blood sugar.

Table 8.4 High- and Low-Glycemic Index Fruits and Vegetables

Low-GI Foods	High-GI Foods
Asparagus	Tubers and roots
Broccoli	Corn
Cabbage	Beets
Cauliflower	Carrots
Celery	Parsnips
Cucumber	Pumpkin
Summer squash	Winter squash
Leafy greens (such as spinach, collards, kale, chard, endive)	Potatoes (yams or sweet potatoes are more nutritious than white)
Zucchini	Watermelon
Green beans	Pineapple
Onions	Cantaloupe
Radishes	Raisins
Tomatoes	Mango
Apples	Papaya
Berries	Banana
Dried apricots	
Grapefruit	
Oranges	
Peaches	
Pears	
Plums	
Cherries	

In the next chapter, we give you guidelines for a very simple whole-food dietary regimen that will incorporate all of the nutritional elements you need to make premium breast milk—and to have plenty of nutrients left over for your own consumption. We will try to preserve the pleasure of eating while reducing the amount of work required to make healthful meals.

9

Putting It All Together: Meals and Recipes

E verything we recommend in this chapter will be easy and quick to prepare. When you have a babe in arms or at your breast virtually around the clock, you don't have the time or energy to be chopping or standing over the stove for long periods, or going to three different markets to buy all of the necessary ingredients. But that doesn't mean you have to live on frozen microwaveable dinners and sports nutrition bars. Perhaps the basic fare we include in our dietary regimen will seem a little bland at first, but your taste buds will adjust, and it can be dressed up with a little creativity.

Each meal should include a protein, at least one low-glycemic vegetable or fruit, and a whole-grain carbohydrate. We won't get too fussy about ratios here, or about exact calorie counts; we'll give you general ideas of portion sizes and let you wing it from there. Overwhelmingly, the evidence shows that *what* you eat will almost entirely take care of the problem of *how much* to eat.

Drs. Walter Willett, Meir Stampfer, and Frank Hu, professors at the Harvard School of Public Health, have created a new "food pyramid" that is supported by solid science. It's a perfect model for nursing mothers to follow.

At the top of the pyramid are red meat and butter, which they recommend be used sparingly; also at the top are white rice, white bread, sweets, and pasta, which they say should also be used sparingly. Alcohol is recommended in moderation (one drink per day); so is dairy (one to two servings per day). Then, there's fish, poultry, and eggs (zero to two servings per day); nuts and legumes (one to three servings); fruit (two to three servings); and abundant vegetables and whole-grain foods at most meals. Plant oils—such as olive, canola, and peanut—are also recommended at most meals. Willett and coworkers recommend multivitamins for most people, and their pyramid sits on top of a broad base labeled "Daily Exercise and Weight Control."

No one diet will work for every person who tries it. This goes for Mom and for baby. Some nurslings seem colicky or fussy when Mom eats certain foods, or to dislike the taste of Mom's milk after she eats foods that have strong flavors. Baby's diarrhea, vomiting, or eczema (itchy skin rash) can be caused by foods Mom eats, as proteins from those foods pass into her milk and into the baby. The following foods might cause a problem for some nurslings:

Broccoli
Cabbage
Cauliflower
Chocolate
Citrus fruits
Cow's milk (and dairy products made from cow's milk)
Cucumber
Eggs
Garlic
Onion
Peanuts
Strong spices
Wheat

The only way to know for sure whether your nursing baby is reacting to a food in your diet is to try to link baby's health complaints with a food you eat and eliminate that food from your diet for at least a week to see whether it helps.

Once a Week: Food Prep

For nontoxic, safe kitchen disinfecting, keep one spray bottle of hydrogen peroxide and another of white vinegar; spray each on surfaces (in any order) and wipe both up at the same time. This technique kills as many bacteria as chlorine bleach.

If you've bought fresh vegetables, prep them for cooking:

- Wash cauliflower or broccoli, dry thoroughly, and cut into florets. Store it in a ziplock bag or other sealable container with a folded paper towel (to absorb extra moisture).
- If you buy fresh spinach or other leafy greens, submerge them in water and then drain; remove stems and store in a sealable container, also with a folded paper towel.
- Use a permanent marker to label the bags with the purchase date, or use masking tape if you're using reusable containers. Be sure to get washed produce as dry as possible before storing it to avoid accelerating spoilage.
- If you plan to make stir-fries, cut veggies very small (no larger than a quarter). The goal here is to be able to reach into the fridge and dump ingredients directly into salads or cooking vessels.
- Dice an onion and keep it in a tightly sealed ziplock bag or resealable plastic container. Although it'll lose some of its flavor, this is not a more formidable problem than having to dice onion while holding a baby or dealing with a toddler (or both). If you prefer to keep your onions whole until you use them, you can buy a handheld dicer that will dice onions with a twist of the wrist.
- Tear up (don't cut) and wash salad greens. Make sure you get them completely dry before putting them in the fridge. If you like other veggies in your salad, add them now, but don't yet add tomato, avocado, or sprouts.

If you buy large packages of meat, poultry, or fish:

- Separate it into single-serving or meal-sized portions.
- Freeze all that you don't plan to use within a couple of days. To prevent freezer burn, try to make packages airtight, and don't stack them until they are frozen solid—instead, spread them out on the freezer shelf.
- If you like to stir-fry, cut meats into small cubes or slices of uniform size and wrap airtight before freezing. To use, thaw in the refrigerator as you would a whole piece of meat.

If you find a great deal on fresh fruit:

- Freeze what you can't use in a few days. Cut larger fruits into pieces to freeze. Pit cherries before freezing.
- To prevent pieces from freezing together, place berries or pieces of cut-up fruit on waxed paper–covered cookie trays and freeze for an hour, then place in ziplock bags or other airtight containers and return to the freezer.

Make salad dressing if needed:

- Combine three parts olive oil with one part vinegar (balsamic and rice vinegars are good) and add seasoning (one-quarter teaspoon of dried herbs or one or two tablespoons of fresh herbs per four servings). A hand blender will emulsify the dressing beautifully.
- Try adding a dollop of Dijon or dry mustard, a tablespoon or two of lemon juice, minced garlic, or shallot. Toss your salads in one or two tablespoons of this dressing just before eating.
- If you prefer a creamy dressing, try this recipe for tahini dressing from Feeding the Whole Family by Cynthia Lair, whole-foods cooking instructor (Seattle, WA: Moon Smile Press, 1997). Place one-half cup tahini, one-quarter cup extra-virgin olive oil, the juice of one and a half lemons, a clove of garlic, a teaspoon of tamari or shoyu, a pinch of

cayenne pepper, and three-quarters cup water in a blender or food processor and blend until smooth; let sit at least half an hour so the flavors can blend. Lair recommends using this dressing for salads, brown rice, vegetables, or noodles.

Additional items:

- Hard-boil some eggs, and peel them if you like.
- Toast some pumpkin seeds, either in a large, heavy skillet or on a baking sheet in a 350°F oven. Wait for a toasty smell and the sound of seeds starting to pop—that's how you know they're done. Keep close track of them; they burn easily.
- Make granola (see recipe later in this chapter) if needed.

When It's Time to Eat

The next time it's time to eat, whether you're pulling out of the drive-through with a double cheeseburger in your lap or sitting down to a home-cooked, veggie-rich meal that happens to coincide with your baby's afternoon snooze, pause for a moment. Look at the food you're about to put into your mouth. Appreciate it. Thank your Higher Power for providing nourishment for you and your baby. Say a brief prayer if you like to do so before eating. Take a breath or two. Even if your baby needs you, even if he's squirming on your lap or crying, take a few moments to be aware of what you are eating.

Take small bites and chew them thoroughly. Food that's incompletely chewed can cause gastrointestinal distress as the friendly bacteria in your digestive system try to finish the job your teeth should already have handled. Roll the food around in your mouth and taste it fully. Take a breath between bites.

When we gobble down our food without appreciation or awareness, we leave the table feeling less satisfied. We're more likely to turn to the intense tastes of sugar or refined foods to try to "top ourselves off." And we set a poor example for our children. With this in mind, let's move on to the actual meal plan.

Breakfast Dishes

First thing in the morning, have a tall glass of cool (not cold) water with a tablespoon of liquid chlorophyll. You can premix the chlorophyll water in a bottle or pitcher and keep it in the refrigerator. Or try a glass of warm water with lemon squeezed in.

We also recommend a powdered green drink with concentrated organic fruits, berries, vegetables, barley grass, chlorella, apple pectin, oat beta-glucan, and probiotics. There are many such powders on the market, but we like one called Greens First that is made by Doctors for Nutrition. It's available in doctors' offices and at firstshake.com and amazon.com. One scoop of this powder, which tastes great, contains the amount of antioxidants found in ten servings of fruits and vegetables!

If you like coffee, have one cup (six to eight ounces), and stick with organically grown beans as much as possible. Decaffeinated varieties should be Swiss water process only; others are processed with harsh chemical solvents like methylene chloride, a known carcinogen. Some research shows a link between coffee consumption and risk of miscarriage and infertility. Pregnant women should have no more than one eight-ounce cup of coffee a day. If you prefer, have tea. Your baby will probably settle down for his morning feeding while you have your water and/or tea and/or coffee.

When your breakfast time rolls around, choose from one of the following options.

- Three-quarters cup of homemade granola (see recipe) stirred into a cup of plain yogurt with as many fresh, frozen, or dried berries as you like, plus a tablespoon of ground flaxseed (grind just before using). If you choose instead to buy granola, find a version that's low in sugar, made with all natural ingredients, and contains no hydrogenated oils.
- Twelve- to sixteen-ounce smoothie made with yogurt; frozen fruit; a spoon of orange, white grape, or apple juice concentrate; half a tablespoon of ground flaxseed; a scoop of whey protein powder; and enough water to reach the desired consistency. Add a tablespoon of greens

powder if you don't mind the taste or color (it will turn your smoothie green or brown) and a tablespoon of desiccated coconut if you don't mind the texture.

- One or two poached, scrambled, or fried omega-3 eggs, preferably organic (use a small amount of butter or canola oil for scrambling or frying). Add liberal servings of spinach, zucchini, tomato, onion, or other vegetable to the oil before scrambling eggs, or eat your eggs with chopped raw vegetables. Have one slice of whole-grain toast with Neufchâtel cheese (low-fat cream cheese), butter, or trans fat-free omega-3 spread. If you do not include veggies in your eggs, have some fresh berries or grapes.
- A bowl of slow-cooked oatmeal with fresh or dried berries. Add a half tablespoon of maple syrup or a pinch of stevia powder to sweeten if needed, and stir in a tablespoon of ground flaxseed and top with a dollop of plain yogurt.

Take morning supplements with breakfast. Taking them with food enhances their absorption.

San Marcos Parent-Child Workshop Recipe for Homemade Granola

Thanks to staffers at this co-op preschool in Santa Barbara, California, for this simple recipe—especially delicious warm right from the oven.

> 1 large (42 oz.) carton old-fashioned rolled oats
> 2 tablespoons cinnamon
> ½ cup brown sugar
> ½ cup honey (since it contains honey, do not feed this to a baby less than one year old)
> ½ cup oil (try canola, extra-light olive, or coconut oil, or a mixture)
> 2 tablespoons maple syrup
> 1 tablespoon vanilla extract
> ½–1 cup fresh chopped apple
> ½–1 cup raisins (organic) or other dried fruit
> ½ cup slivered almonds or other nuts
> ½–1 cup desiccated coconut (optional)
> Sesame, pumpkin, or sunflower seeds (optional)

1. Mix the oats, brown sugar and cinnamon in large mixing bowl. Mix honey, oil, maple syrup, and vanilla in a separate, small bowl. Mix with dry ingredients and add apple or any fresh fruit you are using.

2. Spread over one or two baking sheets. Bake at 325°F for 30 to 40 minutes, stirring often. Cool and add dried fruit, nuts, or coconut. Store in an airtight container or in the refrigerator. If you only need small portions each day, freeze half the batch.

Makes 20 to 30 servings

Balanced Snacks

Try to make snacks balanced, incorporating lean protein, healthful fat, and complex carbohydrate. If you have to skip one part of this equation, make it the carbs. A high-carb, low-fat scone will satisfy your nosh needs in the short term, but will send your blood sugar peaking and crashing within an hour or two. Here are some ideas for balanced snacks:

- One-half cup cottage cheese or plain yogurt with berries or peaches and granola
- Apple slices with one to two tablespoons nut butter or a few small slices of cheese
- Whole-grain bread or crackers with nut butter or cheese
- Cold chicken or other meat wrapped in a lettuce leaf with a dab of canola mayonnaise
- Smoothie (as described in the breakfast section, if you didn't have one for breakfast)
- Celery with nut butter or soft cheese
- Toasted sheet of nori wrapped around rice and salmon or tuna salad
- Toasted corn tortilla with avocado and cheese, sprinkled with garlic salt; add tomato, sprouts, or other veggies if desired

If there's no time for balance, have a protein snack: nuts, pumpkin seeds, a hard-boiled egg, some pieces of leftover cooked chicken or beef, or a slice or two of cheese.

How about commercially available "energy bars"? Many of the more popular versions are loaded with sugar or sugar substitutes and a lot of artificial ingredients. Choose organic bars made from nuts, dates, and other fruits, without refined sugar, like those sold by Oraganics (oraganics.com).

Lunch and Dinner Dishes

If possible, make lunch the largest meal of the day and have a modest dinner. This will help you to shed postpregnancy weight and sleep better. One of the best ways to make sure you have a nutritious lunch every day is to make enough dinner the night before to leave some leftovers. The less you eat late at night, the more easily your postpartum weight will come off. After dinner each night, think about what you'll be making the next day. If you need to defrost anything, now is the time to move it into the refrigerator.

As you'll see from these meal ideas and recipes, the possibilities for simple and nutritious meals are vast. Notice that these recipes contain virtually no processed ingredients. They aren't time-consuming or complicated.

Try these ideas for lunch and/or dinner.

- Put some of your salad greens on a plate or in a bowl and toss with a tablespoon of vinaigrette. Top with toasted pumpkin seeds and salad vegetables, along with no more than three ounces (the size of a deck of cards) of poached salmon, sliced beef, or sliced chicken breast.
- Make a basic soup. Sauté a diced onion and one or two pieces of celery in a couple of tablespoons of extra-virgin olive oil. (Add minced garlic, too, if you like it.) When the onion starts to get translucent, add vegetable or chicken stock, bring to a simmer, and add whatever vegetables you like. Add rice or barley. Try chunks of cooked chicken or gourmet chicken sausage. Coconut milk is a good addition, but if you use it, include minced ginger in the beginning (this combination of flavors is a staple of Thai cuisine). Add salt or tamari and pepper for more flavor. Use the chart of herbs and spices in Table 9.1 to decide which will best complement your brew.
- Make chicken salad, salmon salad, or tuna salad with celery and canola mayo. Add a little curry powder, scallions, grated ginger, or fresh or dried chopped onion for extra flavor. Grapes and celery are great mix-ins for tuna; or try walnuts and dried cranberries in chicken salad. Toss a few garbanzo beans or kidney beans on top for added protein and fiber. If you like a burrito or wrap, try a whole-grain tortilla—or, if it's seafood or tofu salad, wrap it in a sheet of toasted nori seaweed.

- Roast an organic chicken. A three-pound chicken will roast completely in a shallow roasting pan at 375°F within about an hour. Before roasting, wash and dry the chicken and brush with melted butter and sprinkle on salt and pepper. You can add poultry seasoning, thyme, tarragon, or other spices as well. The thickest part of the thigh should be 165 to 170°F when it's done.
- Try a stew made with coconut milk, chicken, and plenty of vegetables (see recipe, "Turkey or Chicken Stew with Coconut Milk").
- Try a stir-fry. Cook some brown rice about an hour ahead of cooking your stir-fry (see recipe, "Simple Stir-Fry").
- Sauté chicken breasts. Dredge boneless chicken breasts lightly in flour with salt and pepper added and sauté in extra-virgin olive oil with some minced garlic or shallots. Add tomatoes or mushrooms to the pan for variety. To make for faster cooking, place the raw chicken pieces between two sheets of waxed paper and pound them thin with a meat mallet before dredging. (If you buy chicken fresh and freeze it, you can pound it before freezing.)
- Sauté fish fillets. Thin, white fish fillets are best for sautéing. Dredge the fish in flour, cornmeal, or fine, dry breadcrumbs with salt and pepper added. Heat a mixture of unsalted butter and extra-virgin olive oil in a skillet or frying pan over medium-high heat. Sauté until fillets are brown and crispy on both sides. Add a squeeze of lemon when they are done.
- Fish can also be poached or baked. When you buy fish at the market, ask the person who sells it to you if she or he can recommend a good way to cook that particular kind of fish. To cook a fillet of salmon, put a half-inch of water in a five- to six-inch frying pan. You can substitute wine, fruit juice, or broth for part of the water if you like. Cover and heat to simmer. Add the fillet and poach it in the water, covered, for four minutes. This will leave the center of the salmon tender, and any skin will wash or scrape off.

- Pan-fry or grill lean beef or pork chops, but do this only once or twice a month; cooking meat at high heat creates carcinogens.
- Try a miso and tahini (sesame seed paste) sandwich on whole-grain bread with sliced avocado and sprouts; add a small amount of mayonnaise or salad dressing.

It's a Wrap: Tortilla Technique

If you have leftover meat or fish, you can make these easy tacos. Pile reheated meat, pinto or black beans, salsa, avocado (if you have it), julienned cabbage or lettuce, and a small dollop of low-fat plain yogurt into toasted taco shells.

If you want to make a "wrap" sandwich or burrito—a convenient to-go option at any meal—try using low-carb, whole-grain tortillas. Soften the tortilla over a burner, in a frying pan, or in the microwave (only takes a few seconds). Put the filling in the center of the wrap in an oval shape. Turn the tortilla so the long edge of the oval is facing you. Fold the sides of the tortilla toward the center, tucking the tortilla firmly underneath the filling where it meets itself.

Then, roll the edge of the tortilla closest to you over toward the other side, tucking it tightly around the filling. Keep rolling it away from you until the whole tortilla is wrapped around the filling.

Miso Soup

5-inch piece wakame
3 cups chicken or vegetable stock
1 or 2 mushrooms, sliced
1 handful chopped spinach or other leafy greens
1 carrot, julienned, or equivalent amount of
    julienned cabbage
Tofu (optional)
¼ tablespoon grated ginger root (optional)
2 tablespoons miso

1. Soak wakame in warm water for 5 minutes and drain.
   Lightly simmer vegetables in chicken or vegetable stock.
   Add cubed tofu or grated ginger root if you like.

2. When the vegetables are cooked through, thin miso in a
   small amount of room-temperature water or stock and add
   to soup. Don't boil or simmer the miso, as this will remove
   some of its nutritional value and taste.

Makes 2 to 3 servings

Turkey or Chicken Stew with Coconut Milk

1 pound boneless chicken or turkey, cut into chunks
½ teaspoon Chinese five spice powder (or a
    pinch each of cinnamon, cloves, and
    ground fennel, mixed together)
½ teaspoon salt
pepper to taste
1 tablespoon coconut oil
2 cloves minced garlic
1 tablespoon minced ginger root
1 can (13.5 ounces) coconut milk
1 can (13.5 ounces) chicken broth
1 head bok choy or Napa cabbage, or 1 or 2 bunches
    of spinach
1 can baby corn or corn niblets
1 14-ounce can chopped tomato, with juice, or 2
    small or 1 large fresh tomato, chopped
¼ cup thinly sliced green onions
1 tablespoon lime juice
Chopped fresh cilantro (optional)

1. Sprinkle the chicken or turkey pieces with five spice
   powder, salt, and pepper and sauté in coconut oil until
   browned and barely pink inside. Set aside.

2. Add garlic and ginger to pan, stir until fragrant—about 30
   seconds. Add the coconut milk, broth, and meat and cook
   for 5 minutes.

3. Add vegetables and cook, stirring, until greens are wilted—
   about 5 more minutes. Add lime juice. Serve immediately;
   sprinkle with chopped cilantro if desired.

Makes 4 to 6 servings, with rice

Simple Stir-Fry

Steamed rice or cooked whole-grain or rice noodles
   (optional)
¾ pounds meat (try beef, pork, chicken, shrimp,
   firm fish) or tofu
1 tablespoon soy sauce or tamari
1 tablespoon dry sherry
4 tablespoons canola or peanut oil, divided
Any vegetable you like, chopped into small pieces.
   (Just about any vegetable can be used! Try
   carrot, cauliflower, onion, bell pepper. Sea
   vegetables are a nice addition to stir-fries.)
1 tablespoon minced garlic
1 tablespoon minced ginger root
Stir-fry sauce or homemade peanut sauce (see recipe
   in Chapter 11)

1. Use a large sauté pan instead of a wok; on a flat stove
   burner, a wok heats unevenly and won't get hot enough on
   the sides.

2. Toss meat in soy sauce or tamari and dry sherry and set
   aside. (If you are using cooked meat, reserve it and add it
   last; skip this step.)

3. Heat the pan for four minutes over high heat. Add 2
   tablespoons oil.

4. Drain and add your chosen meat when the oil begins to
   shimmer and smoke.

5. Stir-fry until about three-quarters cooked—20 seconds for
   seafood, 1 minute for meat or tofu, 2 to 3 minutes for
   chicken. Transfer the food into a serving dish, cover, and
   keep warm.

6. Let pan come back up to temperature (about 1 minute).
   Add remaining 2 tablespoons oil. After oil is heated, add
   the first batch of vegetables. Stir-fry vegetables until they

are crisp and a little bit tender, about 4 minutes. Add remaining vegetables.

7. Once all vegetables have been added, clear the center of the pan and add garlic and ginger. Drizzle a tiny amount of oil onto the spices, then mash them into the pan with back of spatula. Cook for 10 seconds.

8. Remove pan from heat, reduce heat to medium, and with pan off of heat, stir garlic-ginger mixture into vegetables. Return pan to heat. Add cooked meat and stir-fry to coat all ingredients, about 1 minute. Stir in stir-fry sauce and serve immediately. You can serve it over rice or noodles if you like, or enjoy as is.

Makes 4 to 6 servings, with rice

Simple Veggie and Grain Additions

You can serve any of the lunch and dinner options we mentioned with a raw, steamed, or stir-fried vegetable. Hardy greens like kale and collard greens should be boiled. Choose from leafy greens, broccoli, cauliflower, zucchini, cabbage, asparagus, or any others you like, or a mixture. You can add a small pat of butter, powdered kelp or nori with salt, garlic salt, a dash of soy sauce—whatever it takes to bring out flavors you enjoy. Those who dislike vegetables can try the adult version of the old "drown it in cheese" trick that sometimes works with children: finely grate some flavorful cheese over cooked veggies.

Cook some grains in your rice cooker. Try different kinds of rice for variety: brown, white, wild, basmati, jasmine. Try some new grains like barley, quinoa, or millet. Also try a few varieties of whole-grain noodles. In a pinch, you can have whole-grain bread or crackers, or corn tortillas lightly toasted in the toaster oven or on a hot, dry skillet.

Tips on using sea vegetables. Sea vegetables are rich in minerals, detoxifying fiber, and phytochemicals. Here are some ideas when cooking with these foods.

- Nori: for making sushi rolls, toasting over a burner just until phosphorescent green and eating plain, or crumbling over grain dishes or soups
- Kelp: flaked or powdered; try mixing powdered kelp with garlic powder and white pepper as a substitute for table salt
- Hijiki: soak in warm water for five minutes, rinse, chop, and eat raw in salads; try it with peeled sliced cucumber marinated in rice vinegar and a little sugar.
- Kombu: put in soup broths as soon as you add them to the pot; will take about twenty minutes to cook all the way through.
- Wakame: rinse in cool running water, then soak in a bowl of warm water for five minutes before adding to miso soup.
- Dulse: also good for soups; cook in broth with other vegetables.

How to prepare leafy greens. Although raw greens aren't commonly eaten in our culture, and they aren't exactly delicious compared to, say, french fries, they are so nourishing and cleansing that you might just want to try munching them in their raw state. While living in rural Washington state, coauthor Melissa discovered the joys of picking and eating raw dinosaur kale, dandelion greens, and sorrel that grew in the garden of her co-housing community. Even the children enjoyed grazing on the sour sorrel leaves. Avoid cooking greens (spinach, kale, chard, collards, mustard or beet greens) in aluminum or copper pots or pans. The metals react with the sulfur compounds in the greens, yielding unpleasant smells and flavors.

If you are cooking more tender greens, such as spinach or chard, you don't need to remove any but the thickest of the center ribs from the leaves. Remove stems from chard and chop before cooking. These greens can be steamed or stir-fried, or added to soups and stews. Chard should take only a few minutes to cook. Spinach will overcook in only a minute's time when sautéed. Instead, try a spinach salad, tossed with a tablespoon of rice vinegar and some walnuts and dried cranberries. Add sliced hard-boiled eggs for protein. Or lightly steam spinach, or drop leaves into hot soup just before eating.

Hardier greens like collards, kale, and beet and mustard greens will take longer to cook—up to thirty minutes of boiling. You will need to remove the thick, woody center stems from these greens before cooking (you can do this as part of your weekly food prep). You can preboil them for a few minutes and add to stir-fries, casseroles, or sauces. Hardy greens can all be used interchangeably in recipes. Food writer Terra Brockman tells us that these foods are best teamed up with generous amounts of aromatic herbs like garlic, onions, or fresh ginger; meaty, smoky ingredients like bacon or pancetta; sharp and spicy ingredients like vinegar, lemon juice, chili paste, or hot sauce; or with creamy ingredients like heavy cream, sour cream, rich Romano or Parmesan cheeses, or goat cheese. Also, try dandelion greens (very cleansing!), arugula, mustard greens, and chicory raw in salads. The latter three have strong, spicy flavors.

Have Some Resveratrol or Hops with Your Meal!

With dinner, enjoy a glass of red wine or a dark beer. Wine is packed with resveratrol, a phytochemical that's good for you and your baby; it helps to move toxins out of the body and quenches free radicals. The alcohol in one glass of wine or one beer won't harm your baby. Purple grape juice is rich in resveratrol, too, so if you don't want to drink alcohol, add this to your staples.

Red wine and purple grape juice are also rich in proanthocyanidins and polyphenols, both of which reduce free radical damage in the body (better than vitamins C and E) and protect against cardiovascular disease and some cancers. The hops in beer amp up breast milk production by boosting prolactin levels.

Another option for concentrated greens: wheatgrass juice! Most juice bars can juice to order tiny cups of freshly squeezed wheatgrass, which is rich in chlorophyll, vitamins, and minerals.

Delicious Desserts

Try healthful desserts when possible:

- Frozen blueberries or other berries mixed into organic plain or vanilla whole-milk yogurt. A small swirl of maple syrup and a sprinkling of homemade granola, and you've got a parfait. Plain frozen berries, grapes, or other fruits make great hot-weather snacks.
- For antioxidant-rich homemade popsicles, freeze a deeply colored juice—try pomegranate, berry, or cherry—in small paper Dixie cups. When slushy, push a popsicle stick into the center. You can also do this with leftover smoothie.

When you indulge in more decadent sweets—and it's not wise to do so more than two or three times a week—follow these guidelines:

- Only eat the best, highest-quality, richest versions. If you like ice cream, stick with Häagen-Dasz or Ben and Jerry's. These ice creams are loaded with flavor and fat, and you'll be satisfied with less. Don't bother with low-carb, fat-free, or any of that stuff. The jury's still out on a lot of the ingredients in those highly processed foods, and chances are you'll come away still wanting the real thing.
- Indulge in chocolate or cookies or cake made only with real ingredients (butter, flour, sugar, cocoa butter)—no artificial ingredients or hydrogenated oils. Or, if you have the time or inclination, bake your own from scratch. Dad will probably be more than happy to take over baby care for a while if he knows he's going to get homemade cookies or cake! Give some away to neighbors, coworkers, or friends so you don't overindulge over the next day or two.
- Eat sweets slowly. Wait until a time when you can enjoy what you're eating. Take small bites and roll them around on your tongue. Eat small servings; choose the smallest ice cream size, the smallest chocolate bar, or share. Don't do anything else while you eat dessert. You can absentmindedly eat a whole pint of ice cream in front of the television, but if you stay aware, you'll be satisfied with less.

Simple, Sweet, Satisfying
Coconut Macaroons

Remember that your intake of lauric and capric acids from coconut increases the amount in your breast milk.

> 2½ cups shredded unsweetened coconut
> 14-ounce can sweetened condensed milk
> 2 teaspoons vanilla
> 8 ounces dark chocolate (optional)
> 1 pat butter (optional)

1. Preheat oven to 350°F. Mix all ingredients together. Drop the mixture in 1½ inch rounds on a greased cookie sheet and bake for 8 to 10 minutes until they start to turn brown on the edges.

2. If you're in the mood for something more decadent, melt high-quality dark chocolate (antioxidant-rich) with a small pat of butter in a pan over low heat, then dip half the macaroon into the melted chocolate. Allow to cool on waxed paper.

Herbs and Spices: Which to Use and How to Use Them

Table 9.1 gives basic guidelines for using herbs and spices. Generally, when you use dried versions, use one-quarter teaspoon for every four servings. (That's about a "pinch.") If you are using spice blends, use more—two teaspoons to one tablespoon for every four servings. Use less if you aren't sure—you can always add more. Many of the spices in Table 9.1 aren't in our spice cabinet staples list (see Table 8.3), but feel free to add them if you find one you love!

Crush dried herbs in one palm with the fingers of the other hand before adding them to foods. This releases their aroma and flavor. Herbs that are good on just about anything include basil, rosemary, onion, garlic, oregano, thyme, tarragon, and parsley.

Table 9.1 Pairing Foods with Herbs and Spices

Fish/ Shellfish	Meats	Poultry/Game	Vegetables	Soups	Eggs	Salad Dressings
Chives	Allspice	Anise	Anise	Anise	Basil	Caraway seed
Curry powder	Anise	Caraway seed	Caraway seed	Caraway seed	Chives	Cardamom
Dill	Caraway seed	Chives	Chili powder	Cardamom	Dill	Chili Powder
Fennel seed	Cayenne	Cumin	Coriander	Chives	Parsley	Chives
Marjoram	Chili powder	Curry powder	Cumin	Cloves	Pepper	Curry powder
Mustard	Chives	Marjoram	Curry powder	Coriander	Sage	Dill
Paprika	Cloves	Parsley	Dill	Cumin	Tarragon	Fennel seed
Pepper	Cumin seed	Rosemary	Fennel seed	Dill	Thyme	Marjoram
Tarragon	Curry powder	Sage	Marjoram	Fennel seed		Mustard seed
	Dill	Tarragon	Mustard seed	Marjoram		Paprika
	Fennel seed		Nutmeg	Mustard seed		Parsley
	Ginger		Parsley	Paprika		Pepper
	Nutmeg		Pepper	Parsley		Poppy seed
	Paprika		Poppy seed	Poppy seed		Sesame seed
	Parsley		Sage	Sage		
	Pepper		Sesame seed	Sesame seed		
	Rosemary			Sorrel		
	Sage					
	Sesame seed					

Herbs for Improving Milk Production—and Herbs to Avoid

Try these milk-stimulating herbs in the form of tea (allow to steep for at least ten minutes) or as herbal supplements in tincture or capsule form.

- Herbs that can improve milk production: *fennel, fenugreek, garlic, goat's rue, milk thistle, blessed thistle; also liquid chlorophyll, spirulina*
- Herbs for the nursing mother to avoid: *ephedra, aloe vera rind (aloe gel is excellent for soothing the gut and has no adverse effects on mom or baby), comfrey, feverfew, coltsfoot, buckthorn, black cohosh, buckthorn, sage, wintergreen, cascara sagrada, rhubarb, senna, uva ursi, kava, dong quai. Some of these herbs will slow down milk production (sage is prescribed to women who have overabundant milk), and others may pass potentially harmful substances into breast milk.*

While Nursing, Eat for Nourishment, Not for Weight Loss

This is not a weight loss diet, although it will probably lead to gradual weight loss unless you're already at your fighting weight. The nursing months are no time to cut calories. You may not lose all of your baby weight in a matter of weeks, or even months. Eat as much healthful food as you think your body wants during the nursing months or years. If you still feel the need to lose weight once your child is weaned, you can take a more aggressive tack at that point.

Start with a regular exercise program as soon as you can after your baby is born. Three or more times a week, take an hour walk or dance around the living room with your baby to your favorite music, or do whatever else you can fit into your life. Be as physically active as you can from day to day, but keep in mind that the New Breastfeeding Diet is about providing grade A premium breast milk and supplying Mom with enough nutrition to keep up with the demands of motherhood.

10

If You Cannot Breastfeed

Rebecca was committed to nursing her firstborn, but found her milk supply was not adequate to provide all of his nourishment. She tried everything, then resigned herself to supplementing with formula. He nursed happily until he was a year and a half old. When Rebecca's daughter came along, she was fiercely determined: she catalogued everything she'd done wrong the first time and resolved to make it right. A few days after the birth of her daughter, she was confronted with the sad truth that no matter what she did, she would have to supplement. Weeping right along with her, the lactation consultant said, "You're one of that two percent that can't make enough milk. You just don't have enough glands."

Rebecca was ashamed to pull out a bottle in public, admitting to being a "breastfeeding snob." Her husband had caught the snobbery bug too, hiding in the car to mix bottles and otherwise engaging in subterfuge to hide the fact that they were partially formula-feeding. She had wanted to attend La Leche League meetings for support, but dreaded the inevitable torrent of advice she'd get to toss the formula and do this or that or the other thing to bring her milk supply up.

"I wish I could just wear a sign: 'I WANT TO, BUT I CAN'T.' I read every book I could find, and all of them said that 2 percent of mothers can't produce enough milk. But there's no information out there for that 2 percent."

There are steps parents can take while formula-feeding to fortify available formulas in ways that will help give the formula-fed baby some of the advantages of breastfeeding. In this chapter, we'll give you the information you need to bottle-feed successfully and safely: how to choose the right formula, how to feed it to your baby, and how to know when it's time to try another formula. We will also address some of the controversy that is blossoming about soy formulas.

A single chapter about formula feeding in a book about breastfeeding may not be enough. Your pediatrician will be an important resource in your quest to feed your baby the best possible formula on the best possible schedule. If we don't succeed in giving you enough information, consult with your baby's doctor about any problems your baby seems to be having on his current diet and how you might change it to better suit his needs.

The Decision to Formula-Feed

There isn't any conclusive research that tells us the percentage of mother-infant pairs who physically are incapable of establishing a mutually satisfying nursing relationship. If one were to do a survey of women who gave up nursing, it would be hard to determine which women just didn't have adequate guidance, information, support, or motivation, and which women truly could not breastfeed. The most accurate figures we have indicate that only 1 to 3 percent of new mothers actually cannot breastfeed.

If you find yourself having trouble making adequate milk or if your milk comes in late (more than three days postpartum), you could have the following aspects of your medical history to blame:

- Trauma to the breast
- Surgical incisions

- Radiation exposure (x-rays of the chest) during the time when breast buds were developing (prepuberty)
- Hormone imbalances (such as those seen with polycystic ovary syndrome, or PCOS; theca lutein cysts; or an underactive thyroid gland)
- Exposure to chemicals during fetal development or other times
- Type 1 (insulin-dependent) diabetes
- Pain medications given during labor
- Obesity (reduces prolactin production)
- Retention of the placenta (which prevents the drop in progesterone levels that is the trigger for milk to come in)
- Stress (high levels of the stress hormone cortisol can delay the onset of milk production)

Adoptive mothers (although some adoptive moms can and do nurse, with the help of a supplementer and a skilled lactation consultant), ill mothers, mothers who must take drugs that could threaten the baby's health, mothers who have insufficient milk production due to inadequately developed milk ducts, mothers who have had breast surgery or cancer, mothers who have suffered sexual abuse and cannot psychologically handle the breastfeeding relationship, and mothers of infants with physiological problems that prevent them from suckling need good information about choosing a formula and feeding their infants as safely as possible. Thankfully, it isn't a life-and-death choice, as it was in the Victorian era and before when alternatives to breast milk were deadly to babies. But, although formulas are better than they have ever been, anyone who tells you that they are just like breast milk or just as good is not telling you the truth. Even our best scientific efforts are no match for the complexity and brilliance of the human body as it has evolved over tens of millions of years.

Doctors don't learn in medical school (or anywhere else) how to help a nursing woman who is having problems; they tend to advise women to supplement with formula as soon as difficulties come up. This has likely been the case—even for the staunchest breastfeeding advocates—since the middle of the twentieth century, when bottle-feeding became the infant-feeding method of choice in most industrialized nations. And it is certainly understandable: when a baby is going hungry, everyone wants to do what it takes to get her adequately fed, and as quickly as possible.

Counting Our Blessings

It's easy to say that formula cannot compare with breast milk, and that's likely true—but it sure is nice to know that your baby's chances of survival do not hinge entirely on your ability to nurse her. It's easy to forget that in "the olden days," a woman might expect to bear twice as many children as survived infancy. Let's count our blessings, and include formulas among them. They're a safety net mothers can trust when nursing is unsuccessful or inadequate for their babies.

Formulas now contain what may turn out to be an appropriate balance of the fats needed for optimal brain and immune system development. The addition of these fats to formulas is based on what is believed to be their optimal content in breast milk. (It's hard to say what that optimal content is; the range naturally found in breast milk is so broad.) Researchers continue to seek out ways to create formulas that approximate the composition of breast milk as closely as possible, and it's likely that formulas will continue to improve.

Formula Basics

All baby formulas sold in stores or given out in hospitals or doctors' offices have been prepared according to strict Food and Drug Administration guidelines. The FDA guidelines are based on recommendations from the American Academy of Pediatrics' Committee on Nutrition and dictate the formulas' nutrient content and purity from contaminants.

Available Types of Formula

Most babies whose mothers do not breastfeed from the start are given milk-based, iron-fortified formula. If no problems arise, you can give the same formula until the baby is weaned. The following types of formula are available:

The Origins of Formula

By the time the late 1800s rolled around, food chemists were doing their best to try to find better stuff to go into the various feeders that were available at the time. In the 1890s, physician Thomas Rotch derived a system for modifying cow's milk in a detailed fashion according to a child's age. This "formula"—and this is where the term formula *comes from—had to be monitored and supervised by a doctor, with changes sometimes made on a weekly basis.*

This early formula-feeding approach helped to begin a trend where physicians became indispensable to parents. By the 1940s, childbirth almost always involved general anesthesia, forceps delivery, and two-week postpartum hospital stays. After going home with her baby—who may have been almost a stranger to her, having been kept in a nursery away from the mother so that both could "rest"—the mother then relied upon her doctor for managing her baby's feedings. Brilliant marketing for the pediatric profession, but less than optimal for the mothers and babies involved.

Formulas have come a long way since the days of Dr. Rotch, and even since Dr. Rountree learned to mix that corn-syrup-and-evaporated-milk concoction in medical school. The days when a baby without access to breast milk had hardly a chance of survival are past, at least in developed parts of the world.

- Cow's milk–based formula: proteins come from nonfat milk and whey protein concentrate; fats from palm, safflower, sunflower, coconut, soybean oils; carbohydrates from lactose (milk sugars), maltodextrin, corn syrup
- Soy formula: proteins come from soy protein isolate; fats from palm, safflower, sunflower, corn, coconut, soy oils; carbohydrates from corn syrup solids, sucrose (sugar)

- Lactose-free formula (contains no milk sugar, but does contain milk proteins, which may be allergenic to some babies): proteins from whey, casein (milk proteins), nonfat milk with milk sugars removed; fats from palm, soy, coconut, sunflower oils; sugars from corn syrup, sucrose (sugar)
- Premature formulas (available in soy and milk-based forms)
- Formulas supplemented with DHA and ARA (available in all of the above); DHA and ARA are derived from fungus, fish oils, or algae
- Elemental (hypoallergenic) formula: protein from hydrolyzed (predigested) casein; fats from safflower, coconut, soy oils; sweetened with corn syrup, dextrose, or modified corn or tapioca starch; one such formula, Pregestemil, gets its fat from medium-chain triglycerides, a factory-made fat

Follow-up formulas are also available. They are designed for babies aged four to six months and older and contain a slightly different balance of nutrients, with more calcium, protein, and iron than regular baby formulas. As long as your baby is eating solid foods with gusto by six months, the extra nutrients are probably not necessary. Many follow-up formulas are sweetened with corn syrup—the same sugars used to sweeten most sodas. In order to avoid whetting your baby's tastes to favor sweetness, avoid those made with corn syrup if at all possible. A baby who turns his nose up at solids may be a good candidate for a follow-up formula, but his nutritional needs can probably be filled with slightly increased intake of standard formula plus some solid foods that contain calcium and iron.

Breast milk contains high concentrations of a substance called alpha-lactalbumin, which is a rich source of the amino acid tryptophan. Tryptophan has soothing, sleep-inducing effects on the nursling. In the early 2000s, formula researchers recognized that adding a little extra alpha-lactalbumin to formulas could help mimic that soporific effect of breast milk. The extra tryptophan in these formulas has been found to bring formula-fed infants' levels of this amino acid up to match those of breastfed babies.

Competing Brand Advertising: What You Should Know

No one brand of formula is recommended over another by the American Academy of Pediatrics. Although ads for different brands trumpet the ways in which their product is superior, there is no conclusive, non-manufacturer-sponsored research that definitively shows one brand to be better than another. They all have to adhere to strict standards, within which there's little wiggle room for creating something new and noteworthy.

At this writing, it appears that you are best off with a brand that adds DHA and ARA (arachidonic acid) to its formulas. Research isn't yet conclusive on how much these fats in formula help babies' nervous system and visual development. It's said that the addition of these fats to formula makes it just like breast milk, but the biological matrix in which these fats are found in breast milk is not reproducible in formula. It remains to be seen whether adding these fats to formula will make a significant difference in the health of formula-fed babies. There have been numerous reports of explosive diarrhea—somewhat similar to the type of diarrhea seen in people who eat too much of the fat substitute Olestra—in babies fed DHA- and ARA-containing formulas. Olestra isn't absorbed into the body, but passes through the intestines unabsorbed, and if too much goes through at once, diarrhea results. The same thing may happen with babies who don't absorb the formulas' DHA and ARA well.

Organic formulas are now available. They are so new that no one knows whether organic makes a difference, but it would seem that if you can afford them, they're bound to be at least as good as nonorganic versions, and a little purer to boot.

Some homemade formula recipes call for fish or flaxseed oil as an omega-3 source, or for cod liver oil. We can't in good conscience advise you to supplement infant formulas that do not contain extra DHA or ARA with fish oils or flaxseed oil alone, because neither of these oils contains a source of arachidonic acid. As you know if you've read this far, a relative dearth of ARA compared to DHA and EPA can slow a baby's growth. Homemade formula supplementation recipes may call for addition of a soft-cooked egg yolk to contribute this fat; more on this a bit later in this chapter.

Soy Formula Pros and Cons: Making an Informed Choice

Critics of soy formulas call them "worse than worthless" and "a formula for disaster." But soy formulas have a lengthy history of apparently safe use, having been developed in the 1920s. They are currently consumed by 20 to 25 percent of babies in the United States. Multiple studies show that babies fed soy formula grow and develop normally, but in 1996, the AAP's Committee on Nutrition recommended against soy formula for preterm babies because its high aluminum content appears to reduce the mineralization of their bones.

The main current concern about soy formulas is their content of isoflavones. Although these plant chemicals are weakly active compared with the estrogens made in the body, they do have demonstrated hormone-altering activity—in lab studies, in animal studies, and in studies done *in vivo* (in the human body). The research shows that babies whose sole diet is soy formula get a dose about five times greater (by weight) than the dose shown to noticeably alter grown women's menstrual cycles.

We know from long years of experience with soy formula feeding that it isn't causing any dramatic ill effects in children or in the adults they become. Only one study has shown any problems in adults who were fed soy formula as babies compared to infants fed other foods: women who got soy as babies had slightly longer menstrual cycles and more menstrual discomforts. Some researchers postulate that the isoflavones in soy formula are not active enough in the baby's body to act as hormone disruptors.

Some journalists have compared the estrogen exposure from soy formula to the estrogen exposure from diethylstilbestrol (DES), the synthetic estrogen that, when given to pregnant women, ended up predisposing their daughters to a rare vaginal cancer or to infertility. No one knew that the drug was damaging girl babies' reproductive development until young women started turning up with this cancer and some astute scientists put the pieces together. No such thing has happened with soy, and comparisons to the DES disaster are hysterical and inaccurate.

The phytoestrogens have been intently studied for their potential for inhibiting some cancers, including breast and prostate cancers. It is theorized that the phytoestrogens might somehow block the carcinogenic activity of more powerful estrogens. At this writing, the research on this is inconclusive; while many studies show that soy isoflavones slow breast cancer growth, others show a growth-accelerating effect. Currently, women with breast cancer are advised against taking soy phytoestrogen supplements, although they are encouraged to eat moderate amounts of soy foods (tofu, tempeh, miso). Soy isoflavones are also believed to help prevent osteoporosis in aging people (estrogen inhibits bone loss).

The bottom line is this: It was once thought that phytoestrogens in baby formula might actually be a good thing. However, today, the consensus is that soy formulas need to be used with care, only when needed and that the long-term effects—subtle and not-so-subtle—of feeding them to babies should be the subject of much more study. Some parents start their baby out on soy protein because of a family history of allergy or colic. However, the AAP claims, based on current research, that parents in this boat will have more success with hypoallergenic formulas. Soy formula has been found to be ineffective for preventing or remedying colic.

If your baby doesn't tolerate milk-based formulas, you may need to turn to soy formula. But don't make it your first choice, thinking that soy is healthier than milk. As far as we know, for infant nutrition, it isn't.

Formula Preparation Pointers

Formulas are available in powdered, liquid concentrate, or ready-to-drink forms. Powdered formula is less convenient, but also considerably less expensive. Powdered formula is mixed as it's needed, with pure water that has been boiled for one minute. (Bottled water that is marketed for use in mixing baby formulas should also be boiled for one minute; this water only has to meet EPA standards for tap water, and isn't sterile unless the label says so.)

Prepare formula using the exact ratio of water to powder or concentrate described on the label. Diluting it to save money can lead to baby becoming malnourished, while concentrating it to try to help baby put weight on can cause dehydration. In rare instances, when a formula-fed baby is not growing well, a pediatrician might direct you to concentrate her formula by adding less water. Don't do this without a doctor's guidance. Follow the guidelines we suggest in Chapter 6 for ensuring that the water you mix formula with is pure and clean.

Keep opened, unused formula—whether mixed by you or ready-to-drink—in the refrigerator. Bottles mixed from powdered formula should be used within twenty-four hours; those mixed from liquid concentrate can be kept in the fridge for forty-eight hours. A container of powdered formula, once opened, should be covered tightly, stored in a place that's cool and dry, and used within a month. Storing mixed bottles of formula in the freezer isn't a good idea—not because of sterility issues, but because the formula will probably separate and be highly unappetizing when reheated.

Once baby has drunk from a bottle of formula, you'll need to discard the remainder of that bottle, since bacteria from the baby's mouth can get into the formula and multiply.

Choosing a Nipple

If a baby is both bottle- and breastfeeding, choose a nipple that has a wide base to mimic the sensation of nursing at Mom's breast. Using a standard, longer nipple can cause nipple confusion and create a "lazy nurser" who only wants to suck at the end of the nipple rather than opening wide to take the whole nipple and most of the areola. There is no conclusive evidence that so-called "orthodontic" nipples are superior to others, despite what the ads might say.

Boil nipples for five minutes before first using them. If any cracks or tears appear, toss the nipple in the trash, as a piece could come off and cause choking.

Buying and Sterilizing Bottles

Bottles made from polycarbonate plastic are convenient and easy to find, but research has shown that hormone-disrupting chemicals—specifically, bisphenol A (BPA)—readily migrate out of polycarbonate and into the liquid inside the bottle. It seems prudent to find alternatives, and there are a few good ones.

Here's what the Children's Health Environmental Coalition (checnet.org) has to say about safer baby bottles.

- Glass bottles are making a comeback. At this writing, Evenflo is the only company that sells them, and you may need to order them by mail if your local stores don't have them. If you choose to use glass bottles, be vigilant about checking them over for any cracks or chips and discard them right away if you find any.
- If you'd rather avoid glass, buy polyethylene or polypropylene bottles, neither of which is known to leach any hormone disruptors into formula or any other liquid. Polyethylene will have recycling numbers 1 or 2 on them, while polypropylene will carry the recycling number 5. Polycarbonate is recycling number 7. At this writing, Medela, Evenflo, and Gerber make polypropylene and polyethylene bottles.
- If you end up using polycarbonate, keep in mind that the older the bottles get, the more BPA they'll shed. As soon as bottles start to show signs of wear, toss them in the recycling bin.

Soft plastic liners are another option, but they have been known to cause choking accidents. No research thus far demonstrates that these liners release toxic chemicals into formula or breast milk. Rubber nipples have also been called into question for their safety because they have been found to shed nitrosamines, a carcinogenic chemical. Choose bottle nipples and pacifiers made from natural latex or silicone instead. Silicone is clear, while rubber is usually yellow.

You'll probably need about six bottles a day. Follow proper procedure for sterilizing bottles before use:

- Wash in a dishwasher with water temperature of at least 180° Fahrenheit (82° Celsius).
- If you don't use a dishwasher, rinse used bottles and nipples and leave on a clean towel until you are ready to sterilize the next set of bottles.
- Wash with hot, soapy water, using a bottle brush. Rinse completely in hot water.
- Place all the bottle paraphernalia in a large pan lined with a dishcloth and filled with water. Make sure it's all submerged, then boil for ten minutes with the pan covered.
- Turn the water off, let it cool to room temperature, then remove the bottles and nipples from the water with tongs and place them on a clean towel to dry.

Bottle-Feeding

Expect newborns to take an ounce or two at each feeding; one- to two-month-olds, three to four ounces; two- to six-month-olds, four to six ounces; and children between six months and one year of age, up to eight ounces per feeding. Another way to gauge how much she will eat: add three ounces to your baby's age in months. Under one month of age, baby will probably consume less than three ounces per feeding; at one month, four ounces; at two months, five ounces; and so on.

Because formula is more filling than breast milk, baby will probably be fine on a four-hour schedule around the clock until she sleeps through the night. Check to see that the hole in the bottle's nipple is big enough for adequate milk flow. When you turn the unshaken, filled bottle upside down, the liquid should come out at the rate of one drop per second. Older babies get nipples with larger holes; the product packaging will tell you which to buy as your baby grows.

Never prop a bottle or put your baby to bed with a bottle in her mouth. Feeding, whether from a bottle or the breast, should be a time for closeness and cuddling. If you can, hold your baby skin-to-skin while bottle-feeding. Falling asleep with sugary formula in her mouth could cause tooth decay. Milk from propped bottles end up in the middle ear, making the infant prone to ear infections.

Do not warm bottles in the microwave; this can cause "hot spots" that will burn baby's mouth. Warm formula by placing it in a pan of hot water or running it under a warm tap. Shake a few drops on your wrist before feeding to ensure that it isn't too hot.

While feeding, hold baby so that her neck is straight and her head lined up with the rest of her spine. This makes drinking and swallowing easier. Turn the bottle upside down and allow the formula to collect in the nipple and the air to collect at the bottom of the bottle before starting to feed.

A baby's stomach is only about as big as his fist. He won't drain a full bottle every time, and if he eats too much, his tiny stomach will send some of it back out. A baby who drinks too much formula at a feeding may also show signs of colicky pain (tense abdomen, legs drawn up, screaming) and, over time, excessive weight gain. Small, frequent feedings are better than fewer feedings with longer intervals in between. Heed your baby's hunger signals early, and don't press her to drink past the point when she seems satiated.

Your baby might fall asleep while drinking from a bottle. Once the deeper, drinking sucking gives way to little fluttery sucks, take the nipple out of baby's mouth; if he wants to keep sucking for comfort to get to sleep, give him a fingertip or pacifier instead. This will prevent him from getting too much formula in that feeding.

Signs of dehydration or inadequate formula consumption to watch for: slow weight gain (as measured at your doctor's visits), fewer than six to eight wet diapers per day, persistent crying, a depressed fontanel (soft spot on the crown of the head), or skin that looks loose or wrinkly. If you suspect your baby isn't getting enough to eat, check in with your doctor as soon as you can.

Supplementing Store-Bought Formulas

Here are a few steps you can take to make store-bought formulas just a little more nutritionally sound and "alive." Formula companies are now investigating the addition of *probiotics*—friendly bacteria that aid digestion and the healthy development of the gastrointestinal tract—to formulas. In the meantime, you can add your own. It should help to reduce colic and the incidence of upper respiratory infections.

Buy a brand especially for infants that contains lactobacillus and bifidobacterium strains—especially *Bifidobacterium infantis*, the strain most populous in the intestinal tracts of healthy, breast-fed infants. One brand I recommend, Pharmax's HLC Neonate Powder, is made especially for newborns, and at this writing is being researched in a multicenter clinical trial to see whether its early use will reduce incidence of allergies. Pharmax also has a toddler probiotic in handy kid-friendly "straws" and probiotics for adults. (You can purchase Pharmax probiotics at Rockwell Nutrition, rockwellnutrition.com, or at Pharmaca Integrative Pharmacy, pharmaca.com.) Add the recommended amount to baby's bottle or dust the recommended amount on the nipple of the bottle or pacifier once a day. Keep probiotics stored in the refrigerator.

Infant liquid multivitamins containing DHA, B vitamins, and antioxidants are now available. Talk with your pediatrician about adding one of these multivitamins to your baby's feedings. Some multivitamins for babies contain only vitamins A, D, C, and iron; these are not generally recommended for babies who are formula-fed, since formulas must supply adequate amounts of these nutrients.

A pinch of ascorbate powder (the equivalent of 40 or 50 milligrams) may help to improve formula's antioxidant and immune-boosting power. Try it when your formula-fed baby is sick or getting sick.

Formulas can also be supplemented with soft-cooked organic egg yolk. Use DHA-rich eggs, which are now widely available.

To prepare, boil the egg for three and a half minutes, then place in bowl and peel off shell. Remove and discard the white—or eat it yourself. Egg white is allergenic to babies less than one year old. The yolk should be soft and warm, but not hot.

Use your hand blender, a blender, or a whisk to mix it into the formula. Use one yolk per approximately thirty-five ounces of formula—that's about a cup of powdered formula and three and five-eighths cups of filtered water.

Store leftovers in a glass jar or bottles in the refrigerator (boil them first, according to sterilization techniques described earlier in this chapter).

Some sources recommend adding cod liver oil to formulas as a source of natural DHA. If you do so, choose a formula without added DHA. Use only one-half teaspoon per thirty-five-ounce batch, and add it along with the egg yolk.

Homemade Formula: Do Not Use!

The FDA—and most doctors and nutritional experts—advise against homemade formulas. It's difficult to know whether a homemade formula is meeting the nutritional needs of the infant.

Cow's milk proteins are hard for babies to digest unless they have been processed. Evaporated milk was recommended to Dr. Rountree way back when because the evaporation process improves the milk's digestibility somewhat. Goat's milk, also used to make homemade formulas, is low in B vitamins, iron, and vitamin D.

It's not worth the risk to your baby to use homemade formula. Your best bet is to prudently supplement commercially available formulas with safe amounts of nutrients. A lot of babies didn't make it during the years when infant formulas were still being figured out. Don't try to reinvent the wheel!

Today's formulas are the best they've ever been. They are *not* breast milk. They aren't even close. But they come in second place to breast milk, hands down. If you cannot breastfeed, you should use them.

Never use soy milk, rice milk, carrot juice, or almond milk as a replacement for formula or breast milk.

Introducing Other Foods and Liquids to Formula-Fed Babies

Exclusively formula-fed babies may benefit from water from time to time, especially when the weather is hot. Talk to your pediatrician about how often to give water to a formula-fed baby. There is never, ever any reason to give a baby juice or soda in her bottle (yes, we've heard tales of parents putting Coke in their baby's bottle). In fact, you can get through the first year of a baby's life without ever offering him a single drink of juice.

Two exceptions will aid in baby's digestion after the first four months of life: freshly squeezed pressed vegetable or fruit juices (apple, carrot) rich in enzymes. In addition, antioxidant-rich organic juices from purple grapes, pomegranate, cherries, or berries may help boost baby's antioxidant defenses. Give juices in cups, not bottles, and only once baby is four months old or older. Dilute juices fifty-fifty with water. (This advice is only for formula-fed infants. It is best to avoid supplemental juices in breastfed babies until at least six months of age or later.)

There is no reason to add any cereal to formula or bottled breast milk before baby's fourth-month birthday, unless there are reflux issues and your pediatrician advises you to try adding cereal. Regular cow's milk or goat's milk are fine after the baby's twelfth month. It may be better to introduce plain, live-culture, whole-milk yogurt first, then milk. Babies fed formula can just continue with that through their second year. If you have a source of fresh, whole, unpasteurized milk, that's your best bet—but only if you are 100 percent certain that the herds are healthy and that the milk collection environment is pristine; otherwise, unpasteurized milk can bring unacceptable risk of infection. If you use pasteurized, homogenized milk, use organic, and add a pinch of powdered probiotics.

Some authorities recommend introducing solids to formula-fed babies as early as the fifth month of life to try to add invaluable nutrients that may be missing in formula. Insist that the formula-fed baby's first foods be whole foods, preferably antioxidant-rich fresh vegetables and organic meats or egg yolk.

Try strained cooked sweet potato mixed with cooked greens, fortified rice cereal, cooked pureed brown rice or oatmeal, or thoroughly cooked organic chicken or beef. Hand-cranked baby food makers are portable and easy to use and clean.

When Standard Milk-Based Formula May Not Be Best

When a formula-fed baby is chronically ill-tempered, fussy, gassy, colicky, spits up or cries a lot, or has other gastrointestinal symptoms, parents often start switching to different formulas, not realizing that the formula may not be to blame at all. Then, miraculously, the baby's symptoms stop, and the parents think they've finally found the right formula. The same thing can happen with a baby who is breastfed: the mother thinks something in her diet is going into her milk and causing irritation for the baby. She goes nuts trying to eliminate the offending food from her diet. One day, the symptoms stop, and she thinks she's fixed the problem by subsisting on brown rice and baked chicken.

While changes in formula or a breastfeeding mother's diet *can* make a difference, the truth is that babies fuss, get colicky or gassy, or cry for many reasons. One of the most sanity-preserving tenets of parenting is that just before something your child is doing or expressing drives you completely insane, the child's behavior will change. You'll get pushed to the edge of your endurance, and just when you think you can't take it anymore, things change, and suddenly your *impossible* baby is an angel again.

Lactose Intolerance

Lactose intolerance, for example, is probably not nearly as common in children or adults as it is widely believed to be. It runs counter to common sense that an infant would be allergic to the carbohydrate that is specifically designed to feed human babies.

Lactose intolerance and milk allergy are often confused. They are quite different, and unrelated. They don't even involve the same body system. Lactose intolerance is a digestive issue; milk allergy is an immune system problem.

Lactose intolerance is the result of a lack of the enzyme lactase. When lactose is not broken down, intestinal bacteria go to work on it, creating gas and bloating and drawing excess fluid into the intestines, which leads to diarrhea. True lactose intolerance is rare in infants, with an estimated one in every sixty-five thousand babies actually missing the genetic equipment needed to manufacture lactase, the enzyme that breaks lactose down in the digestive tract. Human babies evolved to consume lactose as their first source of carbohydrates.

Problems that could suggest lactose (milk sugar) intolerance include:

- Gas
- Diarrhea
- Abdominal swelling
- Red, burnlike rash around the anus

If you suspect that your baby isn't digesting a milk-based formula, try a lactose-free milk-based formula. Lactase deficiency can be a temporary problem just following an intestinal infection; a lactose-free formula can be used for a brief time to allow the intestines to heal and start making lactase again. Formulas that don't supply sugars as lactose will usually contain corn syrup or maltodextrin—more refined sugars that aren't optimal for growing babies. Lactose is Mother Nature's carbohydrate source for infants, and it's best to stick with that if you can.

Allergy to Cow's Milk Proteins

An allergy to cow's milk protein is a more common issue than lactose intolerance in infants. The baby's immune system reacts to those foreign proteins, causing various symptoms, such as the following:

- Extreme crankiness and lots of crying, particularly around feeding time
- Vomiting
- Diarrhea
- Abdominal pain
- Rash
- Blood in stools

If you encounter these problems, and they're not traced back to an illness, you may be advised to switch to a soy-based formula. Keep in mind that 30 to 50 percent of babies who are allergic to milk proteins often are allergic to soy. You may want to shift directly to a hypoallergenic formula.

Problems Digesting Iron-Fortified Formula

Most formulas are fortified with iron. A nursing infant absorbs about 100 percent of the iron in mother's milk, but the iron in formula is much more poorly absorbed. This can lead to constipation. Formula manufacturers responded to this problem by making low-iron formulas, but then there's the issue of the baby possibly not getting adequate iron. Most authorities on the subject recommend using the iron-fortified formulas, but keep in mind that most babies have enough iron stored up from being inside your body to last the first four months of life—that is, as long as your iron levels were adequate during pregnancy. Babies who don't tolerate iron-fortified formulas well can be given low-iron formulas, with a doctor-prescribed, nonconstipating iron supplement starting at four months of age.

Hypoallergenic formulas usually are far more costly than others, and they don't taste very good compared to other formulas. They are the newest breed of formula, with the shortest history of safe use. Don't think that you can circumvent formula problems up front by starting out with hypoallergenic versions. You should not use them unless they are medically necessary.

Banked Breast Milk

A formula-fed baby who cries inconsolably for long periods, who vomits often, has dark circles under the eyes, frequent or bloody stools, or skin inflammation, despite having been switched from formula to formula, may be formula-intolerant—and an excellent candidate for banked breast milk. Premature infants whose mothers' milk isn't coming in fast enough, or whose mothers can't nurse at all, also may be prescribed some donor milk because the bene-

Spitting Up

Babies spit up often—that is, food comes up from the stomach into the esophagus and out of the mouth, and then possibly onto your nice black shirt or the curtains across the room. It doesn't usually bother baby anywhere near as much as it bothers those who are in the line of fire. Spitting up—medically, known as reflux—*is different from vomiting, which is more forceful and may even cause the baby pain. Often, there's no warning; your happy, full-of-food infant just opens her mouth and an incredible torrent of white stuff comes flooding out.*

Usually, in the first one or two months, spitting up often is just an issue of gastrointestinal mechanics, not a problem with the formula (or breast milk). The usual recommendation is more frequent, smaller feedings to help the baby digest more completely. In rare instances, a baby who spits up often and acrobatically may have a condition called pyloric stenosis, *where the valve that leads from the stomach to the small intestines becomes overly tight. Usually, surgery is recommended for this condition.*

Babies who spit up often will often do so less if fed in an upright position. Burp her every three to five minutes during a feeding, and don't lay her down right after feeding. (Spitting up while lying down on her back could cause her to inhale some of the food, potentially leading to lung infection.) Formulas with added rice may be prescribed to help reduce reflux.

If your baby seems to be spitting up so much that she isn't getting enough nutrition—if she doesn't want to eat, seems to be in pain, or starts to cough—see the pediatrician to find out what to do next. Medicine may be prescribed to help control reflux.

fits of breast milk over formula for fragile preemies are so well established.

Banked breast milk requires a doctor's prescription. There are eight breast milk banks in North America (six in the United States, one in Canada, one in Mexico). At these banks, the breast milk is pasteurized (viruses are killed, but antibodies are left intact), checked for bacteria, and carefully frozen. Women who donate breast milk must get medical clearance to do so. They undergo health screening to ensure that they are free of diseases that can be passed on to the recipient of the milk, including hepatitis B and C, HIV 1 and 2, and HTLV 1 and 2. They need proof of immunity to rubella (either from immunization or from having had the illness) and a negative syphilis test and have to provide their history of tuberculosis or herpes. (The milk bank pays for the testing.) Breast milk donors are given detailed instructions on how to hygienically collect and handle their milk in preparation for donating it.

Although banked breast milk is expensive—around $2.25 an ounce—some insurers will cover it if it is medically called for. You can find breast milk for sale on the Internet for far less, but it hasn't been screened or pasteurized, so there is some risk in using it. You don't know what that mother has eaten, whether she smokes, or whether she takes medications to which you don't want to expose your baby. Listings of breast milk banks can be found in the Resources section in Appendix B, or to start a milk bank in your town, call the Human Milk Banking Association of North America at (888) 232-8809 (toll-free) or (919) 861-4530 extension 226.

If you have a trusted friend or relative who is breastfeeding and you can work out a deal with her to buy pumped milk, or to take whatever extra she has, that may be the best way to add at least some breast milk to your baby's diet.

Wet-Nursing and Cross-Nursing

Cross-nursing is any instance where women nurse children who are not their own, not because the mom is unable to nurse, but because she's not around. It is not officially sanctioned by the medical community or by La Leche League International, mainly because of the risk of passing viral infections such as HIV or hepatitis B through breast milk. A baby older than four months of age is not likely to take the breast of anyone besides her mom under any but extreme circumstances, unless she is already used to doing so.

Wet-nursing is done when the mother cannot—or, as was often the case in the seventeenth century and before, when they choose not to—breastfeed. For many centuries, it was the only trustworthy method for feeding an infant when its mother could not do it herself. Today, it's frowned upon—again, because of concerns of communicable diseases being passed on, or concerns that women who take drugs, abuse alcohol, or otherwise contaminate their milk could do a nursling more harm than good.

Concerns have also been raised about the potential for confusion on the infant's part, as well as possible deprivation of the wet nurse's own nursling in favor of the paying client's. Attachment between the "lactator" and the nursling is intense and deep, and it has been theorized that a wet-nurse's departure could traumatize the baby irreparably. Still, wet-nursing appears to be making a comeback: the Beverly Hills, California, firm Certified Household Staffing has wet-nurses on its list of hirable employees.

Relactation

Let's say you decide to go to formula feeding, but your baby doesn't tolerate it well. After a week, or ten days, or more, can you change your mind? Yes. You can restimulate lactation six months or more after weaning.

Even adoptive mothers who have never given birth can often stimulate the production of at least some breast milk. They may pump for about one hundred minutes a day, fifteen minutes per session, during the weeks before their new baby arrives. Herbs like fenugreek are often used to stimulate milk production, and a drug called domperidone—used for gastrointestinal reflux, but which also increases prolactin production—may be prescribed.

Use of domperidone is controversial. It is by far the most effective drug for stimulating milk production in women whose supply is low. It is classified as safe for nursing mothers to use, with two decades of safe use as a gastrointestinal drug (even for infants) and a thumbs-up from the world's best-known breastfeeding pharmacology expert, Tom Hale. Worldwide, domperidone has been used safely for many years. Studies involving small numbers of subjects found that when used intravenously, domperidone can have some dangerous side effects, but this was at doses well beyond what a woman would take to stimulate milk production. Because of the politics of drug importation and competition, these studies were used to justify banning importation of domperidone into the United States and to forbid compounding pharmacists from making it for those who wish to use it. As a result, it's hard to get. Talk to a lactation consultant if you think you may want to try to get your hands on some.

During relactation (or primary stimulation of lactation in adoptive mothers), the first drops of milk can show up as early as a week after intensive stimulation of the nipples, but milk production won't reach its peak volume until up to twelve weeks of such stimulation. Even then, it is quite rare for adoptive mothers to be able to supply all of the baby's nutritional needs from their own breast milk production. Adoptive mothers who nurse almost always have to use a supplementer, which holds formula or donated breast milk in a bag that can be hung from the neck, with a small silicone tube that is taped to the breast. The end of the tube lines up with the end of the nipple, so that a woman who is partially lactating can feed with her own milk at the same time she feeds with the supplemental formula or breast milk.

Adoptive mothers who fail to lactate at all despite their best efforts may still choose to nurse using a supplementer for the closeness the nursing relationship engenders in both mom and baby.

Relactation is an easier road than adoptive nursing. Surveys show that in women who decide to relactate—who return to nursing after stopping for a period of time—about half return to their full milk supply within a month. Women who've stopped nursing for up to six months, whose children were between the ages of one year and forty-eight months, have been able to relactate successfully with nothing more than stimulation by their nursling.

Other estimates state that the length of time needed for full relactation is about equivalent to the length of time since breastfeeding was discontinued. Some take a little longer, and others require a supplementer through the rest of the nursing months or years. Infants who have been switched to the bottle are likely to be resistant to going back to the breast, but perseverance has been shown to pay off: one survey found that although only 39 percent of women who tried to reacquaint their babe to the breast were immediately successful, the percentage of successful relactation attempts in the group rose to 74 percent within ten days of trying. Babies less than three months old tended to go back to the breast more readily.

Success with either adoptive nursing or relactation strongly depend upon the help and emotional support of a lactation consultant. Ask your pediatrician for recommendations, call your local hospital, or go to the website of the International Lactation Consultant Association (ilca.org) or call them at (919) 861-5577 to search for consultants in your area.

11

Transitioning Children to Healthy Diets

What is a healthy child? The World Health Organization defines health as "a state of complete physical, mental, and social well-being, and not merely the absence of disease or infirmity." Let's overlook, for now, the sobering evidence that there are sorry few healthy *adults* around these days. Let's also overlook the high likelihood that many of today's unhealthy adults are unhealthy due, at least in part, to having been poorly nourished in infancy and childhood—starting with being deprived of the food that was designed for human infants: breast milk.

Reviewing statistics and current opinions on the health of children reveals a paradox. On the one hand, current evidence suggests that most of them are in very good or excellent health compared with the children their grandparents and great-grandparents were. About 83 percent of children were reported to be in very good or excellent health by their parents in 2003. However, all modern Western children are at increasing risk of so-called *activity-limiting conditions*, such as asthma, allergy, learning disability, ADHD, depression, autism, overweight, and recurrent

193

bouts of upper respiratory infection. Children are far more likely to make it to adulthood than they have ever been. But this seeming state of good health involves the use of massive amounts of antibiotics. They are also far more likely to be overweight than children used to be, and the incidence of low birth weight—an indicator of future disease risk, both during childhood and well beyond it (remember the research findings of Dr. Barker?)—continues to creep upward.

The number of infants born at low birth weight—less than five pounds, eight ounces—has gradually increased over the years:

- In 1984, the incidence of babies being born at this low weight was 6.7 percent; by 2003, this figure had risen to 7.9 percent.
- In 2003, about 1.4 percent of babies were born at very low birth weight—three pounds, four ounces—with a small rise in this incidence per year since the mid-eighties.

This rise in low–birth weight babies, who are at increased risk of long-term illness, disability, and death, is believed to be partly due to the increase in the number of twin, triplet, and other multiple births, but it doesn't entirely explain this change. Singletons are still being born at low birth weights more often than ever before.

The bottom line here appears to be that although most children enjoy amazingly good health, there has been a price to pay for using the weaponry of modern medical science to obliterate dangerous diseases, and for the wide availability of delicious junk to eat: a sort of backlash of privilege.

Where once children were at risk from inadequate food, excessive exposure to disease-causing germs, and lack of medicines, many of today's children are born into an overfed, under-germ-exposed, overmedicated, underactive environment. Many are deprived of adequate breast milk as infants, or are given a combination of breast milk and formula that undermines the natural development of their gastrointestinal and immune systems—as does the artificially germ-free environment in which many children grow up.

A Pound of Prevention . . .

Getting a child off to a good start in the dietary department will teach her good habits for the rest of her life. Set the example yourself—you just might make up for your own formula-fed, junk-food-and-TV-intensive childhood.

Recent estimates show that only 60 percent of children participate in any vigorous physical activity, and less than 25 percent eat the recommended five or more servings of vegetables and fruits each day.

To help your child get off on the right foot to a lifetime of good health:

- Don't rush to wean; breast milk is a great addition to baby's diet through the second year of life.
- Limit processed foods, refined carbohydrates, and fats.
- Increase fresh, colorful, antioxidant-rich, high-fiber fruits, berries, and vegetables.
- Use organic foods whenever possible.
- Purify your household's water.
- Avoid synthetic chemicals and plastics whenever possible.
- Judiciously supplement the child's diet with herbs and micronutrients.
- Make a point of engaging your child in vigorous physical activity every day; research shows that overuse of strollers for young children may predispose them to overweight later on.
- Get your kid out into the sun for fifteen minutes at a time, two to three times a week if possible, or use a supplement that supplies vitamin D.

Introducing Solids

A baby ready for solids will start grabbing at your food and watching intently the path your forkful of food takes from your plate to your mouth. Don't rush into trying too many different solids too soon. In a study of 1,265 New Zealand children, feeding four or more different solid foods before four months of age was found to increase the likelihood of the child developing recurrent eczema by 300 percent compared to children not fed solids before four months of age.

As you add solid foods to baby's diet, add them one at a time, and feed them exclusively (along with breast milk or formula) for at least four days to see if your baby has any problematic reactions before adding others.

Avoid giving refined flour products first. It's customary in the United States to give very young babies crackers, O-shaped cereal, bagels, or cookies, but there is some evidence that introducing wheat too soon can promote an oversensitivity to gluten in the baby's immature gut. Also, the intense, almost sweet taste of these foods can spoil baby's taste for more nutritious whole foods. Any refined carbohydrate or sugar can contribute to early tooth decay. If you opt for commercially available cereal, use fortified instant rice cereal and mix it with some breast milk, plain live-culture yogurt, or formula. Offer at least two servings per day of pureed meat or fish, especially to the formula-fed baby.

While nursing mothers may wait longer to add solids, parents of formula-fed infants may wish to start with solids in the fifth month. Give formula-fed babies some raw foods that contain digestive enzymes, such as bananas or other ripe fruit, thoroughly mashed. As a supplement to formula, a baby five months old and up can have freshly squeezed juice from vegetables or fruit to augment her consumption of living enzymes, which are naturally abundant in breast milk. (Avoid citrus juices before the ninth or tenth month, as their acidity can make them irritating to young babies.)

Try pureeing fresh, raw apple and and lightly cooked carrot with a couple of tablespoons of fruit juice and a teaspoon of lemon juice. Mashed avocado, applesauce, peas, and cooked winter squash are all good first foods. If you decide to give juices that are not fresh, dilute them 50 percent with water, and do not serve juice or milk (in a cup) with meals—babies may prefer to fill up on juice or milk instead of food. Choose phytonutrient-rich grape, pomegranate, or berry juices.

The AAP recommends against skim or low-fat milks for children under two. If you have access to it, give fresh, local, straight-from-the-udder milk rather than the pasteurized, homogenized variety—if the cows are healthy and the milking environment pristine.

As your baby begins teething, add chunks of fruit or vegetables to her diet, wrapped in a piece of cheesecloth or other thin, mesh-like cloth that has been fastened in with a rubber band. She can hang onto the tail end of the cloth and chew and suck on the apple, banana, pear, sweet potato, winter squash, or carrot chunk inside, without biting off more than she can manage. If you want to try teething biscuits, choose an organic version without refined sugar.

Always watch an eating baby or toddler carefully. Learn how to handle choking emergencies, just in case. Also, never feed honey to a baby less than one year old; it can cause infant botulism.

Most commercially available baby foods are not organic, and they may contain preservatives and additives. If you crave the convenience of jarred baby food, seek out organic versions, which are available in most supermarkets. Handheld manual baby food makers are an easy way to make whatever you're eating into a ground-up version for baby. Whenever you make extra baby food, freeze leftovers in ice cube trays.

What About Food Allergies?

If your child has displayed symptoms of intolerances to formula or to foods that Mom has eaten and that pass into mother's milk, or has already been diagnosed with asthma or nasal allergies, you may want to avoid allergenic foods until the child is two or three years old. Symptoms of a food allergy include:

- Itching, swelling of the mouth
- Runny nose
- Swelling, itching, or rash anywhere on the body
- Vomiting
- Diarrhea
- Itchy or swollen lips

In addition, some evidence suggests that behavioral issues in children labeled as ADHD may have to do with food sensitivities or allergies. Efforts to eliminate allergenic foods, additives, colorings, and preservatives have proven effective in some cases.

Food allergy is an immune system reaction to some component of a food that results in the formation of antibodies against that component. If that food is eaten again, the body reacts to it as though it were dangerous, producing antibodies designed to do away with it. Allergy is not the same thing as an intolerance, which is usually descriptive of a gastrointestinal problem—like lactose intolerance, where the gut makes inadequate lactase to digest lactose, the sugar found in milk. Celiac disease is not a true allergy to wheat, but an inability to digest wheat proteins (gluten) that causes diarrhea.

True allergic reactions to foods can range from mild to severe, with *anaphylaxis*—sudden onset of rash, asthma-like symptoms, tingling, metallic taste in the mouth, vomiting, diarrhea—the most extreme allergic reaction. Anaphylaxis can be fatal, and can result from exposure to even the tiniest amount of the allergenic food. Treatment usually includes an epinephrine injection (parents of kids prone to anaphylaxis should always have an EpiPen handy, and leave one with the school nurse in case of a reaction there). Benadryl and asthma medicines may also be used, but never as a replacement for epinephrine. Potentially food-allergic babies should avoid cow's milk, citrus fruits and juices, wheat, and soy foods until twelve months of age; eggs until two years of age; and peanuts and shellfish until three years of age.

True food allergy is much less common than most parents think. According to the American Academy of Family Physicians, about 8 percent of children and 1 to 2 percent of adults are food-allergic. Suspected food allergies can be confirmed by an allergist with tests for specific antibodies. The best way to prevent food allergy is to breastfeed exclusively for the first six months of your baby's life.

Eat on a Schedule

Children—even very young ones—thrive on routine. They like to know what to expect and what is expected of them. Sit down to eat on a regular schedule, even if baby doesn't actually eat. Offer new foods several times. A baby might turn his nose up at it eight times, then devour it the ninth! Allow baby to touch, play with, smell, and otherwise manipulate his food. Don't stress about giving a specific amount of each food group each day. As long as breast milk or formula are part of the diet, baby's nutritional bases are probably covered.

Delay the introduction of refined sugars and other sweets as long as you can. Although it's tempting to put a gigantic cake in front of baby on her first birthday or feed her ice cream when she won't eat anything else, the longer you can put off introducing these foods, the less hooked on them she's likely to become.

When Your Baby Can Chew and Feed Himself

Once your baby can chew, pick up food between fingers and thumb, and feed himself, your options for feeding dramatically expand. The foods described below are appropriate for children aged fifteen months and beyond, or for slightly younger kids with enough teeth to chew foods well.

The foods described in the New Breastfeeding Diet are the same foods that will be most beneficial for your young child. Offer her the same foods that are on your plate, made toddler-friendly by cutting them into small pieces. Toddlers love "nibble trays" with a few different choices, set apart from one another. Most toddlers do not like their food mixed up, so whenever possible, use plates with compartments for each food.

Tips for the toddler-friendly diet:

- Use the size of the child's fist as a guideline for portion sizes.
- Steam carrots and other hard veggies and cut them into small chunks.
- Offer soft cooked beans; try pinto, black, or garbanzo beans—great finger foods! (Soak dried beans overnight and rinse before cooking; otherwise, they can be gas-producing.)
- Grapes (organic are best) are chokable and should be cut into pieces.
- Vitamin C–rich fruits like berries, citrus, melon, and kiwi are great toddler foods.

- Nuts aren't a great choice for toddlers because of their chokability. Try nut and seed butters: almond, cashew, sesame seed (tahini), and macadamia nut butters over peanut butter when possible. Peanuts can harbor aflatoxin, a carcinogenic mold. If you suspect your child may be food-allergic (see the section on this), delay the introduction of nuts until after the age of three.
- Try brown rice cooked with plenty of water so that it's sticky enough to mold into todder-friendly balls; if they need extra stickiness, add a dash of rice vinegar. Roll the balls in a mixture of kelp and garlic powder and sesame seeds.
- A half-cup of slow-cooked oatmeal is a healthy breakfast; stir in ground flaxseed and a teaspoon of maple syrup or no-sugar fruit jam.
- Best bets for dairy foods: whole-milk, organic, plain yogurt, organic cheeses.
- Dried fruit is a good source of phytochemicals when fresh fruits are out of season. Choose unsulfured dried berries, apricots, and other brightly colored fruits. Stew and puree them for children who aren't ready to chew dried fruit.
- Make baby's first noodles whole-grain or rice. Breads and cereals made from whole grains are OK too, but read labels to ensure they aren't loaded with sugar.
- Keep processed food and junk foods out of the house completely.
- Don't use sweets as a reward or a method for bribing the child into eating more nutritious food. Offer nonfood rewards for good eating habits: a trip to the playground, a game played with Mom, extra hugs and kisses.

Getting Children to Eat Vegetables and Nag Less for Sweets

If you can grow any vegetables yourself, try to make this part of the time you spend with your kids. Live in an apartment? Try a little herb garden. Sprouting raw nuts, seeds, beans, and legumes (which you can get at your health food store or via mail-order) is a wonderful experience for parents to share with children. Simply place the sprouts-to-be in a colander, sprouting bag, or sprouting jar; rinse daily until sprouts shoot out.

Take young children on outings to farms, pick your own produce, pet the cows, watch the chickens scratch and peck. Show them where their food comes from. Children who see food as a link with nature are more likely to eat natural foods without a fuss.

Eventually, your child will get a taste of sweets and refined, processed, attractively packaged food. If it hasn't happened by the time she's in school, it will once she gets there. Make it clear that those foods are once-in-a-while foods.

Try creating a schedule where your family has a sweet treat one or two days a week. "Oh, you want a candy bar? It's not our sweets day—we'll have one on Sunday!" Show your child those days on the calendar; it's a good way to introduce the days of the week.

Children will naturally clamor for junk foods that are marketed and packaged specifically for them. Don't get in the habit of falling prey to those who profit from marketing directly to children—companies who, in marketing meetings, try to figure out how to optimize "the nag factor" in improving their bottom line. Once your child recognizes that you won't be buying those foods, he'll quit asking for them.

Just before the evening meal, when kids are likely to be most hungry, put out a plate of cut-up raw vegetables with dip. Instead of commercially available salad dressings, which usually contain a lot of MSG and less healthful oils, try a dip such as the following:

- One cup of whole-milk, organic yogurt with a cup of mild mango or peach salsa stirred in
- Cynthia Lair's tahini dressing (see recipe in Chapter 9)
- Organic cottage cheese or light sour cream
- Hummus: one 14.5-ounce can of chickpeas, two rounded teaspoons of tahini, a crushed garlic clove, a drizzle of extra-virgin olive oil, a sprinkling of salt, and the juice of half a lemon, all blended in a blender or food processor

- Warm peanut sauce: combine one-half cup peanut butter (or another nut butter, such as cashew or almond butter) with three-quarters cup water, one-quarter cup maple syrup, a tablespoon soy sauce, and a little grated ginger in a saucepan over medium-low heat; stir often until all ingredients are blended; also great with chunks of chicken, over cooked hearty greens, or in stir-fry

Most kids love ranch dressing; buy organic versions or Newman's Own, which is made with natural ingredients. By the time your child is two or three years old, she should be able to eat the foods you have grown to love while on the New Breastfeeding Diet!

(Relatively) Healthy Treats

Allow healthful treats like smoothie or frozen juice pop; homemade granola; plain organic yogurt with granola, fruit, and a dash of maple syrup; frozen or fresh fruit; trail mix; sulfite-free dried fruit; nuts or seeds; or applesauce during snack times any day. The coconut macaroon recipe from Chapter 9 is a good one to try with the kids—easy to make, and with all the benefits of lauric and capric acids.

If you need something sweet to help get through a car ride or a time when quiet is needed, try sugar-free lollipops made with sorbitol or xylitol. Most health food stores carry them. There are lots of excellent cookbooks that can help you make healthful treats for—and with—your kids. See our cookbook recommendations in Appendix B for ideas.

Nutritional Supplements for Children

A multivitamin and mineral supplement can help ensure that even picky eaters get the nutrients they need to thrive. Choose a supplement that contains no sugar or artificial sweeteners—better options are those sweetened with fruit juices or with stevia. If possible, choose a children's supplement that is made with whole-food ingredients rather than lab-created, isolated vitamins and minerals.

Research shows that taking multivitamin supplements improves children's levels of important nutrients and significantly improves performance on tests of nonverbal intelligence.

You can choose from liquid or chewable vitamins. Also available are multinutrient powders that can be added to applesauce, smoothies, or juices. Talk with your doctor or health food store salesperson to find out which multivitamins for kids come with the highest recommendations. Encourage your child to drink "green water," or purified water with a half-teaspoon or so of chlorophyll added. A green food powder made from spirulina can be added to foods to help a picky eater get her daily dose of greens.

Children who eat any processed foods should also take a probiotic supplement—one that is designed with your child's age range in mind. Pharmax makes a version they call "toddler straws," which the child can open and pour into her mouth or sprinkle into applesauce, yogurt, oatmeal, or milk. (You can buy Pharmax products at Rockwell Nutrition, rockwellnutrition.com, or at pharmaca.com.) When your child has to take antibiotics, she can take a dose of the "good guys" between doses of the antibiotic.

Herbal and Homeopathic Medicines for Children

Increasing numbers of parents are investigating herbal medicines for themselves and their children. Many of the herbs used today have centuries-long traditions of safe use. Ear infection? Antibiotics have been found not to make much difference in the course of this common childhood illness. Drops made from willow and garlic oil, however, can work wonders.

No mainstream drug will make a significant difference in the course of illness in a child with the flu, but elderberry extract can be a useful therapy. Explore the world of homeopathic and herbal medicine when seeking gentle healing for your children. A naturopathic physician, M.D. trained in alternative medicine, or chiropractor can help. This kind of gentle approach works in harmony with the child's developing and constantly changing physiology. It's nice to know the mainstream "big guns" are there when we really need them. Have a couple of good reference books like the following on your shelf to help you use natural medicine for your child:

- *Naturally Healthy Babies and Children: A Commonsense Guide to Herbal Remedies* by Aviva Jill Romm (North Adams, Mass.: Storey Publishing, 2000).
- *Smart Medicine for a Healthier Child* by Robert Rountree, Rachel Walton, and Rachel Zand (New York: Avery Books, 2003).

Concluding Thoughts

IN THE UNITED STATES, poverty and lack of education stand in the way of breastfeeding. The children of women of lower socioeconomic and educational status are more likely to have babies who are not breastfed, who are sick more often, and who have developmental or behavioral problems. In the United States, children of African-American and Hispanic mothers are particularly at risk for low birth weight, prematurity, and chronic illness.

Rarely acknowledged in the "breast is best" conversation is the role of the mother's educational level, socioeconomic status, and intelligence in the health of her baby. The bulk of modern research shows that women who breastfeed exclusively and for longer periods tend also to be more intelligent and more educated than those who do not breastfeed or who combine formula and breastfeeding.

These are hard issues to confront, but solutions are beginning to materialize. Programs like the Special Supplemental Nutrition Program offered by WIC (Women, Infants, and Children) aim to help those who are in need of education and assistance in better meeting their own nutritional needs and those of their children. Peer counselors trained by La Leche League have been successful at encouraging exclusive, extended breastfeeding in growing numbers of low-income mothers.

If you, dear reader, are socioeconomically middle- to upper-class and of high educational status—college or beyond—you are in that privileged sector of society that is most likely to engage in extended nursing and to go to great lengths to try to optimally nourish your children. Indeed, the fact that we'd probably be "preaching to the converted" troubled us as we worked on this book. We knew that women who were at greatest risk of not nursing their kids and of feeding their kids foods that wouldn't support their health would probably not be the women who would read this book and apply the advice it contains. We can only hope that each woman who reads this book can take some action to help promote a culture that supports extended, on-demand nursing.

It's hard to conceive of ourselves as a species that makes food for its young and to be comfortable with having that process in plain view. It smells something like barbarism, something too primitive for us to bother with in all our sparkling modernity. The sight of a breastfeeding woman has been known to cause discomfort in many circles.

Regardless, all across the United States, women are demanding the right to nurse their babies in public places. Any time a nursing woman is shooed away from a public area by store or restaurant employees, several dozen angry lactating women show up and stage a "nurse-in." Several states have established laws that give breastfeeding women the right to nurse in public.

Although we live in a far more breastfeeding-friendly world than we did twenty years ago, we have a long way to go. Public breastfeeding isn't the only challenge faced by women who wish to feed their babies the food made just for them, whenever they are hungry.

Helping to Create a Breastfeeding-Friendly World: What You Can Do

There are other challenges: combining breastfeeding with work, for example. This is a particularly troublesome issue for women who must work full-time just to make enough money to meet their families' needs. Legislation and social action to promote extended, paid maternity leave or government benefits to new mothers are sorely needed to improve the health of American children, starting with the first weeks of life.

You can help improve all children's health by being active in pro-breastfeeding causes as your time allows. Join campaigns to get the toxins out of the environment and out of pregnant and nursing mothers' bodies. Help push politicians to create laws like those in Europe that provide six months' paid leave from work for new mothers. Participate in campaigns to help end the horror of malnourishment and starvation in children and mothers overseas.

On a smaller scale, by breastfeeding exclusively and on demand yourself when you are out in the world, at the mall or in a coffee shop or in front of the supermarket, you can help to make this practice seem normal and desirable—so that a woman who might otherwise have forgone breastfeeding will think twice when it comes time for her to make the formula/nursing choice. Some little girl who has never seen a woman breastfeed will see you and know that this is possible and beautiful. A little boy may have the seed planted in his mind that breastfeeding is natural and that the mother of his children will, someday, put their children to her breast.

The simple action of breastfeeding on demand, wherever you happen to be, goes a long way toward helping to create a more breastfeeding-friendly world. This simple act helps to make the world friendlier, more loving, and more child-centered: a better world, overall.

Appendix A

Hidden Food Sources of MSG (Monosodium Glutamate)

MSG IS ALMOST UBIQUITOUS in processed foods. Even so-called "healthy" or organic foods may contain some version of this chemical. MSG is controversial because it is a source of free glutamic acid, a form of the amino acid glutamine that acts as an *excitotoxin*—meaning that it overexcites nerve cells, sometimes to death. Some people have strong allergic or anaphylactic (an allergic response that is sudden and possibly fatal) reactions to MSG; seizures and irregular heartbeats also have been reported. But there is some evidence that this chemical may have more subtle neurological ill effects. Neurosurgeon Russell L. Blaylock has been a powerful force in the research of the potential harmful effects of MSG. He has described convincing links between MSG overconsumption and autism, Alzheimer's disease, and neurodegenerative diseases like multiple sclerosis.

Currently, there is not widespread acceptance of Blaylock's theories. This is due in part, no doubt, to the fact that MSG is a crucially important ingredient in processed foods. Once all the taste has been processed out, it's added in with this chemical, which "excites" the taste buds and makes even bland food taste great. Without it, food manufacturers would be hard-pressed to find ways to make their products palatable.

Our advice: avoid it when you can. Unless you are highly sensitive, however, it isn't likely to kill you or make you ill if you consume it only very occasionally. Look for the following ingredients on labels and try to avoid most of them. (This table is adapted from the website truthinlabeling.org, which contains many links and references to Dr. Blaylock's work.)

Always Contains MSG	Often Contains MSG (or Creates MSG During Processing)
Glutamate	Carrageenan
Monosodium glutamate	Natural pork, chicken, or beef flavoring
Monopotassium glutamate	
Yeast extract	Bouillons, broths, stocks
Hydrolyzed protein	Flavors/flavorings
Glutamic acid	Natural flavors/flavorings
Calcium caseinate	Maltodextrin
Sodium caseinate	Citric acid
Yeast food	Barley malt
Hydrolyzed corn gluten	Malt extract/flavoring
Gelatin	Soy sauce (not tamari)
Textured protein	"Seasonings" (when not specified)
Yeast nutrient	
Autolyzed yeast	

Hydrolyzed protein—including the whey protein found in protein powders—may contain small amounts of MSG, created during the processing of the protein. Unless you have allergic reactions to even small traces of MSG, our advice to use whey protein to make smoothies a few times a week still applies.

You can find Dr. Blaylock's book, *Excitotoxins: The Taste that Kills* (Santa Fe, New Mexico: Health Press, 1997) in bookstores or at Amazon.com. As you might guess from the title, it isn't a light read, but it is highly informative—the definitive resource on the subject.

Appendix B

Resources

Breastfeeding and Parenting Books

Eiger, Marvin, and Sally Wendkos Olds. *The Complete Book of Breastfeeding*. New York: Workman Publishing, 1999.

La Leche League International. *The Womanly Art of Breastfeeding*. New York: Plume Books, 2004.

Liedloff, Jean. *The Continuum Concept: In Search of Happiness Lost*. Boston: Addison Wesley, 1986.

Sears, Martha, and William Sears. *The Attachment Parenting Book: A Commonsense Guide to Understanding and Nurturing Your Baby*. New York: Little, Brown, 2001. (The books by pediatrician Dr. William Sears and his wife Martha, nurse and mother of seven, are excellent, comprehensive volumes that promote natural parenting, breastfeeding, and the use of baby slings. Look also at *The Baby Book*, *The Family Nutrition Book*, and *The Breastfeeding Book* by these authors.)

Breastfeeding and Parenting Websites

promom.org

The site of a nonprofit organization, Pro Mother's Milk, which provides comprehensive information on and promotion of breastfeeding.

kellymom.com
gentlebirth.org/archives/index.html
The Midwife Archives site—advice straight from experienced midwives, meant as a place for midwives to share information but fascinating and informative for the rest of us too.

http://neonatal.ttuhsc.edu/lact/index.html
The site of Thomas Hale, R.Ph., Ph.D., author of *Medications and Mother's Milk*. Go here to find information on the safety of any medication for lactating mothers.

Breast Milk Banks

If you don't see one near you, call your local hospital to find out whether one has formed.

Mother's Milk Bank
Valley Medical Center
P.O. Box 5730, San Jose, CA
(408) 998-4550

Mother's Milk Bank
Presbyterian/St. Luke's Medical Center
1719 East 19th Ave.
Denver, CO 80218
(303) 869-1888

Mother's Milk Bank of Iowa
Division of Nutrition, Department of Pediatrics,
    Children's Hospital of Iowa
University of Iowa Hospitals and Clinics
Iowa City, Iowa, 52242
(877) 891-5347 (toll-free)
(This milk bank only receives from and gives milk to women who live in Iowa City, Cedar Rapids, and Davenport, Iowa.)

Mother's Milk Bank
Christiana Care Health System
P.O. Box 6001
Newark, DE 19718
(302) 733-2340

Mother's Milk Bank
WakeMed
3000 New Bern Ave.
Raleigh, NC 27610
(919) 350-8599

Mother's Milk Bank at Austin
900 East 30th St., Suite 214
Austin, TX 78705
(512) 494-0800

Canada
Christian and Women's Lactation Services
British Columbia Children's and Women's Hospital
4480 Oak St.
Vancouver, BC V6H 3V4
Canada
(604) 875-2282

Mexico
Banco de Leche
Dr. Rafael Lucio Av Adolfo Ruiz Cortines #2903
C P 91020
Xalapa Veracruz
Mexico
+52 55 14 45 51 or +52 55 14 45 00

Apparel and Accoutrements for the Breastfeeding Mom

Behavioral problems, including depression, lack of impulse control, substance abuse, violence, and even impaired function of the immune system have been found in children who, as babies, were deprived of adequate time "in-arms" the first nine or so months of life. Children who were severely deprived of holding and one-on-one interaction with caregivers as infants have substantial deficits in intelligence and physical development. One study found that children adopted from orphanages do not produce increased amounts of the hormones oxytocin and vasopressin, hormones linked with bonding and feelings of loving connection, in response to interaction with their adoptive parents.

Try not to strap your baby into swings, strollers, or other contraptions when you can hold or carry her instead. Car seats are necessary, but as soon as you get where you're going, if your baby isn't sleeping, take her out. She needs the extra stimulation of being held and carried, her body moved around—not staying in one position for so many hours in the day.

There are many great slings, front packs, backpacks, and hip carriers available these days (we include some listings and merchants here). Or you can fashion your own sling from a big piece of fabric, as women have done for centuries. Instead of placating and tranquilizing your baby, you'll engage him in fascinating sights and sounds as you experience them. The motion of your body will aid in the development of his proprioception and sense of touch. You'll be much more attuned to his needs.

As your baby grows, you will find you prefer different kinds of carriers. The one type that can be used from baby's birth all the way to her third year or beyond is the baby sling. Melissa's favorite is the padded two-ring version, such as the SlingEZee and Over the Shoulder Baby Holder brands. This type of sling may be a bit harder to get the hang of, but it's versatile: it can be used while breastfeeding, for a newborn lying down (you may need to add some padding behind his back if he's very small), for a baby who's sitting up, and for an older baby or toddler who can ride on your hip.

Maya Wrap slings are more unstructured; their fabrics are beautiful, and many moms prefer them. The Baby Bjorn–type front packs are very popular, but some experts don't recommend them. They put pressure on a baby's developing spine, hip joints, and groin and leave his legs dangling. Slings have a more cradling effect, keeping legs gathered in a more natural position in younger babies or creating a padded "shelf" for older babies to sit on when riding on your hip. A better option for the front-and-center position is the Baby Bundler, a long, soft, stretchy piece of fabric that can be wrapped to hold baby in multiple positions, including front-facing. Frame backpacks are good for housework, grocery shopping, or cooking; baby stays out of harm's way (and your way) while you work.

Check out these websites where you can buy fashionable nursing wear:

motherwear.com
babystyle.com

These are sites where slings and other baby carriers can be purchased:

nurturedfamily.com
mayawrap.com
attachedtobaby.com
nursingbaby.com

Cookbooks

Bittman, Mark. *How to Cook Everything: Simple Recipes for Great Food*. New York: Macmillan, 1998. (If you only have one cookbook, this one should be it. The pages of Melissa's copy are stained and stuck together from constant use. An amazing resource for preparing simple, quick, delicious, from-scratch food.)

Lair, Cynthia. *Feeding the Whole Family*. Seattle, Washington: Moon Smile Press, 1994.

Books and Websites About the Toxins Issue

Baillie-Hamilton, Paula. *Toxic Overload: A Doctor's Plan for Combating the Illnesses Caused by Chemicals in Our Foods, Our Homes, and Our Medicine Cabinets.* New York: Penguin, 2005. (Although this is targeted more toward adults, it is one of the best-researched books available regarding the effects of toxins on health.)

Colborn, Theo, Dianne Dumanoski, and John Peterson Myers. *Our Stolen Future.* New York: Plume Books, a subsidiary of Penguin Books, 1997. (This book is billed as a "scientific detective story," and it reads like a thriller. The information it contains isn't easy to swallow, but will raise your awareness about the extent of the toxin problem.)

Erickson, Kim. *Drop Dead Gorgeous: Protecting Yourself from the Hidden Dangers of Cosmetics.* New York: McGraw-Hill, 2002. (Although it is a few years old now, this book is still highly relevant.)

Landrigan, Philip, Herbert Needleman, and Mary Landrigan. *Raising Healthy Children in a Toxic World: 101 Smart Solutions for Every Family.* Emmaus, PA: Rodale Press, 2001. (Written by well-respected researchers, this is an essential, practical guide to simple lifestyle changes that can have a huge impact.)

Magaziner, Allan, Linda Bonvie, and Anthony Zolezzi. *Chemical-Free Kids: How to Safeguard Your Child's Diet and Environment.* New York: Kensington Publishing, 2003. (A well-written, comprehensive review of the impact of toxins on children's health, complemented with lots of solid, useful advice.)

Steingraber, Sandra. *Having Faith: An Ecologist's Journey to Motherhood.* New York: Berkeley Books, 2001. (Informative reading on environmental toxins woven with one woman's personal story of motherhood. Beautifully written and highly recommended.)

http://ourstolenfuture.org

Companion website to Colborn, Dumanoski, and Peterson Myers's book.

checnet.org

Information about toxins and their effects on children's health.

http://www.panna.org/

Pesticide Action Network of North America; Dr. Rountree is a member. Does excellent work, especially regarding children.

http://www.organicconsumers.org/sos.htm

Organic Consumers Association; the link is to a page for its national campaign to get nontoxic and organic products into schools.

http://www.nrdc.org/health/kids/default.asp

National Resources Defense Council, one of the best activist groups around. This link is to its page for issues related to toxins and childrens' health.

http://www.ewg.org/

Environmental Working Group; has sponsored some incredibly helpful research on the body burden of chemical toxins in adults and children. Dr. Rountree can't imagine doing the work he does without them.

Sources for Organic Foods and Supplements

localharvest.org

Web locator for consumer-supported agriculture, farmer's markets, and other sources of locally grown fresh food.

shoporganic.com
sunorganic.com

Two sites where organic foods can be ordered for delivery to your home.

tropicaltraditions.com/virgin_coconut_oil.htm
   Source for organic coconut oil.

naturalacres.com; or call (717) 692-1000
   Source for organic beef, poultry, and dairy.

alvaradostreetbakery.com; or call (707) 585-3293
   The Alvarado St. Bakery sells organic, whole-grain baked goods. Try their sprouted grain bagels—especially the onion poppyseed.

edenfoods.com
seaweed.net
loveseaweed.com
   Three mail-order sources for sea vegetables.

xymogen.com
   Xymogen Professional Products makes a number of nutrients useful for detoxification, including protein powders, encapsulated nutrients for support of phase 1 and 2 liver detoxification, clinically researched probiotic strains, high-quality fish oil, and rosemary. They also have a patented capsule form of sulforaphane, developed at Johns Hopkins University in the Brassica Chemopreventive Laboratory. Xymogen does not sell to the public or on the Internet. What Dr. Rountree recommends is that people call and ask for a referral to a health-care professional in their area that uses its products.

Natural, Healthy Products for Home and Personal Care

Berthold-Bond, Annie. *Better Basics for the Home: Simple Solutions for Less Toxic Living.* New York: Three Rivers Press, 1999.

Steinman, David, and Samuel Epstein. *The Safe Shopper's Bible: A Consumer's Guide to Nontoxic Household Products.* New York: Wiley, 1995.

Siegel-Maier, Karyn. *The Naturally Clean Home: 101 Safe and Easy Herbal Formulas for Non-Toxic Cleansers*. North Adams, Mass.: Storey Publishing, 1999.

greenbuildingsupply.com
    The Green Building Supply Environmentally Friendly Home Center. A good resource for any and all needs for the less toxic home.

grassrootsstore.com
    A source for skin brushes, massage oils, and more—all "green" and nontoxic.

Finding a Detox Physician

functionalmedicine.org
    The Institute for Functional Medicine in Gig Harbor, Washington. Contact the IFM to find a nutritional medicine doctor in your area.

Children's Health and General Family Health

Raffelock, Dean, Robert Rountree, Virginia Hopkins, with Melissa Block. *A Natural Guide to Pregnancy and Postpartum Health*. New York: Avery Books, 2003.

naturalfamilyonline.com
    A site for information on natural family living.

Appendix C

Converting to Metrics

Volume Measurement Conversions

U.S.	Metric
¼ teaspoon	1.25 ml
½ teaspoon	2.5 ml
¾ teaspoon	3.75 ml
1 teaspoon	5 ml
1 tablespoon	15 ml
¼ cup	62.5 ml
½ cup	125 ml
¾ cup	187.5 ml
1 cup	250 ml

Weight Conversion Measurements

U.S.	Metric
1 ounce	28.4 g
8 ounces	227.5 g
16 ounces (1 pound)	455 g

Cooking Temperature Conversions

Celsius/Centigrade—0°C and 100°C are arbitrarily placed at the melting and boiling points of water and are standard to the metric system.

Fahrenheit—Fahrenheit established 0°F as the stabilized temperature when equal amounts of ice, water, and salt are mixed.

To convert temperatures in Fahrenheit to Celsius, use this formula:

$$C = (F - 32) \times 0.5555$$

So, for example, if you are baking at 350°F and want to know that temperature in Celsius, use this calculation:

$$C = (350 - 32) \times 0.5555 = 176.66°C$$

Selected References

Chapter 1

Barker DJP, M.D. *Mothers, Babies and Health in Later Life*, 2nd ed. Edinburgh, Scotland: Churchill Livingstone, 1998.

Eriksson JG, et al. Catch-up growth in childhood and coronary heart disease: longitudinal study. *BMJ* 1999; 318: 427–31.

Eriksson JG, et al. Fetal and childhood growth and hypertension. *Hypertension* 2000; 36.

Eriksson JG, et al. Pathways of infant and childhood growth that lead to type 2 diabetes. *Diabetes Care* 2003 Nov; 26(11): 3006–10.

Eriksson JG, et al. Early adiposity rebound in childhood and risk of type 2 diabetes in adult life. *Diabetologia* 2003 Feb; 46(2): 190–4.

Forsen T, et al. Mother's weight in pregnancy and heart disease in a cohort of Finnish men: follow-up study. *BMJ* 1997; 315: 837–40.

Forsen T, et al. Growth in utero and during childhood and coronary heart disease: longitudinal study. *BMJ* 1999; 319: 1403–7.

Chapter 2

Arita M, et al. Epidemiological research on incidence of atopic disease in infants and children in relation to their nutrition in infancy. *Arerugi* 1997 Apr; 46(4): 354–69.

Auestad N, et al. Growth and development in term infants fed long-chain polyunsaturated fatty acids: a double-masked, randomized, parallel, prospective, multivariate study. *Pediatrics* 2001 Aug; 108(2): 372–81.

Botto LD, Mulinare J, Erickson JD. Occurrence of congenital heart defects in relation to maternal multivitamin use. *Am J Epidemiol* 2000; 151: 878–84.

Chen ZY, et al. Breastmilk fatty acid composition: a comparative study between Hong Kong and Chongqing Chinese. *Lipids* 1997; 32(10): 1061–67.

Connor WE, Lowensohn R, Hatcher L. Increased docosahexaenoic acid levels in human newborn infants by administration of sardines and fish oil during pregnancy. *Lipids* 1996 Mar; 31 Suppl: S183–7.

Czeizel AE. Reduction of urinary tract and cardiovascular defects by periconceptional multivitamin supplementation. *J Med Genet* 1996; 62: 179–83.

Czeizel AE, Dudas I. Prevention of the first occurrence of neural-tube defects by periconceptional vitamin supplementation. *N Engl J Med* 1992; 327: 1832–5.

Davis BC, Kris-Etherton PM. Achieving optimal essential fatty acid status in vegetarians: current knowledge and practical implications. *Am J Clin Nutr* 78(3 Suppl): 640S–646S.

Demmelmair H, et al. Influence of formulas with borage oil or borage oil plus fish oil on the arachidonic acid status in premature infants. *Lipids* 2001 Jun; 36(6): 555–66.

Duchen K, Bjorksten B, Polyunsaturated n-3 fatty acids and the development of atopic disease. *Lipids* 2001; 36(9): 1033–42.

Dunstan JA, et al. The effect of supplementation with fish oil during pregnancy on breast milk immunoglobulin A, soluble CD14, cytokine levels and fatty acid composition. *Clin Exp Allergy* 2004 Aug; 34(8): 1237–42.

Fallon, Sally, and Mary G. Enig, Ph.D. *Nourishing Traditions: The Cookbook that Challenges Politically Correct Nutrition and the Diet Dictocrats.* Winona Lake, IN: New Trends Publishing, 1999.

Hawkes JS, et al. Transforming growth factor beta in human milk does not change in response to modest intakes of docosahexaenoic acid. *Lipids* 2001 Oct; 36(10): 1179–81.

Heird WC, et al. The role of polyunsaturated fatty acids in term and preterm infants and breastfeeding mothers. *Pediatr Clin North Am* 2001 Feb; 48(1): 173–88.

Helland IB, et al. Maternal supplementation with very-long-chain n-3 fatty acids during pregnancy and lactation augments children's IQ at 4 years of age. *Pediatrics* 2003 Jan; 111(1): e-39–44.

Helland IB, et al. Similar effects on infants of n-3 and n-6 fatty acids supplementation to pregnant and lactating women. *Pediatrics* 2001 Nov; 108(5): E82.

Hoppu, Ulla, et al. Breast milk—immunomodulatory signals against allergic diseases. *Allergy* 2001; 56(Supplement 67): 23–26.

Hoppu U, Kalliomaki M, Isolauri E. Maternal diet rich in saturated fat during breastfeeding is associated with atopic sensitization of the infant. *Eur J Clin Nutr* 2000 Sep. 54(9): 702–5.

Hussein N, et al. Long-chain conversion of [13C]linoleic acid and alpha-linolenic acid in response to marked changes in dietary intake in men. *Journal of Lipid Research* 2005 Feb; 46: 269–280.

Jensen CL, et al. Effect of docosahexaenoic acid supplementation of lactating women on the fatty acid composition of breast milk and maternal and infant plasma phospholipids. *Am J Clin Nutr* 2000 Jan; 71(1 Suppl): 292S–9S.

Jorgensen MH, et al. Is there a relation between docosahexaenoic acid concentration in mothers' milk and visual development in term infants? *J Pediatr Gastroenterol Nutr* 2001 Mar; 32(3): 293–6.

Laiho K, et al. Breast milk fatty acids, eicosanoids, and cytokines in mothers with and without allergic disease. *Pediatric Research* 2003; 53: 642–47.

Lindsay H. Allen of the Department of Agriculture, University of California, Davis. Multiple micronutrients in pregnancy and lactation: and overview. ajcn.org/cgi/content/abstract/81/5/1206S, August 27, 2005.

McCann JC, Ames BN. Is docosahexaenoic acid, an n-3 long-chain polyunsaturated fatty acid, required for development of normal brain function? An overview of evidence from cognitive and behavioral tests in humans and animals. *Am J Clin Nutr* 2005 Aug; 82(2): 281–95.

Minda H, et al. Effect of different types of feeding on fatty acid composition of erythrocyte membrane lipids in full-term infants. *Acta Paediatr* 2002; 91(8): 874–81.

Mitoulas LR, et al. Infant intake of fatty acids from human milk over the first year of lactation. *Br J Nutr* 2003 Nov; 90(5): 979–86.

Montgomery C, et al. Maternal docosahexaenoic acid and fetal accretion. *Br J Nutr* 2003 Jul; 90(1): 135–45.

No authors listed. Gamma-linoleic acid supplementation for prophylaxis of atopic dermatitis: a randomized controlled trial in infants at high familial risk. *Am J Clin Nutr* 2003; 77(4): 943–951.

No authors listed. Neurologic impairment in children associated with maternal deficiency of cobalamin—Georgia 2001. *Journal of the American Medical Association* 2003 Feb 26; 289(8): 979–80.

Olafsdottir AS, et al. Fat-soluble vitamins in the maternal diet, influence of cod liver oil supplementation and impact of the maternal diet on human milk consumption. *Annals of Nutrition and Metabolism* 2001; 45(6): 265–72.

Peet M, et al. Depletion of omega-3 fatty acid levels in red blood cell membranes of depressive patients. *Biol Psychiatry* 1998 Mar 1; 43(5): 315–9.

Smit EN, et al. Estimated biological variation of the mature human milk fatty acid composition. *Prostaglandins Leukot Essent Fatty Acids* 2002; in press.

Smit EN, et al. Effect of supplementation of arachidonic acid (AA) or a combination of AA plus docosahexaenoic acid on breastmilk fatty acid composition. *Prostaglandins Leukot Essent Fatty Acids* 2000 Jun; 62(6): 335–40.

Smit EN, et al. Effect of supplementation of arachidonic acid (AA) or a combination of AA plus docosahexaenoic acid on breastmilk fatty acid composition. *Prostaglandins Leukotrienes Essential Fatty Acids* 2000; 62: 335–40.

Spector SL, Surette ME, Diet and asthma: has the role of dietary lipids been overlooked in the management of asthma? *Ann Allergy Asthma Immunol* 2003; 90(4): 371–7.

Terry PD, Rohan TE, et al. Intakes of fish and marine fatty acids and the risks of cancers of the breast and prostate and of other hormone-related cancers: a review of the epidemiologic evidence. *Am J Clin Nutr* 2003; 77(3): 532–43.

Chapter 3

Alberti-Fidanza A, Burini G, Perriello G. Total antioxidant capacity of colostrum, and transitional and mature human milk. *Journal of Maternal, Fetal, and Neonatal Medicine* 2002 Apr; 11(4): 275–9.

Allen, Jane E. Rickets cases on the rise in U.S. *L.A. Times.* August 5, 2004.

Buss IH, et al. Vitamin C is reduced in human milk after storage. *Acta Paediatrica* 2001 Jul; 90(7): 813–5.

Cannell, JJ. Vitamin D and mental illness. cholecalciferol-council .com, accessed October 10, 2005.

Daneel-Otterbech S, Davidsson L, Hurrell R. Ascorbic acid supplementation and regular consumption of fresh orange juice increases the ascorbic acid content of human milk: studies in European and African lactating women. *American Journal of Clinical Nutrition* 2005 May; 81(5): 1088–93.

Duncan, Emma. Spoilt for choice: a survey of food. *The Economist* 2003 Dec 13: 5–15.

Fokkema MR, et al. Plasma homocysteine increase from day 20 to 40 in breastfed but not formula fed low birthweight infants. *Acta Paediatrica* 2002; 91(5): 507–1.

Friel JK, et al. Evidence of oxidative stress in full-term healthy infants. *Pediatr Res* 2004 Dec; 56(6): 878–82.

Greer FR. Are breast-fed infants vitamin K deficient? *Adv Exp Med Biol* 2001; 501: 391–5.

Harik-Khan RI, Muller DC, Wise RA. Serum vitamin levels and risk of asthma in children. *American Journal of Epidemiology* 2004 Feb 15; 159(4): 351–7.

Heiskanen K, et al. Risk of low vitamin B_6 status in infants breast-fed exclusively beyond six months. *J Pediatr Gastroenterol Nutr* 1996 Jul; 23(1): 38–44.

Heiskanen K, et al. Low B_6 status associated with slow growth in healthy breast-fed infants. *Pediatr Res* 1995 Nov; 38(5): 740–6.

Hollis BW, Wagner CL. Assessment of dietary vitamin D requirements during pregnancy and lactation. *American Journal of Clinical Nutrition* 2004 May; 79(5): 717–26.

Hoppu E, et al. Vitamin C in breast milk may reduce risk of atopy in the infant. *Eur J Clin Nutr* 2005 Jan; 59(1): 123–8.

Mangels, Reed, R.D., Ph.D., Vegetarian Resource Group, September 2, 2003, vrg.org/nutrition/b12.htm#reliable, accessed October 12, 2005.

Minet JC, et al. Assessment of vitamin B_{12}, folate, and vitamin B_6 status and relation to sulfur amino acid metabolism in neonates. *Am J Clin Nutr* 2000; 72(3): 751–7.

No authors listed. Does breast milk contain enough vitamin D to prevent deficiency in breastfed babies? 007b.com/vitamin-d-breast-milk.php, accessed October 10, 2005.

Ooylan LM, et al. Vitamin B_6 content of breast milk and neonatal behavioral functioning. *Journal of the American Dietetic Association* 2002 Oct; 102(10): 1433–8.

Preston-Martin S, Pogoda JM, Mueller BA, et al. Prenatal vitamin supplementation and risk of childhood brain tumors. *Int J Cancer Suppl* 1998; 11: 17–22.

Ribiero KD, Dimenstein R. Foremilk and hindmilk retinol levels. *Rev Panam Salud Publica* 2004 Jul; 16(1): 19–22.

Scarlett WL. Ultraviolet radiation: sun exposure, tanning beds, and vitamin D levels. What you need to know and how to decrease the risk of skin cancer. *Journal of the American Osteopathic Association* 2003 Aug; 103(8): 371–5.

Specker BL, Miller D, Norman EJ, et al. Increased urinary methylmalonic acid excretion in breast-fed infants of vegetarian mothers and identification of an acceptable dietary source of vitamin B_{12}. *Am J Clin Nutr* 1987; 47: 89–92.

Turoli D, et al, U of Milan. Determination of oxidative status in breast and formula milk. *Acta Paediatr* 2004 Dec; 93(12): 1569–74.

Walker, Marsha, RN, IBCLC. Supplementation of the breastfed baby. Massachusetts Breastfeeding Coalition, massbfc.org/formula/bottle.html, accessed November 13, 2005.

Wang B, et al. Brain ganglioside and glycoprotein sialic acid in breastfed compared with formula-fed infants. *Am J Clin Nutr* 2003 Nov; 78(5): 1024–9.

Weiss WP, Hogan JS, Smith KL. Changes in vitamin C concentration in plasma and milk from dairy cows after intramammary infusion of E. coli. *Journal of Dairy Science* 2004 Jan; 87(1): 32–7.

Werler MM, Hayes C, Louik C, et al. Multivitamin supplementation and risk of birth defects. *Am J Epidemiol* 1999; 150: 675–82.

Chapter 4

Arem, Ridha, M.D. *The Thyroid Solution.* Ballantine Books, New York, 1999: 305, section entitled "Iodine: A Double-Edged Sword."

Dorea JG. Selenium and breast-feeding. *Br J Nutr* 2002 Nov; 88(5): 443–61.

Dorea JG. Iodine nutrition and breast feeding. *J Trace Elem Med Biol* 2002; 16(4): 207–20.

Harach HR, Williams ED. Thyroid cancer and thyroiditis in the goitrous region of Salta, Argentina, before and after iodine prophylaxis. *Clinical Endocrinology* 1995; 43: 701–6.

Henderson PH 3rd, et al. Bone mineral density in grand multiparous women with extended lactation. *American Journal of Obstetrics and Gynecology* 2000 Jun; 182(6): 1371–7.

Hernandez-Avila M, et al. Dietary calcium supplements lower blood lead levels in lactating women: a randomized placebo controlled trial. *Epidemiology* 2003.

Ortega RM, et al. Supplementation with iron and folates during gestation: influence on the zinc status in the mother and on the zinc content in the maternal milk. *Medical Clinics* (Barcelona) 1998 Sep 19; 111(8): 281–5.

Pizzorno, Joseph, N.D. *Total Wellness*. New York: Prima Publishing, 1998.

Specker B. Nutrition influences bone development from infancy through the toddler years. *J Nutr* 2004 Mar; 134(3): 6915–6955.

Trafikowska U, Sobkowiak E, Butler JA, et al. Organic and inorganic selenium supplementation to lactating mothers increase the blood and milk Se concentrations and Se intake by breast-fed infants. *J Trace Elem Med Biol* 1998 Jul; 12(2): 77–85.

Chapter 5

Crofton, Kevin, et al. Thyroid-hormone-disrupting chemicals: evidence for dose-dependent additivity or synergism. *Environmental Health Perspectives* 2005; 113: 1549–54. Online at http://ehp.niehs.nih.gov/docs/2005/8195/abstract.html.

Dewailly E, et al. High organochlorine body burden in women with estrogen receptor-positive breast cancer. *Journal of the National Cancer Institute* 1994 Feb 2; 86(3): 232–4.

No authors listed. Body burden: the pollution in newborns: the Environmental Working Group executive summary. ewg.org/reports/bodyburden2/execsumm.php, accessed July 14, 2005.

No authors listed. Small study finds chemicals in breast milk. CNN.com, Tuesday, September 23, 2003.

No authors listed. Lead action news. breastfeeding and lead: what mothers need to know. *The Journal of the LEAD (Lead Education and Abatement Design) Group Inc.* 6 (2), lead.org.au/lanv6n2/update002.html. March 7, 2006

No authors listed. Healthy milk, healthy baby: chemical pollution and mother's milk—chemicals: lead, mercury, cadmium and other metals. nrdc.org/breastmilk/lead.asp, accessed August 31, 2005.

Quick, Suzanne. Chemical linked to abnormalities in boys. *JS Online*, jsonline.com/alive/news/may05, accessed May 27, 2005.

Rajapakse N, Elisabete Silva, and Andreas Kortenkamp. Combining xenoestrogens at levels below individual no-observed-effect concentrations dramatically enhances steroid hormone action. http://ehpnet1.niehs.nih.gov/docs/2002/110p917-921rajapakse/abstract.html, accessed September 15, 2005.

Rier, S and WG Foster. Environmental dioxins and endometriosis. *Toxicological Sciences* 2002; 70: 161–170.

Viberg H, Fredriksson A, Eriksson P. Neonatal exposure to polybrominated diphenyl ether (PDBE 153) disrupts spontaneous behavior, impairs learning and memory, and decreases hippocampal cholinergic receptors in adult mice. *Toxicol Appl Pharmacol* 2003 Oct 15; 192(2): 95–106.

vom Saal FS, et al. An extensive new literature concerning low-dose effects of bisphenol a shows the need for a new risk assessment. *Environ Health Perspect* 2005; 113: 926–933.

Xu C, Li CY, Kong AN. Induction of Phase I, II and III drug metabolism/transport by xenobiotics. *Archives of Pharmacological Research* 2005 Mar; 28(3): 249–68.

Chapter 6

Brown MD, Green tea (Camellia sinensis) extract and its possible role in the prevention of cancer, *Alternative Medicine Review* 1999 Oct; 360–70.

Coleman, Eliot. Can organics save the family farm? organic-consumers.org/organic/save090604.cfm, accessed October 21, 2005.

Glei M, Pool-Zobel BL. The main catechin of green tea, (-)-epigallocatechin-3-gallate (EGCG), reduces bleomycin-induced DNA damage in human leucocytes. *Toxicology in Vitro* 2005 Sep 24.

Haramaki N, et al. The influence of vitamin E and dihydrolipoic acid on cardiac energy and glutathione status under hypoxia-reoxidation. *Biochem Mol Biol Int* 1995; 37: 591–97.

Lee JH, Kang HS, Roh J. Protective effects of garlic juice against embryotoxicity of methylmercuric chloride administered to pregnant Fischer 344 rats. *Yonsei Med J* 1999 Oct 1; 72(7): 1285–8.

Mennella JA, Beauchamp JK. Early flavor experiences: research update. *Nutrition Reviews* 1998 Jul; 56(7): 205–11.

Nakano S, et al. Maternal-fetal distribution and transfer of dioxins in pregnant women in Japan, and attempt to reduce maternal transfer with Chlorella (Chlorella Pyroidenosa). *Chemosphere.* 2005 Dec; 61(9): 1244–1255. Epub 2005 Jun 27.

No authors listed. Chlorophyll and chlorophyllin: research summary. Linus Pauling Institute website, http://lpi.oregonstate.edu/infocenter/phytochemicals/chloro-phylls/index.html, accessed November 13, 2005.

Puiggros F, et al. Grape seed procyanidins prevent oxidative injury by modulating the expression of antioxidant enzyme systems. *Journal of Agricultural Food Chemistry* 2005 July 27; 53(15): 6080–6.

Ray SD, Kumar SD, Bagchi D. A novel proanthocyanidin IH636 grape seed extract increases in vivo Bcl-XL expression and prevents acetaminophen-induced programmed and unprogrammed cell death in mouse liver. *Archives of Biochemistry and Biophysics* 1999 Sep 1; 369(1): 42–58.

Takekoshi H, et al. Effect of chlorella pyrenoidosa on fecal excretion and liver accumulation of polychlorinated dibenzo-P-dioxin in mice. *Chemosphere* 2005 Apr; 59(2): 297–304. Epub 2005 Jan 7.

Tattelman E, et al. Health effects of garlic. *American Family Physician* 2005 Jul 1; 72(1): 103–6.

Chapter 7

Foran JA, et al. Quantitative analysis of the benefits and risks of consuming farmed and wild salmon. *J Nutr* 2005 Nov; 135(11): 2639–43.

Hites RA, et al. Global assessment of organic contaminants in farmed salmon. *Science* 2004 Jan 9; 303(5655): 226–9.

Hites RA, et al. The contamination of salmon: where to draw the line. *Science* 2004; 303: 226–9.

No authors listed. Summary: PCBs in farmed salmon. ewg.org/reports/farmedPCBs/es.php, accessed November 10, 2005.

No authors listed. Farmed salmon and rainbow trout as healthy to eat as their wild counterparts. *Communique Universite Laval*, scom.ulaval.ca/communiques.de.presse/2005/mars/farmedsalmon.html, accessed November 19, 2005.

Tsang, Gloria, Ph.D. PCBs—is farmed salmon safe to eat? HealthCastle.com, healthcastle.com/farmed-salmon.shtml, accessed November 11, 2005.

Vallejo F, Tomas-Barberan FA, Garcia-Viguera F, Phenolic compound contents in edible parts of broccoli inflorescences after domestic cooking. *Journal of the Science of Food and Agriculture* 2003 Oct; 83(14): 1511–6.

Chapter 8

Bounous G, Gold P. The biological activity of undenatured dietary whey proteins: role of glutathione. *Clin Invest Med* 1991 Aug; 14(4): 296–309.

Bounous G, Kongshavn PA, Gold P, The immunoenhancing property of dietary whey protein concentrate. *Clinc Invest Med* 1988 Aug; 11(4): 271–8.

Costantino AM, Balzola F, Bounous G. Changes in biliary secretory immunoglobulins A in mice fed whey protein. *Minerva Dietol Gastroenterol* 1989 Oct-Dec; 35(4): 241–5.

Hsieh MH, et al. Efficacy and tolerability of oral stevioside in patients with mild essential hypertension: a two-year, randomized placebo-controlled study. *Clinical Therapeutics* 2003 Nov; 25(11): 2797–808.

Kay, Jane. Legislature considers bill to ban chemical from kids' products: Bisphenol A found in pacifiers, toys and baby bottles. *San Francisco Chronicle*, March 31, 2005.

Lailerd N, et al. Effects of stevioside on glucose transport activity in insulin-sensitive and insulin-resistant rat skeletal muscle. *Metabolism* 2004 Jan; 53(1): 101–7.

Markus CR, Olivier B, de Haan EH. Whey protein rich in alpha-lactalbumin increases the ratio of plasma tryptophan to the sum of other large neutral amino acids and improves cognitive performance in stress-vulnerable subjects. *Am J Clin Nutr* 2002 June; 75(6): 1051–6.

North K, Golding J. A maternal vegetarian diet in pregnancy is associated with hypospadias. The ALSPAC Study Team. Avon Longitudinal Study of Pregnancy and Childhood. *BJU Int* 2000 Jan; 85(1): 107–13.

Sheehan, Daniel M. Isoflavone content of breast milk and soy formulas: benefits and risks. *Clinical Chemistry* 1997; 43: 850–2.

Chapter 9

Brockman, Terra. Overcooked, stinky greens . . . not! conscious choice.com/2003/cc1611/cooking1611.html, accessed July 11, 2005.

Chapter 10

Barrett, Julia R. Soy and children's health: a formula for trouble? *Environmental Health Perspectives* 2002 June; 110(6).

Chen A, Rogan RJ. Isoflavones in soy infant formula: a review of evidence for endocrine and other activity in infants. *Annual Nutrition Reviews* 2004; 24: 33–54.

Irvine CHG, et al. The potential adverse effects of soybean phytoestrogens in infant feeding. *New Zealand Medical Journal* 1995; 108: 208–9.

Mercola, Joseph, D.O. Soy formula kills three babies. mercola.com, accessed November 26, 2003.

Sheehan DM. Isoflavone content of breast milk and formulas: benefits and risks. *Clinical Chemistry* 1997; 43: 850–2.

Raloff, Janet. What's coming out of baby's bottle? *Science News* 1999 July 31, 156(5).

Chapter 11

Benton D, Roberts G. Effect of vitamin and mineral supplementation on intelligence in a sample of schoolchildren. *Lancet* 1988 Jan 23; 1(8578): 140–3.

Borchers AT, Keen CL, Gershwin ME. Hope for the hygiene hypothesis: when the dirt hits the fan. *J Asthma* 2005 May; 42(4): 225–47.

Fergusson D. Early Solid Feeding and recurrent childhood eczema: a 10 year longitudinal study. *Pediatrics* 1990; 86: 541–546.

Nagakura T, et al. Dietary supplementation with fish oil rich in omega-3 polyunsaturated fatty acids in children with bronchial asthma. *Eur Resp J* 2000 Nov; 16(5): 861–5.

No authors listed. Indicators of children's well-being. 2005 Federal Interagency Forum on Child and Family Statistics, childstats.gov/americaschildren/index.asp, accessed November 14, 2005.

No authors listed. Food allergies: just the facts. http://familydoctor.org/340.xml, accessed September 17, 2005.

Williams LK, et al. The relationship between early fever and allergic sensitization at age 6 to 7 years. *Journal of Allergy and Clinical Immunology* 2004; 113(2): 291–6.

Concluding Thoughts

Wachs TD, et al. Maternal education and intelligence predict offspring diet and nutritional status. *Journal of Nutrition* 2005 Sep; 135(9): 2179–86.

Index

Page numbers in *italics* refer to recipes.

About the Authors

Robert Rountree, M.D., has practiced family medicine in Boulder, Colorado, for over twenty-two years. He received his M.D. from UNC–Chapel Hill, North Carolina, in 1980, followed by a family medicine residency at the Penn State Hershey Medical Center in Hershey, Pennsylvania, after which he was certified by the American Board of Family Practice. He is coauthor of *A Natural Guide to Pregnancy and Postpartum Health* (Avery, 2002), *Immunotics* (Putnam, 2000), *Smart Medicine for a Healthier Child* (Avery, 2003), and *A Parent's Guide to Medical Emergencies* (Avery, 1997). He serves on the adjunct clinical faculty of the Institute for Functional Medicine in Gig Harbor, Washington, is a professional member of the American Herbalists Guild, and is a diplomate of the American Board of Holistic Medicine. He has written numerous feature articles for popular health magazines and serves on the editorial boards for *Delicious Living, Alternative and Complementary Therapies*, and the *Journal of the American Nutraceutical Association*.

Melissa Block, M.Ed., has contributed to, ghostwritten, and coauthored many books, articles, and booklets on health, nutrition, and parenting topics—mostly in collaboration with physicians and other scientists. She holds a master's in exercise physiology and has worked as a health educator and yoga and fitness instructor. Before motherhood, she was involved in the performing arts—dance and theater—and hopes to return there someday!

Much of her work has centered around complementary medicine—where the best of the mainstream and alternative worlds merge, giving people a wider range of choices when trying to move toward better health. She also has an interest in writing about how people can better connect with one another and with the natural world, and how that makes everyone healthier.

Melissa, husband Patrick, children Sarah and Noah, and stepchildren Julian and Tristan currently live in Santa Barbara, California.